Pali Metre

MLBD

SACRED BOOKS OF THE BUDDHISTS SERIES

Reprinted Under License from **Pali Text Society**

- **A Buddhist Manual of Psychological Ethics** : Translation of the First Book in Abhidhamma Piṭaka entitled Dhammasaṅgaṇī—With Introductory Essay and Notes by *C.A.F. Rhys Davids.*
- **The Book of the Gradual Sayings** : Translation of Anguttara Nikāya, the Fourth Collection of Sutta Piṭaka **(5 Vols.)**—Tr. by *F.L. Woodward* and *E.M. Hare.*
- **The Book of the Kindred Sayings** : Translation of Saṁyutta-Nikāya **(5 Vols.)**—Tr. ,Ed. & Introduction by *C.A.F. Rhys Davids,* Tr. by *F.L. Woodward.*
- **The Collection of the Middle Length Sayings** : Translation of Majjhima Nikāya, the Second Collection of the Sutta Piṭaka containing 152 suttas. **(3 Vols.)**—Tr. from the Pali by *I.B. Horner.*
- **Compendium of Philosophy** : Translation of Abhidhammattha-Saṅgaha)—With Tr., Introductory Essay and Notes by *Shwe Zan-Aung,* Rev. & Ed. by *C.A.F. Rhys Davids.*
- **Culavaṁśa** : Translation from German Translation by Wilhelm Geiger. A Continuation of *Great Chronicle of Ceylon* (Mahāvaṃśa) : **(2 Pts. in One)**—by *C. Mabel Rickmers.*
- **Dialogues of the Buddha** : Dīgha Nikāya, the First Collection of Sutta Piṭaka **(3 Vols.)**—Translation from the Pali by *T.W. Rhys Davids* and *C.A.F. Rhys Davids.*
- **Dictionary of Pali Proper Names (2 Vols.)**—*G.P. Malalasekera.*
- **English-Pali Dictionary** —*Venerable A.P. Buddhadata.*
- **The Expositor** : Translation of Atthaśālinī, Buddhaghoṣa's Commentary on Dhammasaṅgaṇī, the First Book of Abhidhamma Piṭaka—Tr. by *Pe Maung Tin,* Rev. & Ed. by *C.A.F. Rhys Davids.*
- **Conditional Relations [Paṭṭhāna] (2 Pts.)** Part I : Guide, Part II : Translation of Caṭṭasaṅgāyana Text of the Seventh Book of Abhidhamma Piṭaka—Tr. by *U. Narada Mula Patt Thana Sayadow,* Assisted by *U. Thein Nyun.*
- **The Jātaka or Stories of the Buddha's Former Births (6 Vols. in 3 Pts.)**: Translation from the Tenth Book of Khuddaka Nikāya of Sutta Piṭaka—Ed. by *E.B. Cowell,* Tr. by *Robert Chalmers, W.H.D. Rouse, H.T. Francis* and *R.A. Neil.*
- **Pali-English Dictionary**—*T.W. Rhys Davids* and *William Stede.*
- **Pali Metre** : A Contribution to the History of Indian Literature—*A.K. Warder.*
- **Points of Controversy** (Subjects of Discourse) : A Translation of the Kathāvathu from the Fifth Book of Abhidhamma Piṭaka—Tr. by *S.Z. Aung* and *C.A.F. Rhys Davids.*
- **The Sutra of Golden Light** : Translation of Suvarnabhasottamasūtra—*R.E. Emmerick.*

Pali Text Society
Ancillary Works

PALI METRE

A Contribution to the History of Indian Literature

A.K. WARDER

Professor of Sanskrit and Chairman of the Department of East Asian Studies, University of Toronto, Canada

MOTILAL BANARSIDASS PUBLISHERS
PRIVATE LIMITED • DELHI

First Indian Edition: Delhi, ***2016***

ISBN: 978-81-208-4042-3

Also available at
MOTILAL BANARSIDASS
41 U.A. Bungalow Road, Jawahar Nagar, Delhi 110 007
8 Mahalaxmi Chamber, 22 Bhulabhai Desai Road, Mumbai 400 026
203 Royapettah High Road, Mylapore, Chennai 600 004
236, 9th Main III Block, Jayanagar, Bengaluru 560 011
8 Camac Street, Kolkata 700 017
Ashok Rajpath, Patna 800 004
Chowk, Varanasi 221 001

MLBD Cataloging-in-Publication Data
Pali Metre
A Contribution to the History of Indian Literature
by A.K. Warder
in *MLBD Sacred Books of the Buddhists Series*
ISBN : 978-81-208-4042-3
Includes Bibliography and Index
I. Buddhism II. Indian Literature
III. Pali IV. Warder, A.K.

Published by
Motilal Banarsidass Publishers Private Limited
www.mlbd.com • mlbd@mlbd.com
Printed by Replika Press Pvt. Ltd.

PREFACE

A satisfactory history of the ancient literature of India has not yet been published. The chief difficulty has been the chronology. Despite a certain amount of progress in dating the great *kavis*, our would-be historians have so far preferred the classificatory method of proceeding by types of literature to grappling with the problems of a strictly chronological presentation. It is useful to have essays on the various types, but a collection of such essays is no substitute for a general history of literature. Just as the types of literary composition, such as lyric poetry, epic, drama, the novel, have been segregated, so to an even greater degree literature in different languages or dialects, Sanskrit, " Epic " Sanskrit, Pali, Ardhamāgadhī, Māhārāṣṭrī, Apabhraṃśa and the like, has been rigidly compartmentalized into so many isolated literatures chronologically unrelated.

This compartmentalization has resulted first in the illusion of there being several separate literatures, leading to their being studied in a strange and barren insulation from one another, particularly by more recent writers trained in this artificial tradition. A further and subtler distortion of outlook resulting from the segregated study by dialects and types has been the impression of static literatures, without development, without significant history, seeming to confirm the original bias against historical investigations. The text books of the artificially constituted literatures and types harmonize complacently with the easy and servile (for India) illusion of a static or degenerate society.

The non-chronological study of literature is reflected also in the non-chronological " histories " of Indian philosophy, religion, and other subjects for which the main sources are literary. Some attempts have been made to trace the actual history of philosophy or of various ideological and cultural movements, but in the absence of order in the literary sources the writers have been reduced to arbitrary assumptions as to, for example, the original nature of Buddhism.

The following study has as one of its aims the understanding and appreciation of the metrical techniques of a major and particularly dynamic period in the history of Indian literature. Simultaneously, however, it results from our method of study (of the development of metres rather than of their mechanical classification) that if our understanding is reasonably correct we should have succeeded in establishing the relative chronology of a series of texts. The metrical techniques are in themselves full of interest and delight, moreover in the period studied here we see the origins and early development of the splendid metrical repertoire familiar in its later flowering to the connoisseur of the *kāvya* literature. So far from static was the metrics recorded for us in the Pali Canon that we find some of its essential techniques continuing to generate new metres through many centuries, creating a vital and still popular art medium even for Hindi and other modern literatures. It follows that the isolated study, even of phases in Indian literature which are really as remote from each other as Pali and Hindi, must lose in understanding, much more so those which were nearly contemporary though in different dialects. The continually developing art of metrics, beautiful in itself, may perhaps play the same part in Indian literary history that changing pottery technique plays in archaeology.

The methods here used in analysing metrical data and treating the problems they presented were in great part worked out as the research proceeded. The writer cautiously applied such scraps of scientific method and such more or less intuitive habits of investigation as had come into his possession. He was guided by the empiricist outlook that he was studying some objective reality whose nature should be presumed unknown except in so far as it had been discovered *a posteriori*. He made the further assumption, which is a hypothesis but which appears fruitful, that the phenomena under investigation were related to one another and also to non-metrical and eventually non-literary phenomena : the patterns studied were not chance mechanical occurrences, totally (and metaphysically) isolated and " different " from one another, but constituted a record of change and growth, a continuity in which, however, quite " new " phenomena, hardly predictable even from the most complete knowledge of what had gone before, appear from time to time after what some scientists have called " qualitative " changes. It must be strongly insisted that this guiding assumption is just a hypothesis, found useful in experience as enabling one to spot seemingly significant connections and to suggest new approaches to problems, which may or may not turn out to be capable of solving them, it is not an *a priori* judgment or " law " prescribing any " necessary " framework into which we ought to force our data. One practical methodological consequence of this assumption which appears in this book is that it seemed worth while to devote more attention to the metres which had newly appeared in a given period, as likely to prove most fruitful in revealing the characteristics of that period. This preface is no place for an elaborate discussion of the theory of scientific method: the above sketch should suffice to indicate the general assumptions underlying this study; it is for the reader to decide how far they have been satisfactory.

The writer read various studies by predecessors in the field of metrics in general as well as of Indian metrics in particular. He found no satisfactory general theory of metre which might be applied to any poetry. The progress in the Indian field is reviewed below: it may be noted here, as of general theoretical interest, that this progress seems to the writer to be traceable to a very serious effort from about 1870 onwards to understand Indian metrics, based at first on the deliberate and consistent application of an erroneous general theory; the criticisms of this theory which have arisen from practical study have led gradually towards a more satisfactory theory, at least for Indian metre, which is worked out in this study on the basis of the empirical data.

The present work is a study of the problems presented by the metres in the Pali Canon, seen in their historical setting as representing the Early Middle Indian phase in the development of Indian metrics. During this phase, which is regarded as corresponding to a turning point in the linguistic transition from Old Indian (Vedic) to Late Middle Indian (Apabhraṃśa), a number of new metres appeared and an entirely new technique of versification was developed, differing in principle from the old Vedic technique. The " plot " of our story, we might say, is the conflict between these two contradictory techniques in Pali poetry, in which the new style prevailed: even some of the traditional old metres were assimilated to it, only one epic metre remaining, within narrowed limits of rhythmic variation, as representative of the archaic manner. The new technique was adopted alike for the Sanskrit and Prakrit literature of the following centuries and its understanding should lead to a better appreciation of that phase of Indian poetry too.

The attempt is made to collect and assess all previous contributions to the study of the ancient Indian metres and closely related subjects. The interrelations between these connected fields have been sought, leading to mutual elucidation of problems. The language of the Pali Canon presents many difficulties which have to be investigated before we can tackle the problems of scansion, whilst the linguistic and metrical trends constantly interacted. The most significant feature of the new metres was their close connection with music, the study of which has proved to be indispensable in our research on the history of Indian literature.

In studying Pali poetry we are not concerned simply with the literature of a school of Buddhism or with a "Buddhist" literature. This was not the only literature of the period of the rise of the Empire of Magadha; it is, for whatever reasons, the best preserved representative of that period. The better Buddhist poets of that period, like Aśvaghoṣa later, followed, and perhaps helped to create, current styles which, as far as we can see, were essentially secular styles common to all the dialects of the Indo-Aryan world and to various schools of thought. At most it might be suggested that the Buddhists, as the typical and most vigorous representatives of new ideological currents from about 500 B.C. onwards, would rather naturally use new means of expression, whilst the Vedic or Brahmanical tradition might be expected to have remained conservative. The brahmans, however, were not content to be conservative. If there was to be a new society with new ideals, they would lead it if they could. Indeed they adopted many of the ideals advocated by the Buddhists and other non-Vedic schools, they reformed their rituals and became vegetarians—and in poetry they soon used the new metres. We shall find reason to suppose that in fact it was in Magadha and in the Māgadhī language that the new trend in literature originated. The rapid spread of the trend all over India is probably not unconnected with the expansion of the political power of Magadha (we have not taken up this question in this book), whilst the apparently pan-Indian nature of the succeeding waves of stylistic development would seem to demonstrate a cultural unity of India which was surely furthered by the political unification under Magadha. This cultural unity endured, though the political unification did not, so that in studying the literature of c. 500 to 100 B.C. we are studying the most vigorous formative period of that trend in literature which is often referred to as the " classical ", leading up to the great models of the classical forms which were the legacy of Guṇāḍhya, Aśvaghoṣa, Sātavāhana, Bhāsa, and their now mostly forgotten contemporaries. In Pali literature we see the creation of new forms, a new " poetic " vocabulary, new metres, a new poetics of figurative language, new techniques of story telling and of dramatic dialogue, a new aesthetics foreshadowing the *rasa* doctrine, new subject matter as well as the expression of new ideals ; in a word we see the creation of *kāvya*, the classical standard of literature as a form of art.

After discussing the nature of the literature with which we are concerned, especially as regards its date and authenticity, and the character of the Pali language, the Introduction considers the theoretical problems of this study, including the principles of versification underlying the metres. The first chapters then take up the phonology of Pali in relation to the orthography of the textual tradition, in order to eliminate misreadings (I), the conventions of word junction, treated within the theory of *sandhi* (II), scansion and the question of any effect of " accent " (III) and the limits of rhythmical fluidity and metrical licence (IV). The following five chapters analyse the five main classes of Pali metres. *Mattāchandas* is studied first, and most thoroughly, because it appears to have been the first of the new developments in metre (V). In *gaṇacchandas* the new technique is carried further (VI). Then the metres handed down from the old tradition, the *anuṭṭhubha* or *vatta* (VII) and the *tuṭṭhubha* (VIII) are studied. They do not remain static in our texts but undergo fundamental changes, apparently under the influence of the new technique, so that the knowledge gained from studying the new metres suggests how we should understand new features found in those of the older tradition. *Akkharacchandas* (IX) shows the latest developments within Pali canonical literature, a further range of new metres derived from those already studied. The Conclusion is concerned primarily with the results for the chronology of the literature which emerge from our analysis of the evolution of the metres.

The research reported in this book was carried out mostly between January, 1950, and July, 1951, and partly written up in that period. After a year's interruption due to lack of leisure, a postgraduate studentship awarded by the University of London made it possible to complete the writing up and discussions between October, 1952, and June, 1954, with a view to publication. The work consequently takes account of contributions in its field received by the author up to the beginning of 1954. Under the conditions of lack of encouragement and support for research on Indian literature in the United Kingdom at that time, the author failed to find any sponsor for the publication of the work and so laid it aside, taking up various other research projects, including from time to time the continuation of the study of the history of Indian literature. That this book can now be published is thanks to the interest of the Pali Text Society, which recently has extended the scope of its publication programme to include ancillary works of this kind as well as texts and translations. In preparing the work for the press the author has made only minor changes of presentation and has not attempted any further analysis or discussion. Since 1954 he has not pursued the study of metre further and so has nothing to add on that subject, whilst on looking over the work he still feels able to stand by the conclusions arrived at in it, which he has meanwhile applied in studies in related fields. It is to be hoped that others will continue the metrical analysis of texts, perhaps with the advantage of computers, which promises to be so fruitful for settling chronological problems. Finally the author records his *kataññutā* and *kataveditā* to his wife, Nargez, for help at various stages in the preparation of the book.

1966 A. K. WARDER.

CONTENTS

INTRODUCTION

The Problem of Pali Metre and the Significance of its Solution

§ 1. The study of Pali is at present seriously handicapped by a difficulty which is only slightly felt in that of Vedic and Epic Sanskrit, whilst it is not encountered at all in the " Classical " Sanskrit literature. The verse texts of the ancient Pali literature contain such a large proportion of lines which apparently do not scan that it seems only a matter of chance if *pādas* coinciding in structure with the familiar Sanskrit metres sometimes occur. Moreover the Pali Canon, largely as a result of this metrical confusion, has the appearance of so teeming with corruptions as to be of very poor value as a historical document.

Some of the poems in more complex metres contain only a minority of apparently scannable *pādas* in the editions now in use, and in some cases the metres were not recognized by the leading Pali specialists and editors for many years. Thus of the *Isidāsīgāthā* in the *Therīgāthā*, edited in 1883 by Pischel, who clearly did not suspect that his text was in the *ariyā* (*āryā*) metre, Mrs. Rhys Davids in a footnote to her translation twenty-six years later (1909) remarks: " I am unable to classify the metre throughout this poem, from the first line . . . to the last " (*Psalms of the Sisters*, p. 163), whilst even in the *pāda* index published by the Pali Text Society in its *Journal* for 1924–7 the metre of the *ariyā* poems remained unidentified (consequently some of the *pādas* are wrongly divided). As a matter of fact Leumann had recognized the metre of the *Isidāsīgāthā* by 1900 and pointed it out to Hardy, who most commendably applied metrical considerations in his attempt to define the date of the *Nettippakaraṇa* in the Introduction to his edition of that text (1902, p. xxiii), yet the fruitful possibilities thus suggested were unaccountably ignored by others. One motive for the present piece of research arose from the frustrating experience of reading Pischel's *Therīgāthā* as a set book.

§ 2. The conviction that the Pali Canon is not a document of poor value, but on the contrary of the very greatest value for the history and appreciation of Indian literature—not to mention its interest in connection with the early history of Buddhist philosophy—inspired the undertaking of a general study of its position as representing an important phase in the development of the literature, including the relationships of that phase to others, especially to that of " Classical " Sanskrit. Remarkable affinities could be found between the literary styles of various works in Pali and in Sanskrit (from the *Brāhmaṇa* phase down to the Classical literature), yet up to now the histories of literature had in general treated the two literatures in isolation from one another, only a few tentative speculations on their comparative chronology and stylistic relationships having been made, chiefly by Oldenberg, Winternitz and La Vallée Poussin. As for the development of philosophical and religious thought, the absence of any satisfactory chronological basis had reduced the historians to guesswork and personal tastes in their attempts to explain the relationships between Buddhism and the *Upaniṣads* or the Sāṃkhya and Yoga schools, or to trace the doctrinal tendencies of the various schools among the Buddhists.

Surely it is the responsibility of those who specialize in Pali to find the keys to this most formative period in the history of Indian literature—from the time of the Buddha to that of Aśvaghoṣa.

§ 3. Through the tangled text of the Canon preserved in the Mahāvihāra at Anurādhapura it seemed possible to divine the characteristics of the literature of India as it was in Asoka's time and in the centuries leading up to that great crisis in Indian history. The corruptions present in the text even when Buddhaghosa and Dhammapāla studied it appeared not as obstacles and tokens of an inferior tradition (and certainly not as marks of late fabrication) but as guarantees of antiquity which, in the very process of being eliminated, would enable us to ascertain many of the literary techniques of that period.

The origins of the Classical Sanskrit literature are obscure, the early works having been almost entirely lost, but in the Pali literature we find the beginnings of the new forms and techniques—epic > *mahākāvya*, story-telling > *kathā*, early dramatic performances > the Classical theatre, the growth of the Classical lyric, the development of theories of poetics and aesthetics and the conscious application of these in literary creation, most clearly of all the rise of the new metrics—in a more comprehensive collection and, which is more important, in a much purer state than in the Epics, the Sanskrit translations of the *Bṛhatkathā*, or the early Jaina literature. Moreover the Pali texts offer the possibility of approximate dating, owing to their more direct relations with historical events.

The investigation which follows forms part of a wider plan for the study of this period of the history of Indian literature and aims at laying the foundations for such a study by exploiting the criterion of metre in interrelating the texts and approximately dating them.

The Authenticity of the Pali Canon

§ 4. To go beyond the mere impression of authenticity, as a collection of documents composed during the Moriyan period or earlier, which we derive from the present state of the Pali texts, we require more tangible evidence for the approximate date of these texts and for the reliability of the tradition which preserved them.

It has been shown by Dr. Adikaram (1946, pp. 3, 11, etc.) that the Commentaries on the Pali Canon as edited in the 5th century A.D. are almost entirely Indian in tradition (and in fact North Indian), although this edition was based on a translation from the Old Sinhalese recension of the *Aṭṭhakathā*, collated with South Indian recensions. Of the Buddhist *theras* mentioned in the Commentaries for their views on the interpretation of points in the Canon, the latest belong to the 1st century A.D. A list of the *theras* who handed down the *Vinaya* "up to the present day" has no *thera* later than the 1st century A.D. Adikaram therefore regards the Sinhalese Commentaries as a continuation of the Indian Theravāda (Sthaviravāda) tradition, into which new material was incorporated down to the 1st century A.D., after which time it became closed.

The orthodox tradition in Ceylon is that these Commentaries were brought from India in the 3rd century B.C. with the

Canon, and written down (but in Old Sinhalese, not in Pali) at the same time as the Canon (1st century B.C.). The former date may be slightly exaggerated in antiquity (it represents perhaps rather the beginning of the introduction of Buddhism into Ceylon than the completion of the process—but no time is more likely than that of Asoka for the most decisive events in the establishment of the new religion in Ceylon), but the latter falls in a less legendary period of Ceylon history and is probably correct. The reason given for the writing is that in this period of invasion and famine (the 1st century B.C.) many monks were killed, or starved, and the oral tradition was thus threatened with the destruction of some of its texts.

§ 5. Now, if even the Commentaries were preserved in North Indian form (although translated into the local dialect in order to make the Canon more accessible to Sinhalese monks), the Canon itself should represent at the latest a form and dialect belonging to the period immediately preceding the establishment of the tradition in Ceylon. This form and dialect cannot then be dated later than the end of the 2nd century B.C. Only a few verses not commented in the *Aṭṭhakathā* (as noted by its 5th century A.D. editors) may be later additions to the Canon, together with the *Parivāra*—a kind of index to the *Vinaya* which refers to Ceylon and must have been composed there between the 2nd century B.C. and the 1st century A.D.

The Formation of the Canon

§ 6. We have now to ask whether the Canon in its present form contains material older than the 2nd century B.C. Here we can compare the language with the dated linguistic records of the period—mainly inscriptions.[1] We can also note references in the Canon to historical events.

A comparison with the Prakrit inscriptions shows that the Pali language is closest to the earliest records (e.g. preservation of intervocalic consonants, without voicing), and it may therefore be regarded as having flourished in and probably before

[1] See Mehendale (1948) for a useful survey of Prakrit historical linguistics from the earliest inscriptions (5th or 4th century B.C.) to the 4th century A.D.

the Moriyan Period.[1] The Canonical texts, as we shall argue below (Chapters I, II, IV), have the appearance of standing close to a living language rather than of being artificial productions in a dead language, like their Commentaries, and therefore would seem to belong to the period when that language flourished.

Some indirect indication of the literary tendencies of the period may be gleaned from the sculpture, as pointed out by Professor Codrington in *The Legacy of India* (London, 1937), pp. 78–9. The loss of the names of the "godlings" and the decrease in the number of *jātakas* from thirty at Bharhut to six at Sanchi seem to reflect the literary transition from the Pali Canon with its precise knowledge of the "godlings" and many hundreds of *jātakas* to the confused or vague Buddhist Hybrid Sanskrit conceptions of the various classes of supernatural beings, and to the limited and standardized collections of *jātakas* selected to illustrate the "perfections", such as may be found in one of the latest texts of the Canon itself, the *Cariyāpiṭaka*, and in the *Jātakamālā*.

§ 7. The formation of the Canon is associated historically with at least two assemblies or "rehearsals", the second of which is recorded in a chapter which appears to be a later addition to the *Vinaya*, at which monks from different parts of India compared their versions of the teaching of the Buddha. Certain versions were afterwards approved, others rejected, by the various groups or schools, which gradually increased in number. Each school tried to establish a definitive canon, as authentic as possible within the limits of its doctrines and practices. Under the stabilizing influence of the Moriyan Empire at least three such canons were established: Theravāda, Sabbatthivāda (Sarvāstivāda), Mahāsaṅghika—of which the former two were closely related.[2] The Pali Canon preserved for us by the Theravāda tradition no doubt grew up gradually, during the whole period of formation of canons, around a kernel of ancient texts of various types—long, medium or short *suttas*, *gāthās*

[1] Slight modifications may have resulted from the use of a later Southern orthography when the Canon was written down—on this see Chapter I.

[2] On the rise of the various schools see especially Przyluski (1923 and 1926–8) and Lin Li-Kouang (1949, Ch. IV).

(poems), songs (*geyya*), *jātakas*, *udānas*, and so on—just as did the other canons, which contained the same categories of texts.

We shall see in our study of the metres, especially in Chapter VII on the *vatta* (*vaktra*) (see also §§ 20–1 of this Introduction) that the study of whole collections of texts as found in the Canon (arranged according to these categories), such as the *Theratherīgāthā* or the *Jātaka*, leads to confused results. Only individual poems and small groups of poems show clearly defined usages consistent with composition at a particular stage in the evolution of literary techniques. Of the large collections we can say only that some of them contain a preponderance of older (e.g. Sn) or of later (e.g. Dh) texts, indicating a greater popularity of that form of composition at a particular period, whilst others, such as Th and J, give approximately the same results, when analysed, as the entire Canon or any large random selection of texts from it. If, however, we take, for instance, the *Dhammacariyasutta* or the *Pabbajjāsutta* of Sn, we find homogeneous and very old *vatta* techniques, with which we may contrast the *Vāseṭṭhasutta* and *Dvayatānupassanasutta* of Sn, as examples of homogeneous and late *vatta* techniques (cf. Conclusion).

§ 8. Although we cannot say whether any Pali verses in their present form date back to the time of the Buddha (i.e. circa 500 B.C.), on the one hand the changes in technique within the Canon imply a considerable period of development prior to the 2nd century B.C., and on the other hand the formal similarities between the Canon and those of the other early schools indicate a common origin of the original " kernels " in a period before the sectarian divisions had separated them too far. Here, however, we find ourselves on merely subjective ground and can go no further until we can support our conjectures with more precise conclusions, derived from our analysis, on the internal chronology of the Canon.

To the end of the period of the formation of the old canons the traditions of the early schools assign the rise of the Mahāyāna. Both Northern and Southern texts, such as the Mahāvaṃsa, associate the production of all sorts of heretical treatises of the Mahāyāna with the time of Asoka or of the

Moriyas generally. It is not likely that these traditions would exaggerate the antiquity of their opponents' traditions, so we may perhaps look for a late Moriyan dialect in the oldest Mahāyāna texts as far as their original language can be restored from the Sanskritized versions which have been preserved. In fact this dialect does not appear to have been very different from Pali, as we should expect from the chronology we have sketched.

The Pali Language

§ 9. Having established that the Canonical Pali texts were composed in the period which saw the rise of the Magadhan Empire, we may go further and try to localize their language and to define its position amongst the Indian vernaculars of that period. Pali does not appear to have been simply the vernacular of a particular region, although as we have just said it stood close to one of the vernaculars, on which it was based. Here we must refer to and stress the conclusion of Lin Li-Kouang (1949, 216 ff.), which seems finally to settle the old question concerning the language in which the Buddha is said to have enjoined his disciples to recite his teaching.[1]

This conclusion is " le principe de l'adoption de langues locales par les bouddhistes ", which he derives from several non-Pali traditions, thereby elucidating the Pali tradition, which had seemed equivocal and had been variously interpreted. The correct interpretation of the tradition recorded in Vin II, p. 139, is that each disciple should repeat the teaching in his own dialect. From this practice arose the plurality of dialects in which the Buddhist Canons were preserved.[2]

The 3rd century B.C. inscriptions provide an authentic linguistic survey of India. The variations of dialect show that the language of the Magadhan administration had not become a standard completely overriding the local vernaculars. Although the dialect which we may call Old Māgadhī had, following the Magadhan political supremacy, overlaid to some

[1] On this see also M III, 234 : dialectal variants : in each region use the word which is understood there.

[2] Edgerton, in his *Buddhist Hybrid Sanskrit Grammar*, just published, is in agreement with this conclusion (pp. 1–2).

extent the dialects of the regions radiating outwards from Magadha as far as the Upper Yamunā (Topra), Sanchi, and Kaliṅga, and even that of Mysore (" Kiṣkindhā " ?) (Bloch, 1950, p. 44), this process had not gone far enough to spoil our picture. It would appear that the imperial administrations in Ujjenī and Takkasilā retained the local dialects of the West (Avantī) and the North-West (Gandhāra).[1]

Pali is closest to the Western dialect (Āvantī) and closest of all to the Girnar inscriptions (Bloch, 1934, p. 6, and 1950, pp. 44–5).[2] It agrees generally with all the dialects in regard to the pronouns, intervocalic consonants (e.g. *ṭ* in *paṭi-*, *h* in *dahati* (from *dhā*), *lahu*, *-ehi*, *hoti* ; Pali *-rasa* for *-dasa* or *-ḍasa* in the numerals is exceptional, but the variation *r*/*ḍ* in Indian dialects is not found to be constant and is not regarded as very significant), and the (presumably emphatic) initial *h* as in *hevaṃ*. With the Girnar dialect the identity extends to the whole declension (e.g. Ablative in *-ā*) and to the wavering between *ch* and *kh*. On the other hand Girnar allows a long vowel before a conjunct, which in Pali is allowed only exceptionally as a result of a few *sandhi* combinations.

§ 10. The distinctive features of (Old) Māgadhī, final *-e* in the masculine nom. sing., and *l* for *r*, are found only exceptionally in Pali : a few quotations of Māgadhī speakers using the nom. in *-e* (and perhaps the gen. pl. in *-uno*), and *e* for *o* or *l* for *r* in the following words : *s(u)ve*, *antepura*, *puretaraṃ*, *pure*, *bhikkhave*, *seyyathā* ; *pali-* (for *pari-*), *lujjati* (= *rujyate*), *elaṇḍa*, *daddula*, *taluṇa*, *ludda* (= *raudra*), *antalikkha*, *peyyāla* (= *pariyāya*), etc.[3]

[1] We may compare with the Asokan data the regional (said to include languages, but also dress, manners, etc.) map given in the *Nāṭyaśāstra* (XIV), which probably rests on ancient traditions : Āvantī from Sindhu to Vidiśā ; Dākṣiṇātyā in Mahārāṣṭra, Āndhra, Kaliṅga, and elsewhere in the South (" between the Vindhya and the Ocean ") ; Pāñcālī from Śūrasena to Bālhīkā (Bactria) ; and " Odramāgadhī " or " Ardhamāgadhī " from Vatsa to Kaliṅga and everywhere east of that line.

[2] Brāhmī inscriptions everywhere fail to represent double consonants, which evidently were understood by the reader—see Geiger, 1938, p. 41.

[3] It is remarkable that the formulations of the *Kathāvatthu* appear to preserve some Māgadhī : *vattabbe* (1 ff.), *ese*, *dunniggahīte* (3, 6), *niggahetabbe* (4, 7), *se tena hi ye kate niggahe se niggahe dukkate, sukate paṭikamme, sukatā paṭipādanā* (4, 7), *ke* (24 f.).

§ 11. Taking into consideration the history of the Theravāda school as traced by Przyluski, with its main centre originally at Kosambī and important subsidiary centres at Ujjenī and other western cities, we may suggest that the Pali Canon originated as a western recension of the Buddha's teaching, having, however, a fair sprinkling of Māgadhī words reflecting either characteristic expressions of the Buddha himself (*bhikkhave* ... *seyyathā* ...) or at any rate the eastern, Old Māgadhī, recension which we may infer was repeated by the great majority of his disciples, who were easterners (... *peyyāla* ... very probably originated among them). As we now have it the Canon is probably a fairly good copy of the Ujjenī recension, in a form of the Āvantī dialect with the Māgadhisms just mentioned and certain peculiarities to be discussed in the next paragraph, although it cannot be ruled out that it may be in the main the old Kosambī recension itself and its dialect that of the Vatsa country. Of this dialect we know little. The *Nāṭyaśāstra* includes it in the eastern (Māgadhī) region and the Kosambī column of Asoka is in the same eastern dialect as all six columns bearing the six " Pillar Edicts ", at Topra and Mīraṭh (Upper Yamunā), Nandangarh and Araraj (on the east bank of the Sadānīrā or Gandak), Rāmpurvā (about 30 miles N.E. of Nandangarh), and Kosambī itself (Bloch, 1950, pp. 25–7 and 161). This may be due merely to a temporary ascendancy of Māgadhī over the local dialects in the Kuru and Vatsa countries, thus it is possible that the true Vatsa dialect resembled Āvantī except for the Māgadhisms as found in the Pali Canon, i.e. that it stood between Māgadhī and Āvantī, but was closer to the latter. Attractive as it might be to believe that our Canon was in the language of Udena and Naravāhanadatta, it is more probable that it is " approximately " in Āvantī. We may note, however, that Kālidāsa says *prāpyāvantīn udayanakathākovidagrāmavṛddhān* ... " having arrived in Avantī where the village elders are well versed in the Story of Udayana ... " (which Vallabhadeva equates with the *Bṛhatkathā*), and conclude that in the literary history of India Vatsa and Avantī were especially closely connected. Our conclusion, then, is that Pali is in all probability approximately Āvantī, or the result of a process Māgadhī > " Vātsī " > Āvantī.

§ 12. It has been observed by several writers [1] that in both Asoka's inscriptions and the language of the Pali Canon "archaism" plays a part. De La Vallée Poussin speaks of the "māgadhī officielle" opposed to the ordinary vernacular in which the titles of certain Buddhist texts are quoted (thus the dialect of the administration would be more archaic than the scriptures from which it borrowed its ethical doctrines, which, presumably in accordance with Lin Li-Kouang's principle, had moved with the times), whilst Bloch on the contrary remarks "le caractère simple et fruste...empreint de solennité officielle et peut-être de hiératisme ; qui sait par exemple si nombre de redites ne proviennent pas d'emprunts aux textes de l'ancien bouddhisme ? On a en tout cas retrouvé en certains passages l'écho du canon pali". Lin Li-Kouang suggests that a process of "palisation" took place in the Canon analogous to the Sanskritization in other Buddhist texts. He presumably has in mind that at a certain stage the "principle of adoption of local dialects" gave place to a principle of the antiquity of the tradition resisting further change and seeking to restore an archaic garb to the scriptures. Geiger (1916) and others long ago pointed out the archaisms in the Canon, especially in the *Therīgāthā*, and these seem to betray rather later texts deliberately made to look old than the earlier strata of the Canon.[2] As noted above, we have to make a further reservation about Pali as a vernacular dialect. It was a vernacular modified (i) by certain Māgadhisms and (ii) by certain archaisms. That is, by the time the Canon became fixed, it represented to some extent an attempt to restore a more ancient form of the vernacular in which it was handed down.

[1] De La Vallée Poussin (1936, p. 201), Lin Li-Kouang (1949, p. 215), Bloch (1950, p. 7).

[2] Examples of "archaism": in the inscriptions: *abhivādetūnaṃ* (Bairat) ; in the Canon: *kātuye* (Th II—apparently an old gloss incorporated in the text before the 1st century A.D.), the orthography *brāhmaṇa* for *baṃhaṇa*, *etase* (= *etuṃ*) (Th II), *hetuye* (Bv), *chaḍḍūna* (Th II), *apakiritūna* (Th II), etc. It is noteworthy that these archaic infinitives in *-uye* and *-ase* and the gerund in *-tūna* are confined to some of the latest canonical texts. This indicates clearly the nature of the development taking place in Pali from a living dialect to an artificial literary language.

However, this theory of "archaism" should be treated with reserve, since we find *-tūṇa(ṃ)* in Māhārāṣṭrī. See also § 52 below for "middle" forms.

§ 13. It must be said that all this distinction of dialects amounts to very little when we consider the history of this literature as a whole. The " translation " of a text from one dialect to another involved only very slight changes, which would affect the metre, for instance, only in a tiny minority of cases. A text could thus be taken over from Māgadhī into Āvantī without altering its original character and metre: it was merely a question of substituting *r* for *l* and *o* for *e* in a large number of words and a few other equally slight modifications in a very few words. The point to make here is that we may without danger assume that we are studying the general history of Indian literature rather than the particular history of literature in one dialect, since the dialects were not isolated. If we say that a certain text in the Pali Canon was composed in the 5th century B.C., for instance, we are probably referring to an original Old Māgadhī text, although we are actually studying perhaps an Āvantī version made in the 3rd century B.C., which, however, is 98% faithful to the original in metre and still more faithful in reproducing the content of the original *gāthā*. The local peculiarities of style or metre, and of content or doctrine, which we find in the literature, are secondary phenomena within the general process of evolution (see for instance the evolution of the *tuṭṭhubha* (*triṣṭubh*) suggested in §§ 282 ff. of Chapter VIII).

§ 14. No important changes seem to have taken place during the further migration of the Canon to Ceylon, either directly (legend of Mahinda, connected with Ujjenī, etc.) or indirectly, by stages, via the Godāvarī valley and the Coḷa country. Such confusions as might be anticipated from the use of new scripts,[1] and eventually of the modern Sinhalese and Burmese, which at first sight appear very liable to cause copyists' errors, were limited to sporadic corruptions, and do not seem to have produced any general substitution of new spellings. A good test

[1] The Brāhmī script remained in use in Ceylon for inscriptions during the period 200 B.C.–A.D. 400. The script derived from the Grantha of South India had been introduced by the 4th century A.D. (Geiger, 1938, pp. 1–4). This is of great significance: the Canon was firmly established in North Indian from before the introduction of a new script.

for the reliability of the tradition is the preservation of the authentic instrumental plural in *-hi*, as found in the Asokan inscriptions, against the tendency to archaise to *-bhi* which appears sporadically and is allowed by the Medieval grammarians. The letters *h* and *bh* are very similar in both Sinhalese and Burmese, but this did not lead to substitution even in this most favourable case.

§ 15. To conclude this section we shall note the traditional views of the Pali grammarians on the nature of the language, and also on their susceptibility or resistance to the influence of Sanskrit, with its enormous literary prestige even in Ceylon and Burma. As an example we may take the best of them.

Aggavaṃsa (12th century A.D.), the most comprehensive and detailed writer on Pali grammar, was aware of the fundamental differences between Sanskrit and Pali, and of the non-validity of Sanskrit rules in the latter language, which he no doubt regarded as older (as the original from which all other languages were derived). He strove to present Pali grammar purified of Sanskritisms, supporting every statement by quotations from the Canon itself.[1] On p. 621 of the *Saddanīti* he says : *yathāpāvacanaṃ vidhi. imasmiṃ pakaraṇe pāvacanānurūpen' eva ādesādividhi bhavati*, " . . . in this work the rules for substitution, etc., are laid down according to the Canon." We can go beyond Aggavaṃsa only by comparing the Pali tradition with results derived from the study of other material, such as inscriptions and other Buddhist traditions, most of which was not available to him. Aggavaṃsa was further limited, however, by the absence of historical linguistics, of a theory of regular historical changes of forms, from the grammatical science of his day, which regarded Pali or " Māgadhī " as the unchangeable *mūlabhāsā* or fundamental language spoken by the Buddha.

§ 16. Yet Aggavaṃsa was too acute and rigorous in his

[1] Interesting discussions on Pali and Sanskrit, Sd pp. 92, 510, 923–4, many other comparisons between the two scattered throughout the work. Aggavaṃsa was no doubt criticizing the older school of Pali grammarians founded by Kaccāna, who failed to break away sufficiently from the Sanskrit tradition (or rather failed to apply the linguistic science properly) to give a good description of Pali, merely trying to adapt the *Kātantra* to the language he was studying.

analysis of texts not to discover historical changes in operation in spite of this tradition. Thus he explains that the adjective *yevāpanaka* was acquired by *anukaraṇa*, " imitation " (CPD), i.e. in this case " repetition ", from the phrase *ye vā pana* (Sd pp. 261–2). This phenomenon is classified as *rūḷhibheda* (see Chapter IV). Apart from such a process at work in the Canon itself, Aggavaṃsa was clearly aware of the difference between Canonical Pali and the later language of the *kavis*. Probably he attributed this only to the difference between the individual usage of the Buddha and the *kāvya* style suited to the polished contemporary literature in both Classical Sanskrit and " Classical " Pali, since he remarks that in previous incarnations the Bodhisatta had sometimes been a *kavi* and utilized the polished style which as Buddha he rejected. An example of this difference, which Aggavaṃsa gives, is that in the Canon a compound may not be split between two *pādas* of verse, even *sandhi* between *pādas* occurring there only in certain exceptional cases. The Bhagavant is said not to have split his compounds between *pādas* because (i) this was against the usage of " Māgadhī ", to which he conformed, and (ii) he wished to avoid making his meaning obscure (Sd pp. 631–2).[1] In general, however, Aggavaṃsa stresses the view that " the Bhagavant " was above worldly usage and was able to disregard the latter at will, for instance in regard to metre (see the passages quoted below, Chapter IV).

§ 17. This is the traditional explanation given for irregularities not understood by the medieval writers, and the traditional misconception of the nature of Pali which is characteristic of even the best of the old Sinhalese and Burmese grammarians. The language is regarded as above human rules, as the creation of a superhuman being, and as not evolving. Nevertheless we must acknowledge that it is most fortunate that the ancient and medieval guardians of the texts and tradition in Ceylon and Burma had this special respect for the Canonical text they

[1] Two other rules given by Aggavaṃsa, which apply " in the world " (presumably in " Medieval Pali ") but not in the Canon, are (i) that a pure vowel (*ă*, *ĭ*, or *ŭ*) is not elided before *ādi*, but (ii) that in an *upapadasamāsa* any vowel immediately preceding the *upapada* is elided.

received and regarded it as it stood as the final authority on all questions and as being above the control of ordinary grammatical rules. Had they attempted to correct or restore the texts with the inadequate means available to them, Canonical Pali would have been irretrievably lost.

Previous Research on Pali Metre

§ 18. The treatises on metrics of the medieval writers on Pali expound the techniques of " classical " *kāvya* composition, and those which have so far been published do not add to the interpretations of Canonical usage given in the grammars. It is evident from the treatment of the texts by the Commentaries as edited (by Buddhaghosa, etc.) in the 5th century A.D., and from the poetic compositions in Pali made in Ceylon, that the old metrical techniques of the Moriyan period had already been lost and replaced by those of the classical literature. Reference to the Jaina tradition shows that there too the metrics of the Moriyan period had been forgotten by the beginning of our era. Both the Theravāda and Śvetāmbara Canons preserve corruptions accepted by the earliest extant commentaries which could easily have been rectified by anyone acquainted with their metrical usages, and it appears that this partial interruption of the traditions took place in about the 1st century B.C. In Ceylon, at least, this interruption may have coincided with a period of war and famine, which threatened the loss of the texts through the deaths or dispersal of the monks. As we have already mentioned, this resulted in the taking of emergency measures such as writing down the texts, and we may suppose that it was at that time that the old metrical tradition of the reciters was interrupted and ceased to preserve the texts from corruption—a task which was henceforth undertaken by writing. Writing was safer than the old technique in that manuscripts last longer than " repeaters " and were perhaps easier to make copies of, but the dead, de-rhythmized, written words and *pādas* could be mutilated by careless scribes, who copied with the eye only : the leaves on which they wrote, like the rain god, did not distinguish good from bad and preserved all forms alike.

§ 19. In order to restore the old metrics it is necessary to refer to other phases of development of Indian metre, since we are concerned with one stage of the single process of evolution from Vedic to the modern vernaculars. For this reason it might be better to describe our subject as " Early Middle Indian metre ", taking the Pali texts as a sample for analysis. Professor Helmer Smith has said (1950a, p. 2) : " Or, tandis que la belle époque de l'indianisme européen nous a légué une métrique védique (Oldenberg, Arnold), une sanskrite (dogmes de Piṅgala, élucidés par Jacobi et son école), une apabhraṃśa (*Prākṛtapaiṅgala*, *Chandonuśāsana* de Hemacandra, d'autres traités encore, vérifiés et mis au point par Jacobi et MM. Schubring et Alsdorf), seule la versification du moyen-indien ancien (techniques Bauddha et Śvetāmbara) n'a pas, sauf erreur, été jugée digne d'un traitement d'ensemble..."

Our task is to fill this lacuna between Vedic and Sanskrit metrics, taking Jacobi's well-known 1884 article as a starting point. Helmer Smith in his Index volume to the *Saddanīti* (1949) takes a more or less synchronic view of the canonical Pali metres, his terminology completed by that of the classical metres enumerated by the *Vuttodaya*, beside which he has since placed an analysis of the Buddhist Hybrid Sanskrit texts as a later stage (1950a, 16 ff.) and, which is most important, attempted to distinguish two phases, which he calls P′ and P″, in the development of Buddhist metrics. In the present study we take on the other hand a predominately diachronic view of the metres, tracing their historical development, which seems to offer the possibility of a better understanding of their interrelationships and of their actual rhythmical nature. The previous contributions to our subject and those related to it have been collected in the Bibliography and will be referred to as we proceed with the study. There are, however, certain general topics, and principles of methodology, which require discussion in this Introduction.

The Evolution of a Metre as the Key to the Relative Chronology of a Series of Texts

§ 20. In connection with the historical conclusions on the date of the Pali Canon given above, we may refer to the discussions of Oldenberg and others on the history of the *vatta* (*vaktra*)[1] metre (the " epic *śloka* ") and the position of the Pali *vatta* in relation to the *vatta* of various Vedic and Sanskrit texts. The details will be found at the beginning of Chapter VII, but the two important conclusions arrived at by Oldenberg should be stated here :—

(i) The Pali *vatta* is close in structure to that of the *Brāhmaṇas* and early *Upaniṣads*, and apparently a little later in date, whilst it appears to represent a stage a little earlier than that of the *Bṛhaddevatā* ; the chronological sequence is then continued by the *Mahābhārata* and afterwards by the *Rāmāyaṇa*.

(ii) The *vatta* of the *Aṭṭhaka* and *Pārāyana*, the last two *vaggas* of the *Suttanipāta*, appears older in structure than that of the *Jātaka*, *Theratherīgāthā* and *Dhammapada*.

§ 21. These conclusions are in harmony with our conclusions above, since the approximate dates generally accepted for these Sanskrit texts do not contradict our chronology for Pali. Macdonell places the *Bṛhaddevatā* in the 5th century B.C., which may be a little early, since it would suggest that the great majority of *vatta* texts in the Pali Canon were composed not later than about 400 B.C. Hopkins assigns the " main composition " of the *Mahābhārata* to the 2nd century B.C., whilst the *Rāmāyaṇa* in its present form probably represents a period having its " centre of gravity " not earlier than the 1st century B.C. (See Johnston's introduction to his translation of the *Buddhacarita*, xlvii ff., and S. Lévi : " Pour l'histoire du Rāmāyaṇa " in JA, 1918, p. 149.) The *Upaniṣads* are often associated with the early Buddhist period. In connection with the *Brāhmaṇas* we may support Oldenberg by pointing out the similarity between the laconic but repetitive prose styles of the *Śatapathabrāhmaṇa* and the *suttas* of the *Dīghanikāya*.

[1] After some hesitation, the Pali forms of the names of metres have normally been used, as most appropriate for a treatise entitled *Pali Metre*. The more familiar Sanskrit equivalents are given in brackets at the first mention and occasionally elsewhere, and in the Index. In the next section dealing with the works of various scholars on the Vedic and Sanskrit *triṣṭubh*, it seemed more natural to retain the Sanskrit forms of the names, and this has been done elsewhere when discussing Vedic or Sanskrit metres.

Our conclusions on the internal relationships of the Pali texts confirm Oldenberg's partial conclusion. We have already said something on this subject above, §§ 6–8, and more detailed results will be summarized at the end of this study.

The Nature of Indian Verse

§ 22. The discussions on the *triṣṭubh* have been much more extensive than those on the *anuṣṭubh*, but the results are much less satisfactory. The complex and baffling structure of the *triṣṭubh pāda* led to arguments about its nature already in the early days of European research on the metres, but the results are still unsatisfactory owing to the uncertainty as to the way in which the *pāda* evolved. As for the Pali *tuṭṭhubha* in particular, much less work has been done on it than on the Pali *vatta* and very few verses have been analysed. On account of the general vagueness prevailing about the *triṣṭubh* and the difficulty of understanding its evolution, it has been left to a later stage of this study and then taken up for analysis in comparison with the development of the other metres.

The *triṣṭubh* was selected—as if it were felt to be the most characteristic Indian metre—as the battlefield on which the theoretical principles of Indian metrics should be contested, so that in addition to the analysis of texts on a statistical basis we have long discussions, sometimes of a fanciful nature uncontrolled by reference to Indian criteria for the interpretation of the metre, on the theoretical rhythmical elements composing the *pāda*.

The " foot " is not in Indian (or in European) metrics a " division " of verse in the same sense as the *pāda* or strophe. The *yati* or caesura does not necessarily coincide with a boundary between two feet, or *gaṇas*, and word-endings are likewise independent of foot or *gaṇa* divisions. The foot or *gaṇa* can be only an abstraction intended to describe a unit (indivisible) of rhythm or a " measure " in the verse. Such a foot can be isolated in more than one way, but the usual convention, and the only really satisfactory one, is to find an " ictus " and make it the beginning of a foot, like the beat at the beginning of a bar in music. It will be shown below, however, that the " ictus " (in the European sense) is very far from being a universal feature of Indian verse, so that in the majority of metres the whole scheme of division into " feet " is left hanging in the air and can serve no purpose whatsoever. In the Indian *mātrāvṛttas* [1] (used in Pali, Sanskrit, Apabhraṃśa, Hindī, etc.) the *gaṇa* is a useful abstraction reflecting the rhythmic structure and bearing an " ictus " (*graha* or *sam*), but in the older metres, and particularly in the *triṣṭubh*, a different mode of description must be found.

§ 23. Kühnau's book, *Die Triṣṭubh-Jagatī-Familie* (Göttingen, 1886), is the bulkiest of all the contributions to the *triṣṭubh* debate, and since it marks a turning point in the development of the study of Indian metre, it will be convenient to begin with it. Kühnau's was the first attempt at a deep and thorough historical analysis, on scientific principles, of ancient Indian metrics, and his failure was the first step towards a proper understanding of Indian verse, since it exposed most thoroughly the misconceptions on which Westphal's (1860) pseudo-science of " comparative metrics " rested, with the result that no one afterwards attempted to apply it. Only in analysing the musical *gaṇacchandas* did Cappeller (*Die Gaṇachandas*, Leipzig, 1872) have some success with this " science ", since there the strophe is organized in *gaṇas*, or " feet ", as had long been recognized by the Indian theory itself.[2] It was not from the lack of an Aristoxenus, as Westphal thought,[3] that the Indians failed to find a universal principle of division into *thésis* and *ársis* in their metres : the Indian theoreticians were acute enough, and do not deserve reproach for not discovering something which evidently was not there. When the musical division, the *gaṇa*, did appear in certain metres, the Indian theory recognized it, and when the ictus itself (the *graha* of the musical theory and

[1] The term *mātrāvṛtta*, Pali *mattāvutta*, includes *mātrāchandas*, *gaṇacchandas*, *tālavṛtta*, etc.

[2] On Cappeller, see Chapter VI on *gaṇacchandas*.

[3] Rossbach and Westphal : *Metrik der griechischen Dramatiker und Lyriker*, volume II part 2 (1865), by Westphal : *Allgemeine Griechische Metrik*, p. 227. On the other hand Rossbach's principles for the study of ancient Greek metre, avoiding imposing preconceptions arising from modern (classical) European music, especially song, as expounded in his Introduction to Vol. I of their work (1854), seem excellent ; in the same way we should approach ancient Indian rhythms guided by ancient Indian ideas.

the *sam* of Hindī metrics) came to play an important part (with the development of the stress accent),[1] it too was recognized.

§ 24. The difficulty for European scholars trained in the school of Aristoxenus was to acquire a correct feeling for metres whose rhythm is engendered purely by the quantitative oppositions of the long and short syllables. The result of Oldenberg's efforts to correct or improve the ictus schemes of Kühnau was in the end to associate an ictus with every long syllable (1915, pp. 492–6 and 524–5 ; he is doubtful about the first syllable of *pādas*, but this in the older metres was anceps and could be "heavy" or "light").[2] This is the reductio ad absurdum. Oldenberg had studied the "Vienna Phonograms" obtained by Felber, and had half-discovered that the modern Indian recitation of Sanskrit verses was based on the simple opposition of longs and shorts, every long being "heavy".[3] To say that the "heavy" syllables carry an ictus is superfluous and misleading.

§ 25. In the case of the "semi-musical" *mātrāchandas* it is interesting to note that Kühnau's ictus scheme (1886, pp. 178–9 and 206) in fact coincides with that arising from the *gaṇa* division we have determined in our analysis of those metres (see Chapter V). Like Cappeller dealing with fully musical metres, he there had material before him which was governed by an ictus, probably of musical origin, and succeeded in the main in scanning it correctly. Unfortunately the scansions he applied (pp. 40–1) to some varieties of *mātrāchandas*—those we have called "syncopated": *pavattaka* (*pravṛttaka*), etc.—were entirely fanciful, and the "fruitfulness" (p. vi) which he attributed to this particular phase of his research led him far astray in his study of the *triṣṭubh*.

[1] See the section of Chapter III on the accent.

[2] It is appropriate here to refer to the Indian terminology of "heavy"—*garu* (*guru*)—and "light"—*lahu* (*laghu*)—for long and short syllables, which was probably associated with a feeling for a quasi-ictus similar to Oldenberg's.

[3] The recordings made recently by Pandit Kapīndra at the School of Oriental and African Studies, London, confirm this recitation, which probably derives from old tradition. In the *akṣaracchandases*, such as *upajāti* and *vaṃśasthā*, the rhythm springs from the metre, and is not derived from a *tāla* even in the musical renderings.

§ 26. Kühnau further raises the question of a hypothetical transition from " syllabic " to " quantitative " metrics in a proto-Vedic period. Vedic metre, however, is already fully " quantitative " in the sense of Westphal and Kühnau, since the rhythm is based on the opposition of short and long syllables. The transition we are in fact confronted with, but in the post-Vedic period, is the substitution ⏕ allowed within certain limits in all Pali metres, and generating *mātrāchandas* and ultimately *gaṇacchandas*, in which almost any long syllable may be resolved in this way. This transition is the central topic of the present study.

This introduction of a new form of variation of rhythm within the *pāda* was by no means a new departure in Indian metrics. On the contrary, it should be stated that such variation was an essential and characteristic feature of Indian versification at all periods, only the means to attain it having changed. Contrary to the belief of Kühnau, there was no fixed recurring ictus precisely in those ancient metres in which variation could be achieved only by the substitution of one short for one long syllable, and it was only in the later metres, where two shorts must alternate with one long, that the ictus could arise—the " beat " became regular and variation was realized in a new way: the system of " Taktgleichheit ", " equality of measures ", i.e. equivalence in length of the *gaṇas*, within which variations and cross rhythms could most effectively be introduced. In Classical Sanskrit, where except for the *vaktra* and the *āryā* all the metres have fixed syllabic schemes, variation is usually achieved by another method, the mixture, at strophe and at canto level, of a wide range of different metres.

§ 27. Oldenberg, criticizing Kühnau, rejected the " comparative metrics " theory based on Aristoxenus (" ...die Tatsachen des Veda auf das Prokrustesbett aristoxeneischer Theorie zu spannen... " 1915, p. 491).[1] As we have said, however, he retained the ictus with reservations (partly influenced by Fox Strangways—see e.g. 1914, p. 14), seeking better ways of scanning the *pādas* by dispensing with the *thésis—ársis* system.

[1] See also 1887, p. 196.

This compromise method of analysis—the ictus without a foot—did not in itself throw any fresh light on Indian versification, but in spite of it Oldenberg made substantial contributions to the historical understanding of both *triṣṭubh* and *anuṣṭubh* (see his articles 1896, 1909, 1915). His freedom from Aristoxenian preconceptions enabled him, despite the encumbrance of the ictus, to lay the foundations of the study of Vedic metre in his " Prolegomena " (vol. I of his edition of the *Ṛgveda*) published in 1888. Thus on p. 21 of that work he suggests that the rhythm might go " against the quantity " (sic), but nevertheless arrives at the fruitful conception of a normal or fundamental " rhythm " for each type of metre, from which variations have arisen. What we find is not : " rhythm against quantity," but : " variations of quantity = variations of rhythm." He is thus working in harmony with the fundamental Indian variation-technique we have just discussed, which we might call the *pathyā—vipulā* technique partly recognized by the Indian theory.

§ 28. Immediately after the " Prolegomena ", Zubatý's article " Der Bau der Triṣṭubh- und Jagatī-Zeile im Mahābhārata " was published in the ZDMG (1889). His criticism of Westphal—Kühnau, which had appeared in several articles from 1886 onwards (1886, 19 ff., 1888a, p. 185 ; 1888b, p. 56), goes further than Oldenberg's, since he gives up ictus schemes altogether except in so far as he occasionally uses ictus-marks (′) simply to show how he would recite a particular *pāda* (e.g. 1889, p. 645—it will be observed that this " ictus " again falls on all the long syllables).

Next we come to Arnold, who in his *Vedic Metre* (1905) uses methods very similar to and largely derived from those of Zubatý. He says of *anuṣṭubh* verse (p. 151) : " A division into feet of two syllables is not traceable in the Rigveda, and therefore the usual terms applied to the Greek and Latin classical metres are unsuitable. There is some practical convenience in speaking of an *ictus* which falls normally on the even syllables, but is transferred from the second to the third in the ' syncopated ' form : and also in speaking of the ' general iambic rhythm ' of the verse as a whole : but it must not be assumed that the ideas which these words connote were present to the Vedic poets." The " practical convenience " here is not very clear, and Arnold's very rare use of these terms in his book does not add anything to his exposition, moreover the danger he himself sees in reading in ideas foreign to the Vedic poets is one which must be avoided at all costs if we are to understand the poetry. Arnold goes on to say that the division into " members " of four syllables each " seems to be fully established ", and of course his whole study presupposes the ancient distinction of " dimeter " and " trimeter " verse. Such a division, with important variations from four syllables to three or five, certainly seems to be inherent in the structure of Vedic verse, but the basis and significance of this " Indian foot " have not been explained.

§ 29. Since the time of Oldenberg and Arnold the only important contributions to the analysis of the *triṣṭubh* have been those of Professor Edgerton, whose method is approximately that of Arnold, but without any discussion at all on the ideas of " ictus " or even of rhythm. This " schematic analysis ", as Kühnau would disparagingly have called it, is in fact quite adequate for the material concerned and leads to excellent results, especially since Edgerton improves on the traditional Indian theory—and on the valueless tables of Hopkins—by following the natural divisions and internal relationships of the *pāda*, and is thereby able to separate the different historical strata in the Epic *triṣṭubh*.

§ 30. The standpoint of the present work is more independent of the traditions of Greek scholars than these other contributions, or those of Helmer Smith, have been. There appears to be no reason to suppose that the Indian rhythms had any special resemblance to the rhythms of Greek metres. On the contrary the impression of the present writer is that those Western scholars with a Western Classical education who read, for example, (" Classical ") Sanskrit poetry according to the habits of scansion they acquired when studying Greek poetry, thereby destroy the beauty, the variety and especially the syncopations of the Indian rhythms. Indian scholars do not recite Sanskrit poetry in that manner. Their renderings encouraged the present writer to follow his inclination as a music lover (with more training in music, Western and Indian, than in Greek and Latin), fascinated by what appeared to him to be the musical rhythms of, in particular, the *akṣaracchandases* ("fixed syllabic" metres), to take the Sanskrit patterns in a strictly "measured" manner. Instead of reducing them to the regular feet of Greek metrics, through anceps, "drag" and the like, he thus realized an immense variety of different rhythms. If the scansion of all these *akṣaracchandases* should be limited to a few trochaic, dactylic, etc., patterns as in Greek, why are there so many of them in regular and carefully contrasted use? If the complex patterns of the *akṣaracchandases* are not fixed, what are they? As will be suggested below (Chapter IX), the *akṣaracchandases* appear mostly to be built out of particular rhythms (often of some length) which may occur in the clearly musical metres *gaṇacchandas* and (less often) *mātrāchandas*. If this is so, we should expect them to preserve the rhythmic values of their musical basis, with two short syllables exactly equal to one long (⏑⏑ = -), *l'égalité* as some call it. Every short has exactly half the value of a long and every long is a "true" long, with all that this implies by way of syncopations, not to be slurred over by looking for anceps. The whole line (*pāda*, quarter verse) becomes the rhythmic unit here, which repeats in the *samavṛttas*, not the "bar" (*gaṇa*, or pair of *gaṇas*) of the musical metres. The long, complex *pāda*-rhythm of an *akṣaracchandas* is fixed by its fixed pattern of long and short syllables, whereas the *gaṇa*-rhythm of *gaṇacchandas* is internally variable, only the total value of the bar being fixed. (One might suppose that a *gaṇacchandas* singer accompanied by a musical instrument would have been subject to the same principle which even today governs Indian musicians, as when a *vīṇā* and *mṛdaṅga* are played together: the two must coincide in rhythm on the beat (ictus, *graha*) at the beginning of each bar of their *tāla*, although within the bar they are free to go their own separate ways). The discussion of *akṣaracchandas* is not central to the present study, though of great interest for the reading of *kāvya* literature, arising only at the end of it. This brief note may serve, however, to underline the nature of the approach of the author to *gaṇacchandas* and *mātrāchandas* as well as *akṣaracchandas* : his original supposition, which seems justified by this study, that in the later Indian metres ⏑⏑ = - (exactly) and that the basis of rhythmic variation is ⏑⏑/-, contrasting with the ancient variation ⏑/- of the early metres (surviving in the *vaktra*).[1]

The Scope of this Study

§ 31. It is now possible to trace the general history of Indian metrics and to describe the transition from the old metres to the new musical rhythms, governed by the ictus, which led up to the medieval *tālavṛttas*. This is connected with the history of the language : the transition from Vedic, with its preponderance of long syllables and musical accent, to Apabhraṃśa, with its preponderance of short syllables and stress accent. In studying Pali metrics we shall be concerned with the crucial phase of this transition.

We must first attempt to clarify the metrical interpretation of the Pali texts : the relationship between the orthography of the manuscript tradition and the phonology of the Canonical language, the *sandhi* usages of the Canonical poets, *pāda*-building, the fluidity of the language in so far as it affects versification and the kinds of metrical licence current.

The study of the various classes of metre found in the Canon follows. *Mattāchandas* (*mātrāchandas*) and *gaṇacchandas* are taken first, in accordance with the aim of studying the metrical transition which begins in the Pali literature. They may be felt to have a special relationship with a dialect very close to that of their origin, and to exemplify the general poetic usages of the period in a higher degree than the other metres. The other metres, in fact, were found to be impossible of full understanding in their Pali phase without reference to *mattāchandas* (especially the *tuṭṭhubha*) and *gaṇacchandas* (especially the *vatta*). These two chapters contain the central discussions of this book. The solution of these problems is facilitated by

[1] The suggestion for elaborating this standpoint came from Dr. H. N. Randle in the course of an interesting correspondence with the author during the summer of 1955. *bhavati subhagatvam adhikaṃ vistāritaparaguṇasya sujanasya* | *vahati vikāsitakumudo dviguṇarucim himakaradyotaḥ* || Subandhoḥ ||

reference to Indian music, and it is hoped that this research will in turn throw light on some early phases in the history of the music. The chapters on the *vatta* and the *tuṭṭhubha* attempt to collect and interpret the previous work on these metres and to extend it to cover representative parts of the Canon and give greater precision to the descriptions and a better understanding of their evolution in the light of (i) a better understanding of their language, (ii) the results of the study of *mattāchandas* and *gaṇacchandas* and (iii) comparison with recent successful studies in Buddhist and Epic Sanskrit. The *akkharacchandases* (*akṣaracchandases*) appear first in the later parts of the Canon and find their natural place at the end of our study, where their affiliations to the other metres can be worked out. They are of great interest as products of the transition process and on account of the special rôle they play later in the "Classical" Sanskrit literature. "Classical" Sanskrit itself, as a kind of synthesis of the old and the new (Middle Indian in the garb of Old Indian, drawing its literary and metrical techniques from both), might be regarded as a special product of the transition period. In conclusion we review the results of the research from the point of view of the history of literature.

Chapter I

ORTHOGRAPHY AND PHONOLOGY

The Problems

§ 32. In order to scan Pali verses, it is first necessary to ascertain the relationship between the orthography of the manuscript tradition and the phonology of the original language of the Canonical texts.[1] The Commentaries and medieval grammars, the 3rd century B.C. inscriptions and the ancient phonetic science of the *Prātiśākhyas*,[2] comparison with the related phenomena in Vedic, Ardhamāgadhī, and Buddhist Sanskrit, all help to some extent in this task, but the decisive test in all cases arises from the metre itself. This is not a circular argument based on the mere probability of certain rhythms in the *pāda* : the cadence of the *vatta pādayuga* (" half-strophe ") in the period we are studying was invariably ⏑–⏑× and the cadence of the *tuṭṭhubha pāda* was invariably ⏑–(⏑)× (both inherited from the earlier metrics). By collecting examples of doubtful cases in these positions it is possible to discover their rhythmic values.

The main problems to be solved here are :

(i) whether *e* and *o* may be short in an open syllable ;

(ii) in words containing a *svarabhakti* [3] vowel (or a *yama*), this vowel frequently does not seem to count as a separate syllable : in each of these words the correct rhythm has to be ascertained ;

(iii) alternative forms, with assimilation of the consonant cluster concerned, existed for some of the words with *svarabhakti*, and the tradition may in some cases have

[1] cf. §§ 9–17 of the Introduction.

[2] cf. Dr. Allen's valuable work : *Phonetics in Ancient India*, London, 1953.

[3] Pali equivalents, **sarabhatti* and *yama*, do not seem to have existed, as the medieval grammarians apparently did not understand these phenomena : see Sd p. 621, § 69 for a statement that such alternatives as *cetiya/cetya* existed (in the orthography), with " loss of vowel ", but without any explanation. The *sarabhatti* form is regarded as normal, and the (rarer) alternative is classified as a case of *saralopa*.

substituted one form for the other (contraction of vowels may also be noted here, as a parallel phenomenon) ;

(iv) in a few words syncopated forms (with loss of a short vowel) existed, and again one form may have been substituted for another ;

(v) the process of *samprasāraṇa*,[1] or its absence, resulted in alternative possibilities in one or two words, with possible effect on the quantity of the preceding syllable ;

(vi) certain conjuncts sometimes do not make position.

Of these phenomena the most important are the second (*svarabhakti*) and the sixth (conjuncts not making position), which are of very frequent occurrence and are responsible for the majority of apparently non-scanning *pādas* in the Canon.

§ 33. It may be noted that almost all the phenomena of this type concern the semi-vowels (including the nasals), which historically and grammatically had given rise to alternations of vowel and consonant forms. No doubt our difficulties result from the uncertainty in representing these sounds in the early days of evolution of a script. The ambiguity of the semi-vowels, with their imperfect occlusion, confused the opposition of vowel and consonant and the demarcation of syllables (see Allen's discussion on the *Prātiśākhya* theories of *svarabhakti* and *yama*, 1953, pp. 73–8), and absolute clarity was not attained until the general practice of writing[2] had, by the artificial elimination of all fluidity, classified each phoneme of the language as unambiguously vowel or consonant, and assigned one letter to represent each phoneme. Furthermore, every syllable needed to be classified as either long or short. Evidently, the Pali tradition in the Canonical period, oral and written, had not attained such fixation. Our task is to infer as nearly as possible the correct, or the usual, pronunciation of

[1] This process also does not appear to have been studied by the medieval Pali grammarians.

[2] Or, in the Vedic tradition, an exact system of pronunciation worked out for ritual purposes which supplied an alphabetic fixation equivalent to a written system (again with a certain amount of distortion).

each word, and further to ascertain the extent of the fluidity which still existed.[1]

(i) *e* and *o*

§ 34. According to Aggavaṃsa (Sd p. 608, lines 19–21; cf. the 19th-century Burmese *Nissaya* on this passage quoted by Helmer Smith in the footnotes) *e* and *o* are normally short before a conjunct, e.g. *ĕttha, sĕyyo, ŏṭṭho, sŏtthi*. He also says (p. 614, lines 7–9) that *e* and *o* are not normally produced before a conjunct in *sandhi* (since they are long vowels), *i* and *u* being retained: *yass'indriyāni, lok'uttaraṃ*. On the other hand, he gives two examples in which he says they are long before a conjunct, both in *sandhi*: *cē tvaṃ, puttō ty āhaṃ*. Of course the syllables are long in any case (unless, cf. (vi), the conjuncts here do not make position), but these remarks and the existence of short *e* and *o* in Pali according to the tradition lead us to ask whether they may sometimes be short also in an open syllable, which would have serious repercussions on our metrical studies.

§ 35. On investigation we find indeed the word *gehe* in the *Petavatthu* (III 4.3) in such a position (*vatta* cadence: *natthi etaṃ mămā gĕhē*) that the first *e* is required to be short by the metre. The verses in which this example occurs are, however, somewhat confused and irregular, so that this exceptional case may be the result of corruption (*mamā* m.c. is allowed in Pali, but its conjunction here with *gĕhe* raises suspicions). A possible explanation, however, would be that since *e* stands here for a historically original *ṛ* (*gṛha*) it may be short, or that we should take the form *gaha*, which also exists in Pali (in compounds). In a survey of all the *vatta* cadences in the *Suttanipāta* for this study, *e* was found in open syllables long except for one case only: *mĕdassa* in verse 196 (restoring with Fausbøll: *sedassa* ⟨*ca*⟩ *medassa ca*). Here the Sanskrit equivalent also has *e*

[1] When in Ceylon and Burma Pali acquired an absolutely fixed system of phonology and writing, used by the medieval poets, this system was an artificial one sometimes differing from the Canonical usage, and reflecting the shortcomings of the old orthography. Thus *ācariya* in the Canon counts as three syllables, whilst in medieval verse it counts as four.

(*medaḥ* m. or *medas* n.), although the root is *mid* and a form **midassa* might have existed. The verse, however, is again not above suspicion, and moreover it belongs to a meditation on the foulness of the body very different in spirit from most of Sn, in which the attempt to include all the thirty-two constituents of the body (cf. Kh III) enumerated by contemporary medicine probably interested the versifier more than poetic style and metrical correctness.

We may conclude that *e* is regularly long in an open syllable.[1] *o* is too rare, except as a final, to permit such a test : as final it is in any case sometimes shortened m.c., as we shall see in Chapter IV. As finals, both *e* and *o* may be shortened m.c., in which case they are generally altered to *a*, *i*, or *u*.

(ii) *Svarabhakti*, *yama*, etc.

§ 36. Whereas original conjunct stops[2] were assimilated to each other in Pali, a semivowel, nasal or fricative was frequently retained in a conjunct with a stop or with another semivowel. This peculiarity, in opposition to the " true " consonants, resulted from the indeterminate nature of the presumed original " semi-vowels " (*sonantes*, meaning semi-vowels and nasals) in Indo-European, which were articulated as consonants or as vowels according to their context.[3] This distinction in pronunciation, essential for clarity in quantitative metrics, was not fully attained in the Indian languages in the period we are studying, and fluctuations took place, such as : Vedic *tuam* > Classical Sanskrit *tvam*. The indeterminate nature of these phonemes persisted in Pali (it could only be eliminated by artificial rules, as in Classical Sanskrit), to the effect that the same phoneme might be pronounced as a vowel

[1] Jacobi (1893b, p. 579) mentions *eva* " with short *e* " in Ardhamāgadhī, in explaining the presumed shift of the accent to the preceding word. Cf. Section (vi) below on *-eyy*.

[2] It may be noted that Aggavaṃsa, in opposition to the *Saddasattha* (= Sanskrit Grammar), states that in Pali the term *aphuṭṭha*, " non-occluded," is applied to the non-aspirate stops. The Sanskrit term *spṛṣṭa*, " occluded," applied to all the stops, has no equivalent in the Pali tradition.

[3] That *svarabhakti* was a tendency present already in the Indo-European stage of the languages, is suggested by Meillet (1903/1949, p. 117), who quotes Vedic : *d⟨u⟩vā́u*, *j⟨i⟩yā́*, and Greek : *bi⟨y⟩ós*.

or as a consonant in the same word on different occasions of utterance, and clearly there was a strong tendency for the phoneme to decompose into the vowel articulation followed or preceded by the consonant articulation. This decomposition was often reflected in the orthography, thus *tvaṃ* was sometimes written *tuvaṃ* (vowel + consonant) and **arhati* was written *arahati*, which doubtless represents a pronunciation **arṛhati* (consonant + vowel).

§ 37. This problem of the semivowels and nasals in conjuncts was investigated in the *Prātiśākhyas*,[1] which are perhaps contemporary with the Pali Canon (500 B.C.–150 B.C. according to Varma, *Critical Studies in the Phonetic Observations of Indian Grammarians*, Introduction). In the transition from semivowel to stop or fricative they found that contemporary speakers inserted a " fragment of vowel ", *svarabhakti*, equal in length to one-half, one-quarter or one-eighth of a short vowel in different cases, and in the transition from stop to nasal they found a similar fragment of nasality which they termed *yama*, regarding it as a nasalized " duplication " of the stop. Both these " prosodies " are reflected in the orthography of the Pali Canon, and even the variation in length of the *svarabhakti* seems to be reflected in the greater frequency of writing *r* + fricative (*-rah-*) with *svarabhakti* as compared with the other cases, such as *r* + semivowel (*-riy-*) and *r* + nasal (usually assimilated).[2]

§ 38. According to Dr. Allen, it appears that *svarabhakti* was limited in the *Prātiśākhya* theory to cases of *r* + consonant and *yama* to stop + nasal, to which we may add the case of fricative + nasal. In Pali we find similar *svarabhakti* vowels in the junctions of stop + semivowel (e.g. *kilesa*), *v* + semivowel (e.g. *viyākar-*), fricative + semivowel (e.g. *siyā*), and nasal + semivowel (e.g. *anveti* = ⏑⏑–⏑, Sn 1103), which we may group together as " consonant + semivowel " generally.

[1] Allen, 1953, pp. 73–8.

[2] As examples of *yama* we have: *paduma* (= **pad*$^{\tilde{a}}$*ma*), *sukhuma* (= **suk*$^{k\tilde{h}}$*ma*, or **sukh*$^{\tilde{v}}$*ma* ?—Allen, 1953, 3.123), *gini-* (= **g*$^{\tilde{o}}$*ni*), *supina* (= **sup*$^{\tilde{v}}$*na*). On Allen 3.123 cf. also Pali: *sineha* (= **s*^{t}*neha*).

We may say that in Pali any conjunct containing either a semivowel or a nasal (i.e. an original " semi-vowel ", *sonante*) is liable to this prosody, since any *semi-vowel is liable to decomposition. In the cases of nasal + consonant, however, the phenomenon appears in the form of the *niggahīta* (*anusvāra*), leading to metrical difficulties through the possibility of metrical shortening to *anunāsika* of the preceding vowel, which we have to consider in Chapter III.

§ 39. We now have to determine the extent to which, in Canonical Pali, this peculiar prosody of semivowels and nasals had given rise to additional syllables in some words, changing their metrical value. We find that there is no general rule, no invariable relationship between orthographic *svarabhakti* and metrical, or syllabic, *svarabhakti* : it is therefore necessary to study individual words so far as we can find them in positions where their metrical value is certain. We also find that in some cases the metrical value of a word varied, thus *ariya* is usually

— ˘ - ˘ ˘ ˘ ˘ ˘

ariya (*ar*^{i}*ya*), but sometimes *ariya* and occasionally even *ariya*. This may be due in part to dialectal variations within the Canon, but sometimes such variants appear within a single poem of apparently homogeneous composition. It must therefore be stated that certainty of scansion in all cases is not possible in Canonical Pali ; that the language was not completely fixed but, being not far removed from a living dialect, had a certain amount of fluidity.[1] Our statistical counts of *pāda* structures will therefore be approximate only in most cases, although it seems possible to reduce the uncertainty, on the average, to not more than about 1%. In this connection we note here, anticipating section (iii), that a number of words had alternative forms with *svarabhakti* or with assimilation, having different metrical values.

§ 40. After the partial interruption of the tradition in about 100 B.C., which we have discussed in the Introduction, it appears that the written language became the final authority on all questions. The current orthography was one which had

[1] See the Introduction and Chapter IV on the fluidity of the language.

been preserved with very little change from the 3rd century B.C. or earlier, as we see from comparison with the inscriptions, but, when the written Canon after the disasters of the 1st century B.C. became the sole authority (the oral tradition in so far as it was still maintained being no longer trusted, or rather being made dependent on the written texts), the written text came to be interpreted not according to the old usage but simply as it appeared to the unwary reader, every vowel indicated by the orthography being counted as the kernel of a separate syllable. In this way all the *svarabhakti* vowels shown by the written forms of the words acquired full syllabic value in the tradition, and in all the medieval poetry they must be scanned as separate syllables (some forms written with conjuncts were also current, such as *cetya, tulya, Sakya*).

§ 41. According to the present investigation of the words in positions where their metrical value is certain, in the following cases the *svarabhakti* group counted metrically as a conjunct (for comparison with AM see Pischel, 1900, § 131 and Jacobi, 1877, 594 ff. ; for comparison with BHS see Edgerton, 1953, *Grammar* pp. 29–30) :

brahmacar^{i}*ya* (Sn 267, 274, Dh 267, U 1.4, 8.6, J IV 33 ; AM has *bambhacera* beside the form in *-cariya*, evidently metrically equivalent).[1]
ācar^{i}*ya* (Bv II 19 ; *ācera* occurs in Pali, e.g. J IV 248 and J VI 563. *ācărĭyē* ? S I 178—corrupt verse)
dhammacar^{i}*ya* (Sn 263)
ekacar^{i}*ya* (Sn 821—a very interesting *pāda* ! Scan : *ekacariyaṃ daḷhaṃ kayirā*)
-car^{i}*ya* in any other compound (Sn 700, J IV 362, 422, 483)
kay^{i}*ra-* (Sn 728, 821, 844, 1051, Th II 61, S I 100, U 4.3, 7.9, Dh 117–8, 292, etc., J IV 218)
pay^{i}*rupāsati* (Dh 64–5, Th I 1236, 1238)
(the " metathesis " form *-y*^{i}*r-* is more definitely a conjunct in pronunciation than the normal form *-r*^{i}*y-/-riy-*)

[1] The reading at A II 68 = III 46 is uncertain but apparently should be plural : one would expect *brahmacārino*.

ir^{i}ya- (Sn 1063, 1097)
acchar^{i}ya (J IV 197 ; cf. *acchera*)
macchar^{i}ya (Sn 863 ; cf. *macchera*)
tur^{i}ya (Th II 139 ; AM has *tuḍiya*)
atitar^{i}ya (Sn 219)
anupar^{i}yagā (Sn 447, S I 124)
avakir^{i}yati (Pv p. 172 of Cy. Edn. ; see also CPD suggesting this metrical value in several examples)
antakir^{i}yāya (Sn 454, 725 ; AM : *kir^{i}ya*—Pischel, 1900, § 131)
par^{i}yā̆ya (Sn 581, 588, J IV 218, 426—where the correct reading was suggested by Fausbøll ; cf. *peyyāla*. The normal rhythm is evidently *par^{i}yăya* as in Epic Sanskrit)
par^{i}yanta (Sn 577)
par^{i}yesanaṃ (U 7.9)
gar^{a}ha- (Sn 313, 913, etc., the substantive, however, has the conjunct divided : *garahāya*, in Sn 141, where we also find the gerund with metathesis : *gārayha*. Note that *ar^{a}ha* usually has the conjunct, but with some exceptions : we should therefore not be surprised to find **garaha-* as the verb stem if enough examples could be found ; AM has *gar^{a}hio*, Pischel, 1900, § 131.)
r^{a}hada (Sn 467)
car^{a}ṇavā (Sn 533, 536)
(a)tul^{i}ya (Sn 85 ; usually written *tulya*)
cet^{i}ya (Dh 188)

§ 42. In the following cases the *svarabhakti* counts as a separate syllable :

⏑– ⏑ ⏑
viyañjana (S I p. 38 ; often spelt *vyañjana*, e.g. Sn 1017 ; some other words beginning with *vy* similar—J IV 227, 371, etc.)
viyākar- (Sn 513 in *opacchandasaka* cadence, 1052, 1075, Bv IX 13, J IV 116)
viya (otherwise *(i)va*) (Dh 334, Bv XVIII 27)
siyā (Sn 716, 944, Dh 160, 206, 218, 231–3, 302, 305, 376, U 6.2, J IV 156, 435, Th I 585, 982, etc.)
siyuṃ (U 7.9)
kilesa (Sn 348)

supina (otherwise *soppa*) (J IV 84)
gini (Sn 18–19 ; AM has *ag*^{a}*ṇi*, Pischel, 1900, § 131)
veluriya (Vv VII 7, J IV 352 = 404, Pv II 7.5)
(·)

⏑ ⏑ –
havyaṃ (Sn 463 ff. refrain = 490 ff. ; not in the cadence, but the rhythm seems certain)

⏑ – – –
vyakkhissaṃ (Sn 600)

⏑ – – –
vyākhyātā (Sn 1000)
ātumānaṃ (when so written) (Sn 782)
pāpuṇāti (Sn 324) (otherwise *pappoti*, A III 40)

§ 43. In the following cases the metrical value is variable or uncertain :

ariya
- *ar'ya* (Sn 230, 330, 353, J IV 292 ; many more cases could be added, in the light of Chapters VII and VIII, when the word is initial in the *pāda*)
- – ⏑ ⏑ *ariya* (Sn 535, Dh 236, Th I 959) (⏑ ⏑ ⏑ *ariya* appears only in Medieval Pali)

anariya
- *anar'ya* (Sn 664 in *vegavatī* cadence)
- ⏑ – ⏑ ⏑ *anariya* (Sn 815, J IV 178 ; perhaps under the influence of the " law " of de Saussure, this rhythm seems to be commoner than the alternative, whereas in the positive *ar'ya* is commoner)

viriya
- *vir'ya* (Sn 68, 184, 353, 422, 528, J IV 357, Th II 161, Th I 818)
- – ⏑ ⏑ *viriya* (Dh 7, 8, 112, 144, Th I 962 ; AM writes *vīriya*)

kariya- *akāriyaṃ* (Dh 176)

⏑ ⏑ ⏑
carahi (Sn 988, 990 ?, 999)

araha-	usually *ar*^{a}*ha-* (Sn 765, etc., Dh 9, 10, 230, S I 129, J IV 192 twice, Th I 500, 969 ff.) ⏑ ⏑ ⏑ – *arahataṃ* (*Na-vipula* : Sn 186) ⏑ ⏑ ⏑ – *arahato* (Sn 590—late ?) ⏑ ⏑ – – *arahantaṃ* (Sn 644—very late ?) ⏑ ⏑ ⏑ *araha-* (also S I p. 51) (AM has *ar*^{i}*ha-*, Pischel, 1900, § 131)
bhariya	normally *bhar*^{i}*ya* (J IV 319, 422, 428, 461, probably Sn 290) sometimes *bhariya* (Th II 225)
sineha	*sineha* (Sn 66, 209, S I 134) *s*^{i}*neha* (J I 190 line 6, Sn 36 not making position)
n(a)hātaka	(Sn 518 and 521, in *opacchandasaka*, apparently *nhātako* not making position)
nahāru	(may be *n*^{a}*hāru* not making position at Sn 194)
paduma	*pad*^{u}*ma* (Sn 71) *paduma* (Vv VII 7), *padumī* (Sn 53)
suriya, "sun" (cf. *sūriya*, "valour")	*sur*^{i}*ya* (Th II 87, Sn 687, S I 51 line 5, J IV 139, 338–9) *suriya* = –⏑⏑ meaning "sun" (S I 51 line 3, line 6, J IV 61 line 8) *suriya* = ⏑⏑⏑ (Bv XVIII 27)
dve, duve	usually pronounced as written (Sn 48, 896, A III 346 = Th I 693)
sve, suve	probably also as written (e.g. Dh 229)
hirī	(Sn 77, 253, 719)
sirī-	*s*^{i}*rīmato* (Vv VII v. 22) ⏑ ⏑ *siri-* (Sn 686)
tvaṃ *tuvaṃ*	usually as written (Th II 237–8, etc.), but there are ⏑ – several exceptions : *tvaṃ* (Sn 508, 833, J IV 48 line 6)

˘ ˘-˘
anveti (Sn 1103)
issariya apparently -˘˘- at Sn 112 and U 18
pasāriyaṃ ˘-˘- at J IV 371

kadariya { *kadar*[i]*ya* (Dh 177, Pv II 7.7)
{ *kadarīya* ?? (Sn 133, 362) (or *kadāriyă* ?)

hadaya { *had*[a]*ya* ? (Sn 938 d = Th II 52 b, J IV 419, 420)
(may be for *hṛdi* > **hadi*)
{ *hadaya* (J IV 127 line 18, 296 line 12)
paṭh[a]*vī* ? (Sn 307)
paṭhavī (Sn 1097, Dh 41)
car[a]*to* ? (Sn 823)

§ 44. Other words liable to *svarabhakti* seem usually to be pronounced as written (except words beginning with *vy*).

It is possible that both dialectal variants and historical variants exist within the Canon in some of these cases (e.g. *araha-* ?). The lists could be considerably extended and further clarified by a complete survey of the Canon, and knowledge of the metres will reciprocally increase our knowledge of the pronunciation of words of this type, but the above collection is sufficient for our present purpose of studying the metres.

§ 45. Whilst it cannot be asserted that in every single case in Canonical verse these pronunciations must be restored, they nevertheless make metrically comprehensible many hundreds of *pādas* which otherwise would be inexplicable. Adopting Arnold's principle of admitting simple devices of interpretation which convert mere prose into verse on a large scale (1905, p. 8, §§ 8 and 9), we may believe, despite the many corruptions in our texts, that it is possible to discover the original system of metrics by thus reducing the area of uncertainty to very much smaller proportions than before, and that eventually it will be possible to make satisfactory editions of the verse parts of the Canon.

(iii) Assimilation and Contraction

§ 46. Sometimes we may restore a reading which agrees with

the metre by substituting a form with assimilation for one with *svarabhakti*, one with contraction for an extended form such as -*aya*-, or vice versa. In some such cases the change is illusory, however, as in *ar^{i}ya/ayya*, *ācar^{i}ya/ācera*, except in medieval Pali (cf. the preceding section, §§ 39 ff.). In some cases the unassimilated conjunct exists alongside the *svarabhakti* form. Examples of *svarabhakti*/assimilation :

rājin-	*raññ-*
supina	*soppa*
gini	*aggi*
mātiya	*macca*
Kātiyāna	*Kaccāna* (and *Kaccāyana*)
kāviya (and *kāveyya*)	*kabba* (and *kabya*, *kavya*)
tikhiṇa	*tikkha*
kasira	*kiccha*
suva-	*sa-* (*ssa-*)

Examples of *svarabhakti*/conjunct :

Sākiya	*Sakya*
(most others are metrically equivalent : *tul^{i}ya*, etc.)	
tasiṇā	*taṇhā* (partial assimilation)
also *pāpuṇāti/pappoti* (m.c. at A III 40)	

The following forms are liable to contraction as shown. Several have appeared already as *svarabhakti*, which is a closely related phenomenon :

aya/e (especially causatives)
aya/ā
ayi/e (including *ācar^{i}ya* > **ācay^{i}ra* > *ācera* where no metrical change occurs)
iya/ī
iya/e
āya/ā
āyi/e
āyi/ī
oya/o
ayū/o

uri/o (*purisa/posa*: confusion quite common in the Canon)
ava/o
avi/e
āva/o
avā/ā
upa/ū
apo/o

(iv) Syncopation (and Haplology)

§ 47. A few unimportant alternatives appear in this category:

sarasara/sassara
bharabhara/babbhara
ciṭiciṭāyati/cicciṭāyati (cf. the confusion in Th II 24, where the possible original *cicciṭi cicciṭī ti* preserved in some Sinhalese manuscripts (not noted by Pischel) has become corrupted into *vicchindantī* ⟨⏑⟩, the reading printed by Pischel. This is an example of the most difficult problems confronting the editor of a Pali text: the metre may be *gīti* (first case) or *uggīti*: the preceding strophe, although even more corrupt, suggests the former.)
khalu/kho
udaka/oka (cf. Th II 236–245) (?—from Geiger. But there is of course *uda*.)
-mahe/-mhe

—haplology:
gacchissasi/gacchisi (?) (Th II)
sossasi/sossi (J)
pavisissāmi/pavissāmi
viññāṇānañcāyatana/viññāṇañcāyatana

(v) *Samprasāraṇa*, etc.

§ 48. In connection with *svarabhakti* on the one hand and with conjuncts not making position on the other, the phenomenon of *samprasāraṇa* has to be borne in mind when dealing with certain cases. We commonly find *vīti-* for *vyati-*, for instance, which we presume have different metrical values. Now, in the cases we noted above, under *svarabhakti*, of words beginning with *vy*, we found the possible rhythms: *vyākkhissaṃ* (cf. *viyākar-*) and ˘*vyāhariṃ*. In the second case, and in others like it, we appear to find a conjunct not making position (cf. the next section), but it is also possible that originally there was *samprasāraṇa* here too: **vīhariṃ*.

The alternation *dvi/du*, with possible effect on the quantity of the preceding syllable, may be noted here.

(vi) Conjuncts not making position

§ 49. Certain conjuncts in Pali appear sometimes not to make position. These are: *br, vy, nh, sn, tv, dv*, and possibly *yy* and others with *-y*. *ḷh* is not a conjunct.

br is the most important of these, and together with *vy, tv* and *dv* it was studied by some of the 19th-century writers on Pali, in particular by Simon, 1890, pp. 94–5. Conjuncts with *-r* sometimes fail to make position in the Epics [1] and even in Classical Sanskrit. These cases, however, belong to a discussion on metrical licence rather than here, although in Buddhist Hybrid Sanskrit and probably to some extent in the Epics we are concerned with an archaizing or Sanskritizing orthography which misrepresents the original pronunciation. In Pali (where *br* is the only representative of this class [2]) as in BHS the phenomenon is a regular feature of the language, belonging to the discussion on phonology and orthography, and does not appear sporadically as licence (based apparently on a vague recollection of old pronunciations).

Simon found that *br* made position in *brahā, brahmā, bravīti*, and *brūheti*, and derivations and combinations of the latter,

[1] Note also in the *Kaṭhopaniṣad*, I 25d: *mā 'nuprākṣīḥ* as *triṣṭubh* cadence, and in the *Śvetāśvataropaniṣad*, II 15a: *yad ātmatattvena tu brahmatattvam*, where the 7th syllable could be long but very likely is short, making a regular *upajāti*.

[2] The others are represented by assimilated conjuncts which are further simplified in most cases when initial (e.g. *pr* > *pp* > *p*). As a rule they make position medially and in the seams of compounds, but initially, and sporadically in seams, the single consonant appears. This conforms to the rule in MI that only a single consonant can appear initially, but in close union with the preceding word, and especially in compound with it, the doubled consonant may reappear.

except *anŭbrūhaye.* He also found that *brāhmaṇa* did not lengthen the syllable which preceded it. In this latter case he suggested reading *baṃhana, baṃbhana* or *baṃhmana* as in the Asokan inscriptions at Khālsi, Dhauli and Girnar.

This suggestion is probably correct, in view of the abnormality of a conjunct appearing initially in Pali, and one may add that the " restoration " of *br* here may well have resulted from the tendency to archaize in the early stages of the tradition (discussed already in the Introduction). According to Bloch (1950) the forms *bāmhaṇa, bhaṃbhana, bābhana, baṃbhana, bamhaṇa, baṃhmana* occur in the Eastern, Central, Western and Southern inscriptions, *bramaṇa* [1] is restricted to the extreme North-West, but *brāmhaṇa* and *bramhaṇa* occur once each at Girnar (pp. 98–9), which thus again shows a specially close connection with Pali. Girnar, however, fairly frequently preserves *r* in *pr, tr* (sometimes found in Pali : *tatra,* etc.), and *sr.*

In connection with the other words quoted by Simon, it has been found in the collections made for this study that *br* regularly does not make position in *anubrūhaye* and *brūhi.*[2] Elsewhere, as in *subraha* [3] and in *abravi, abravuṃ* [4] from the same root *brū* as before, *br* regularly makes position.

§ 50. *vy, nh, sn.* These conjuncts liable to *svarabhakti* sometimes fail to make position, as if in *svarabhakti,* even when there is no *svarabhakti.* The case of *că nhātako* Sn 518 is doubtful, since there is a reading *ca nahātako* which we could adopt by omitting *ca.* In *bhavantĭ snehā* Sn 36, however, there seems to be no alternative (*nh* being originally *sn* might be expected to have the same metrical value). Note that *sineha* occurs in the very same poem, *Khaggavisāṇasutta,* Sn 66. We have discussed *vy* in the sections on *svarabhakti* and *samprasāraṇa.* Here we may add the examples of conjunct not making position : *sŭvyāvato* J III 315, *khīṇăvyappatho* Sn 158–9 (there

[1] Once : *bamaṇa* ; once : *braṃana*—misprint ?
[2] e.g. J IV 459.
[3] e.g. J IV 111.
[4] Both in Sn (430, etc.), J and Bv.

are, however, many variants here: this one was adopted by Andersen and Smith, but without any certainty, and the interpretation of the whole compound is very doubtful—see PED s.v.).

§ 51. *tv* and *dv* very rarely do not make position. Simon gives J II 178 d,[1] J III 81 a and J IV 62 b and no further examples have been found. In the words *t*[u]*vaṃ* and *d*[u]*ve* these conjuncts are liable to *svarabhakti*, and they may therefore be compared with the preceding group.

§ 52. Aggavaṃsa gives a rule (Sd pp. 614–5, § 41) that long *ā* may be formed in *sandhi* before the conjuncts *yy*, *ññ*, *ggh* and *ss* in certain words. In all the cases he gives the conjunct stands for an original consonant + *y*, which suggests that position was not strongly felt before such conjuncts, even after assimilation. Compare with this his rule referred to in the section on *e* and *o*, where these vowels may be "long" before *tv* (see above) and *ty*. In other connections we find the position of *yy* felt to be weak, and perhaps *īy* > *iyy* > *eyy* (Geiger, 1916, § 10) illustrates this.[2] Occasionally it may seem desirable to scan *ĕyy* instead of the normal *ēyy*, but usually some alternative form may be substituted. Thus in M I, p. 386 line 21, we might scan
-| ˘ ˘ -| ˘ ˘ -| ˘
-assa veyyākaraṇassa, but here *vyāk-* might be substituted,
| - -|
scanning *-avyā*,[3] whilst the metre (*gīti*) seems normally to insist
| ˘ — ˘ |
on | ˘--˘ | here, i.e. *-a veyyak* with metrical shortening. In Sn 152 we find the variants *vinaya/vineyya* together with *-seyyaṃ* in a verse which is very difficult to scan satisfactorily. On the whole, after spending considerable time on these *gaṇacchandas* verses, and still more time on those of the *Tuvaṭakasutta* (Sn 915–34), the present writer thinks we have in fact to accept *-ĕyy* in most cases, but it appears that the

[1] His references are to *nipātas* and verses, not volumes and pages.

[2] Examples such as *padīpeyya* > *padīpiya* (PED, s.v.) can be found in later texts (Vv and medieval literature: the Vv example here is in a *vatta* cadence and may be presumed to be metri causa).

[3] cf. AM *vāgaraṇa*.

doubtful pronunciation of this syllable may have been partly responsible for the corruption and uncertainty in the tradition preserving these texts. Both here and in the case of *e* generally (cf. section (i) above) it seems that in the original texts *e* was invariably long, although when final it might alternate with *ĭ* for metrical convenience (even this is quite rare in Pali: see Chapter IV; such forms as *ramāmasĕ* (middle) are almost certainly mere archaisms for original *-i*).[1] In the context of Prakrit dialects developing a regular *ĕ* beside *ē*, however, the Pali tradition wavered at times, and its guardians who spoke such dialects were liable to introduce *ĕ* into the Canon.

The orthography *ḷh* does not represent a conjunct, but aspirated *ḷ* in place of *ḍh*. Evidently lacking a letter *ḷh* the scribes wrote the digraph *ḷ* + *h*. As in the word *dăḷha* (Sn 228, 357, 701, Th I 764, etc.), it does not make position, which is perhaps shown also by the possibility of writing a long vowel in front of it, as in *rūḷha*, *mūḷha*, etc.

It may be noted here that in Pali *ch* need not make position (in Sanskrit it invariably makes position and is consequently written *cch*); examples: Sn 42, 387, etc. *cch* is, however, much commoner.

[1] However, the Girnar inscriptions of Asoka show a fair number of middle forms whereas the inscriptions elsewhere have very few (Katre: *Historical Linguistics in Indo-Aryan*, Bombay, 1944, pp. 89–90). Such forms may therefore be a dialectal feature of Girnar (and Āvantī generally ?) and Pali (or some phase of Pali), the affinity between which has been noted in our Introduction above (§ 9).

Chapter II
SANDHI

§ 53. A detailed study of *sandhi* in Pali would not yield any very definite criteria for textual criticism, since clearly the usage was very fluid—in almost every case alternatives existed either of which might be used at will by the poets. Some account of Pali *sandhi* going beyond the incomplete or vague statements of the modern grammars is of interest here, however, in order to give a rough idea of the usage within which we may consider emending particular cases of orthography which seems unmetrical.[1] This can conveniently be taken from the twentieth chapter of Aggavaṃsa's *Saddanīti*, which is based on a very thorough study of the Canonical texts. Any correction or limitation of these statements of the usage in the Canon, such as that a certain combination was preferred by the poets in the great majority of cases, can come only if and when we succeed, through a knowledge of the metres, in restoring the original texts as a sound basis for a statistical analysis of *sandhi*. Only occasionally can we add a point of detail from forms in the cadence of a *vatta pāda* or elsewhere where we are certain of the rhythm and of the text.[2] We should also consider the " new *sandhi* rule " deduced by Jacobi on statistical grounds (1912–3, 211 ff.).

Sandhi in Pali was evidently very simple and natural, as in a living language. (cf. Mayrhofer, 1951, I, p. 72.) The existence of alternatives freely substituted for one another resulted in the tradition being careless of *sandhi*, and very frequently it seems necessary to alter our texts in order to restore the rhythm.

§ 54. Aggavaṃsa considers the whole field of phonology under the heading of *sandhi* (we have already had occasion to refer

[1] With the account based on Aggavaṃsa given in this Chapter, together with some historical discussion, we can now compare the account of the prevailing usages in Canonical prose, based on the *Dīgha*, in our *Introduction to Pali* (London, PTS, 1963, pp. 213–8, also 73, 166, 255, 269, 336, 353, 370–2).

[2] Thus a consideration of Sn 352a and 790d suggests that *tava-y-idaṃ* and *na-y-idha* should be pronounced *tavedaṃ* and *nedha*.

to some of his statements on phonology), and his discussion leads up to the question of metrical licence, which we shall take up in Chapter IV. He begins by stressing the fundamental importance of *sandhi*, which he likens to the salt in a curry, and then sets out the alphabet and describes the manner of production of the various sounds (*sadda* > *vaṇṇa* > *akkhara* ≏ sound > phoneme > letter). Short and long syllables are defined, and one consonant reckoned at half a short syllable in length.[1] Consonants (*vyañjana*) are " dependent on " (*nissaya*) vowels (*sara* = *svara*) (cf. Allen, p. 80—same doctrine), but in turn " protect " or " cover " (*paṭicchādeti*) them.

§ 55. *Sandhi* in the narrower sense is then analysed into the following ten elements or " instruments " (*upakaraṇa*) :

{ *pubba* (the phoneme which precedes)
{ *para* (the phoneme which follows)

lopa (elision)

āgama (transition phoneme, which replaces one elided, or is inserted in addition)

saññoga (conjunct)

cf. the " two fundamental rules " below {
viyoga (the separation from its following vowel of the " dependent " consonant before making *sandhi*)
paranayana (the guiding of a consonant by the phoneme which follows it)

vipariyāya (metathesis, = *viparīta* of NŚ quoted by Allen, p. 77, f.n. 9. Not the same as *viparyaya* of the *Atharva Prātiśākhya*, Allen, p. 74, f.n. 2, meaning " more back ")

{ *vikāra* (modification by union with another phoneme)
{ *viparīta* (change into another vowel or consonant without such union)

[1] As in the Vedic tradition—see Allen, 1953, p. 84. This " natural " length must be carefully distinguished from metrical length : the terms for the former are *rassa* (*hrasva*) and *dīgha* (*dīrgha*) (Sd p. 605), those for the latter are *lahu* (*laghu*) and *garu* (*guru*) (Sd p. 632).

To these might be added the following, which perhaps are intended to be deduced from them :

ādesa (substitution—cf. *lopa* : these two terms are frequently mentioned together as typical *sandhi* processes.—
ādesa = *lopa* + *āgama*)
nimitta (the cause : the phoneme which determines the application of one of the ten elements or instruments)
sabhāgatta (assimilation, = *saññoga* + *vikāra*)
dvitta (doubling—by *vikāra*, as in *ās* > *ass*)
visaññoga (simplifying)
ṭhānantaragati (displacement : the transfer of nasalization from one syllable to another [1])

§ 56. Some general definitions are given :

The four kinds of discourse :

gajja (prose),
pajja (verse),
geyya (mixed),
kaccha (commentary) ;

The three (or four) classes of *sandhi* :

vowel *sandhi*,
consonant *sandhi*,
mixed or general *sandhi* (including euphony, stress of metre, etc.),
(*niggahīta sandhi*—otherwise included in the preceding class)

(Aggavaṃsa selects the threefold classification) ;

The purposes of *sandhi*, defined as *sampatti* (" success ", " happiness ") in sound, meaning, metre, and in *alaṅkāra* (figures of speech, or poetics generally), which (*sampatti*) is " delightful " (*manorama*) ; as the protection of metre, in verse ; and as " euphony " (*sukhuccāraṇa*, " ease of pronunciation ") in other kinds of discourse ;

[1] Only one case of this exceptional phenomenon is given : *iṃsu* > *isuṃ*, which is regarded as *sandhi* because the form regarded as normal is changed under stress of metre in the examples quoted. Sd p. 635.

The dichotomy into external (*pada*) and internal (*vaṇṇa*) *sandhi*.[1]

Before setting forth the individual rules according to the threefold classification Aggavaṃsa lays down two fundamental general rules :

1. In order to make *sandhi*, the (following) protected vowel must be separated from its (preceding) dependent consonant, so that the vowel may be determined by another phoneme which follows it (*viyoga*).
2. When *sandhi* is made, a consonant is guided (determined) by the phoneme which follows it (*paranayana*).

—in other words the syllable is split into its component elements, consonant(s) + vowel, before *sandhi* can take place (it takes place at the level of phonemes, not of syllables), and *sandhi* is " progressive ".

Vowel Sandhi

§ 57. This is defined as the " substitution or elision of vowels ". Aggavaṃsa examines the sixty-four possible cases of the collision of vowels : elision of the preceding (*pubba*) vowel is the commonest result. Where the vowels are dissimilar the following (*para*) vowel may instead, but only exceptionally, be elided (the only regular cases of this are the loss of initial vowel in *iti*, *idāni*, *iva*, etc., where it is perhaps more correct to say that *ti*, etc., were in Pali independent words freely used, whilst the full forms were in fact rare survivals of older forms gradually dying out ; the rule of lengthening a final vowel preceding *ti*, however, could be cited, in support of Aggavaṃsa, to show that the older form was still alive behind the new and that the new could be regarded as merely a *sandhi* form of the old).[2]

[1] In this chapter we need not concern ourselves in detail with internal *sandhi*. Aggavaṃsa, deriving the forms synchronically from Pali roots, lists the apparently irregular cases found in " internal *sandhi* ", together with dialectal curiosities, after the more regular combinations of external *sandhi*. We may ignore those rules here, since in a historical study they belong to the discussion of phonology and in particular to the evolution of Pali out of " Old Indian ".

[2] Very exceptionally a similar following vowel may be elided after the prefix *pa*- (very doubtful : the only cases given are from the Commentary on the *Jātaka*, not from the Canon).

§ 58. When the preceding vowel is elided, the following vowel " may " (not " must ") be lengthened, except before a conjunct. Sometimes when a preceding *ā̆* is elided a following *i* or *u* becomes *e* or *o*, but *iva* never becomes *eva*, *iti* never becomes *eti*, and *o* is never elided before *iti*. In certain exceptional cases long *ā* may be produced before a conjunct :

-*na* -*mā* -*dā* -*vā* -*smā* -*tra* -*ṇhā* -*tvā*	+	*ayya* *añña* *aggha* *assu* *assa*	> > > > >	-*āyya* -*āñña* -*āggha* -*āssu* -*āssa*

—this might be given as evidence that these conjuncts with, or (historically) originally with, *y* as second consonant were not strongly felt to make position (cf. the discussion in Chapter I, section vi). We also find, however :

sa + { *anta* > *sānta* ; *attha* > *sāttha* }

§ 59. Sometimes :

e > *y*
o > *v*
u > *v*
ti > *cc* (not before *ī*)
i > *y*
ā + *eva* > *ariva*
g appears as " transition phoneme " after *putha*, *pā* (> *pǎg*), when a vowel follows
bhi > *bbh*
dhi > *jjh* (not before *ī*)

The " *sandhi* consonants ", *y*, *v*, *m*, *d*, *n*, *t*, *r*, *ḷ*, *h*, are used as transition phonemes.

Before consonants, vowels normally retain their original forms.

Consonant Sandhi

§ 60. " The substitution or elision of consonants." In Pali this is limited to the behaviour of the consonant in the case of vowel + consonant, together with a few complications when a vowel becomes a consonant. Aggavaṃsa here gives a long list of sporadic consonant changes, most of which, as we have said, belong to the wider field of phonology or to internal *sandhi*. Thus he considers the case : when three consonants come together in a conjunct, one of them (one of the same *vagga* as one of the other two in preference to one of a different *vagga*) is usually elided ; exceptionally a cluster of three stands, e.g. *tthy*.

The most important rule in this section is that after a vowel a consonant may be doubled. In fact in the Canon this is limited to cases where a historically original initial conjunct has been simplified, but where in close union with the preceding word or, more especially, in compound with it, the original (metrical) value of the conjunct is restored. Although he gives correct examples of this Aggavaṃsa apparently was not aware of the reason for it, or rather we should point out that he could not admit the possibility of the historical formation of Pali, which for him was the " original language ". In the same way he notes, without explanation, that after the prefixes *u*, *du*, *ni*, a consonant may be doubled. In this way the historically original metrical value was again restored, which resulted from these prefixes being originally " closed syllables " : *ud*, *dur*, *nir*, forming conjuncts with following consonants.[1]

A similar phenomenon is the restoration or preservation of original rhythmic values by vowel lengthening before a consonant, as in *samma* > *sammā* (for historically original *samyak*).

§ 61. Both these processes are important from the point of view of the study of metre, since by analogy doubling of an initial consonant or lengthening of a final vowel were occasionally produced by stress of metre where there was no historical justification. These cases, together with the shortening of a final vowel, which Aggavaṃsa also notes here,

[1] cf. the case *m* + *p* > *pp* in *cirappavāsiṃ* and *hatthippabhinnaṃ*.

will be considered in Chapter IV. (Aggavaṃsa himself notes that many of the cases discussed here and under "mixed *sandhi*"—to which he adds some of the historical forms—were produced by stress of metre.) We must mention here, however, that *sa* (and *esa*) occurs quite regularly in Canonical verse as opposed to the regular prose form *so*, especially when followed by a consonant (as Aggavaṃsa observes, but further on, § 187, he argues that these cases of *o/a* are not, strictly speaking, *sandhi*), historically original *visarga* before surds being lost without compensation, and the resulting form being gradually extended in use to cases where a sonant or even a vowel follows.

§ 62. In this section Aggavaṃsa also gives the following:

dy > *jj* in *yajj evaṃ*;
ti (*ty*) > *cc* in *jāti-*;
adhi > *ajjha* (only doubtful cases derived from *ajjhāvasati*);
adhi + √*bhū* > *addhabhūto*, *addhabhavati*, etc.;
evaṃ viya kho > *evaṃ vyā kho* (and several other cases of loss of a *svarabhakti* vowel);
putha + consonant > *puthu* + consonant;
o appearing as "transition phoneme"[1] before a consonant, as in *parosahassaṃ*, *sarado sataṃ*, *pago-*, *pāto-*;
neuters *taṃ*, etc. > *ta*(*d*)(*a*), etc., in verse.

Mixed Sandhi

§ 63. This includes everything which could not easily or conveniently be described under the other two headings, and especially the substitution or elision of *niggahīta*. Further, it includes *vuttasandhi*, defined as the protection of the number and quantity of syllables in verse and as euphony in prose, which is attained by means of elision, transition phonemes, etc.

Vuttasandhi belongs to Chapter IV. The *sandhi* of *niggahīta* is as follows:

§ 64. Sometimes:

ṃ > *ṅ*, *ñ*, etc., before *k*, *c*, etc.;
ṃ + *l* > *ll*;

[1] We are again concerned with historical "survivals" here (e.g. *sarado* acc. plur. on the consonant stem).

$$\text{ṃ} + \left\{\begin{array}{l} e \\ h \end{array}\right. > \text{ñ} + \left\{\begin{array}{l} e \\ h \end{array}\right. \text{as in} \left\{\begin{array}{l} \textit{taṃ eva} > \textit{tañ ñeva}\text{ [1]} \\ \textit{evaṃ hi} > \textit{evañ hi} \end{array}\right. ;$$

$$\text{ṃ} + y > \text{ññ} ;$$

Usually :

$$\text{neuter} \quad \left\{\begin{array}{l} \textit{yaṃ} \\ \textit{taṃ} \\ \textit{etaṃ} \end{array}\right\} + \text{vowel} > \left\{\begin{array}{l} \textit{yad} \\ \textit{tad} \\ \textit{etad} \end{array}\right. ;$$

$$\text{masculine, feminine} \quad \left\{\begin{array}{l} \textit{yaṃ} \\ \textit{taṃ} \\ \textit{etaṃ} \end{array}\right\} + \text{vowel} > \left\{\begin{array}{l} \textit{yam}\text{ [2]} \\ \textit{tam} \\ \textit{etam} \end{array}\right. ;$$

$$\text{all three genders} \quad \left\{\begin{array}{l} \textit{yaṃ} \\ \textit{taṃ} \\ \textit{etaṃ} \end{array}\right\} \text{in compound} > \left\{\begin{array}{l} \textit{yad} \\ \textit{tad} \\ \textit{etad} \end{array}\right. ;$$

—in various other cases *ṃ* > *m* (in the Canon, before vowels, but only optionally), or, in compound, *ṃ* may be assimilated to a following consonant. Otherwise it is occasionally elided altogether (usually under stress of metre). On the other hand it may be inserted as a " *sandhi* consonant " (" transition phoneme "). Finally, a following vowel may be elided after *niggahīta* (in which case a following conjunct may, exceptionally, be simplified).[3] It is very important to note that this elision of a vowel after *niggahīta* is the only case in Canonical usage where *sandhi* is allowed between the prior and posterior *pādas* of a *pādayuga* (with one possible exception in the *Buddhavaṃsa*, one of the latest additions to the Canon) ;

ṃ may always remain before a consonant.

[1] This is no doubt due to the alternative form *yeva* for *eva*, the *sandhi* being *ṃ* + *y* > *ññ*. In Burmese manuscripts *ñ* is frequently written for *ññ*, so that Aggavaṃsa perhaps had the result *tañeva* in mind and regarded it as having a single consonant.

[2] Historical feminines *yām*, etc., are not restored. A few cases of *-aṃ* > *ām* in *sandhi* do exist, however, such as : *vaḍḍhatām eva* (Geiger, 1916, § 126, see also § 71, end), *mām iva* (Mayrhofer I p. 73). A further example is *arahatām iva* (D II 265), dative plural, with the variants *-aṃ* and *-aṃm*. The metre, of course, is unaffected, and we should perhaps regard these cases as Māgadhisms, cf. AM *-ām eva*, Pischel, 1900, § 68.

[3] An example of this in prose is A II 197, 198 : *evaṃ sa* (= *evam assa*).

§ 65. In this section Aggavaṃsa collects various other rules, including the following :

Sandhi is not made where the result would not be euphonious, or where the meaning might be obscured (this is the fundamental rule of fluidity in Pali usage—the usage of a natural, living language) ;

metathesis sometimes occurs in *sandhi*, as in *payirudāhāsi* (*pari-* > *payir-*) and in *bahuābādho* > *bavhābādho* ;

after a pure vowel, *iti* becomes *ti* preceded by a slight pause (this rule is not observed in medieval Pali) ; [1]

some ambiguous combinations are noted, thus *sāhaṃ* may be (i) *sā ahaṃ*, (ii) *so ahaṃ*, (iii) *cha ahaṃ*, " six days ", *digu* (*dvigu*) ;

when hiatus is left between two vowels, the result may be written as one " word " (*saṃhitāpada*, i.e. any connected unit of speech such as *tatrāyaṃ*), as in : *suāgataṃ*, or as two " words " (*padas*, including prefixes), as in *tatra ayaṃ*.

§ 66. To Aggavaṃsa's doctrine modern scholars have added a few observations. Geiger (1916, § 68) notes that *sandhi* is applied especially to words which are closely connected syntactically : a further demonstration of the naturalness of the language. The historical origin of such phenomena as the *sandhi* consonants has been demonstrated (Geiger, 1916, § 72), but still more stress might be laid on Geiger's remark (1916, § 67) on the origin of many compound words in an older period. It seems likely that the majority of compounds current in the language were a legacy from " Old Indian ", and they should therefore be explained according to the phonological transition from Old to Middle Indian, not according to " internal *sandhi* " in Pali itself. It is for this reason that Geiger finds that on the one hand " internal *sandhi* on the whole follows the rules of Sanskrit " (1916, § 67), whilst on the other " external *sandhi*

[1] This interesting statement suggests that in the older manuscript tradition a final vowel before *ti* was not lengthened as in the extant manuscripts, and the present usage crept in from the practice of the medieval poets. The " slight pause " equivalent to making a long vowel may well be the original pronunciation : a fine point slurred over by writing a long vowel to indicate the quantity of the syllable.

in Pali is fundamentally different from that of Sanskrit " (§ 68). True internal *sandhi* in Pali, in the minority of compounds which were new formations in the language, follows the usage for Pali external *sandhi*, selecting, very naturally, those alternatives which give the closest union between the *padas* concerned.

§ 67. Jacobi has demonstrated a special factor at work in Prakrit *sandhi*, including Pali, namely the influence of the new penultimate accent.[1] A long penultimate syllable weakens the final syllable involved in *sandhi* by reason of the stress which falls on it. In Ardhamāgadhī and Jaina Māhārāṣṭrī the *sandhi* vowel is regularly short after a long penultimate, even where a long vowel would be the normal result of the *sandhi*, whilst the long *sandhi* vowel appears when the penultimate is short. It must be noted that in these two languages a short following vowel is not lengthened to compensate for the elision of the preceding vowel, so that the rule applies only to the remaining cases in which a long vowel may be formed. In Pali this compensatory lengthening is the rule, but it is balanced by the effect of the penultimate accent, so that in the case of a long penultimate followed by a *sandhi* vowel which normally would be long, the probabilities are about equal that it may be long or short. In such a case the metre may decide the quantity.

[1] See 1912–3, 211 ff. The problem of the accent will be investigated in Chapter III.

Chapter III

SCANSION

§ 68. The rules of quantity in Pali are those obtaining generally in Old and Middle Indian, the peculiarities of the orthography having been allowed for as described in Chapter I :

A syllable having its vowel short and followed by not more than one consonant is short (*lahu*) ;

A syllable having its vowel long, or followed by a conjunct, is long (*garu*).

It must be added that the short vowels are *a*, *i*, *u*, and the long vowels *ā*, *ī*, *ū*, *e*, *o*, and, normally, *aṃ*, *iṃ*, *uṃ*. We have already investigated the problems connected with *e* and *o* (Chapter I, (i)), but some further notes are necessary here, together with a clarification of the question of the nasal vowels, if we may use this term for *aṃ*, *iṃ*, and *uṃ*, which seem really to be vowels followed by nasality.[1]

§ 69. These problems are complicated in Middle Indian by the effect of the so-called " Law of Morae ", according to which a syllable should contain not more than two morae.[2] Undoubtedly there was a very strong feeling amongst Middle Indian speakers tending towards this simplification of the language by making the " natural " length of the syllables correspond exactly to the metrical length.[3] Geiger's statement (1916, § 5) that a syllable in Pali can never contain more than two morae is exaggerated, and his description of the exceptions as " learned orthography " (§ 7) cannot be justified. Whilst there was a strong tendency to conform to this " law ", it never became absolute in Pali, and the usage recorded in the manuscript tradition seems quite natural. We have seen in Chapter I, (vi), and elsewhere, that Pali was never completely subjected to absolute, artificial

[1] See Dr. Allen's interesting discussion on this point, 1953, pp. 39–46.

[2] i.e. " natural " morae. There is no question here, of course, of a syllable counting metrically as three morae.

[3] This tendency may be connected with the metrical transition to a system of exact quantitative oppositions.

rules, and the uncertainty whether some conjuncts made position shows the futility of trying to decide whether a syllable was allowed to contain three morae and whether in such a case it represents learned orthography. It would follow from the " law " that *e* and *o* must be short in a closed syllable. Again this was undoubtedly a tendency in the language, but hardly a general rule, and it had not as yet given rise to an " independent " short *e* or *o* appearing in open syllables.

§ 70. In § 5 of his Pali Grammar (1916) Geiger says that long nasal vowels do not occur. He means to say that long vowels are not found followed by *niggahīta* in the traditional orthography. This orthography is part of the general usage of not writing long *ā, ī, ū* before a conjunct, or, as one should say to be precise, in a closed syllable: *niggahīta* makes a closed syllable whether or not a consonant follows it. It is understood from this usage, and found in scanning the texts, that *niggahīta* normally makes a syllable metrically long.

As stated in the Chapter on *sandhi*, *niggahīta* usually becomes the consonant *m* when followed by a vowel. The syllable then becomes metrically short except in those very few cases where an Old Indian *-ām* is restored. Quite frequently, however, *niggahīta* is retained before a vowel and the syllable remains long. The poets appear to have been free to make a final *am/aṃ, im/iṃ* or *um/uṃ*, followed by a vowel, long or short as convenient.

Whilst the normal practice, representing presumably the older usage derived from an earlier stage of the language, treated *niggahīta* as a nasality following the vowel, i.e. as *anusvāra*, we find in the Pali Canon the earliest examples of the short " nasal vowel " of Apabhraṃśa and the modern languages, which became a true nasal vowel, *anunāsika*, and was probably pronounced as such already in Pali. There is no special orthography for this vowel in Pali, and the syllable is written either with *niggahīta*, as in the case of ordinary *anusvāra*, or without it, as if the nasality were lost completely. This loss of nasality metri causa (and the " short nasal vowel " in Pali seems to appear only under stress of metre) was perhaps the origin, and the original pronunciation, of the " short nasal vowel", the nasality having first been lost and afterwards retained in a different form by "colouring" the vowel itself instead of merely following it.[1] In Indian Prakrit manuscripts the new sound came to be represented by the *candrabindu*, which is now usually transliterated by a tilda over the vowel in place of *ṃ* after it.[2]

Accent

§ 71. Besides clarifying the rules of quantity with a view to the scansion of Pali verse, it is necessary to enquire whether any other feature of the phonology may have been at work in determining the position a word might occupy in the *pāda*. There is only one such feature: the accent. In the Vedic language there appears to be no connection between the pitch accent, or "tone", and metrical rhythm. A great deal of discussion has taken place, however, on the question of whether, and, if so, when, a stress accent replaced the Vedic accent at some time during the development of the Indo-Aryan languages after the Vedic period. Such a stress accent might affect versification, and we must therefore examine the results of previous investigations of this question and endeavour to define the situation in the Pali period.

§ 72. Westphal's attempt to found a science of "comparative metrics" of the Indo-European languages on the basis of Aristoxenus,[3] alongside their comparative linguistics and comparative mythology, resulted in the efforts of several Sanskritists to analyse Vedic, Pali and Sanskrit verse on the assumption that it was governed by the recurrence of an "ictus", so that the *pādas* could be subdivided into feet composed of *thésis* and *ársis*.

Both the stress accent and the ictus have been rejected by some Sanskritists as not existing in the Indo-Aryan languages

[1] On the origin of the true nasal vowel in Indo-Aryan cf. Allen, 1953, p. 40.

[2] We cannot adopt such a convention in editing Pali texts. It is only a hypothesis that *ăṃ* in Pali was ever pronounced like *ã* in Late Middle Indian. Where the short quantity is certain the editor may mark it as a guide to the reader.

[3] "Aufsatze zur vergleichenden Metrik der indogermanischen Völker" (1860). We have already discussed this theory in §§ 23 ff. of the Introduction.

and metres. If they do exist, however, they are likely to be interdependent ; that is, the ictus is likely to be carried by a stressed syllable. Let us summarize briefly the development of the stress and ictus controversies.

§ 73. In 1883 G. Bühler described the modern pronunciation of Sanskrit in India, with a stress accent dependent on the penultimate syllable, in his *Leitfaden für den Elementarkursus des Sanskrit.* Jacobi (1893b) traced this stress accent back to Pali, Prakrit, and Epic and Classical Sanskrit on phonological evidence such as the shortening or weakening of vowels. An initial or " expiratory " stress was also assumed to play a part. Enclitics were shown to behave as single word-units with the preceding word. Grierson (1895 and 1896) supported Jacobi by collecting evidence from the modern languages. In the Pali grammars of Geiger (1916 in German, 1937, revised, in English) and Mayrhofer (1951) the Jacobi accent is accepted.

Jacobi was opposed by Pischel (1897 and 1899), who maintained that the Vedic tone still existed in Prakrit, or that at least the accent, whatever its nature, occupied the same positions as the old tone. This, he claimed, gave a more satisfactory explanation of certain phonological phenomena in Prakrit. (On the possible phonological influence of the tone in Vedic itself see Zubatý, 1888b, p. 136 on accent and metrical lengthening in the *Ṛgveda.* The statements that greater effort or greater tension were involved in producing a higher tone suggest a possible stress effect of the musical accent.)[1] By 1900, however, in his Prakrit grammar (§46), Pischel had retreated from his former position and conceded a penultimate accent in Śaurasenī, Māgadhī and Ḍhakkī whilst maintaining his Vedic accent in Māhārāṣṭrī, Ardhamāgadhī and Jaina Māhārāṣṭrī.

[1] cf. Allen, 1953, p. 90. Modern phoneticians, e.g. Chiba : *A Study of Accent*, Tokyo, 1935, seem to regard the two kinds of accent as essentially related and as mutually exclusive as the predominant accentual feature of any language. On the influence of tone on quantity see also Arnold (1905, p. 145). Note also that the tone is often associated with a " strong " syllable, as when in verbs the strong stem is used when the tone falls on the stem, Whitney, *Sanskrit Grammar* (2nd edn., Harvard University Press, 1889, 1941 reprint) § 556. Some modern stress accents in Indo-European languages occupy the place of the old tone, e.g. : Greek, Russian, Lithuanian (the latter two retaining a rise in pitch). cf. now Kuryłowicz, 1952.

§ 74. Jacobi published a further article (1912–3, " Über eine neue Sandhiregel im Pali und im Prakrit der Jainas und über die Betonung in diesen Sprachen ") in which he announced the new *sandhi* rule which we have referred to in Chapter II, whereby a long penultimate syllable weakens, through the stress which it carries, a *sandhi* vowel which follows it. That this rule is not fully, but only 50%, offset in Pali by the special rule that a short initial vowel may be lengthened after the elision of a final vowel he regards as confirmation of the theory.

Bloch [1] rejected both theories, saying that nothing was known of any stress accent in ancient times (§ 33) and even that there was no stress in the modern languages (§ 34) : a position which he still maintained in 1934 (pp. 47–9), stating that the accent disappeared entirely after Pāṇini and that the facts adduced in favour of a stress could be explained in other ways. One wonders, however, what he understands by the expression " sommets rythmiques " on p. 45.[2] He had used this term earlier (1920, p. 50) : in Marāṭhī the final syllable is the " sommet rythmique " of the word, important in poetry on account of rhyme. He held also that the elements preceding the " sommet " lose their quantity. Perhaps the difference of opinion or of feeling in regard to the accent between these German and French investigators is indeed due to the nature of their own languages. English investigators of Hindī (Greaves, Kellogg) noted that, contrasted with the English accent, there is in Hindī either no accent or an accent " quite subordinate in importance to quantity " (Kellogg, 1893, § 35). Until accurate measurements are made, using instruments, the discussion must remain subjective. In 1916 Professor Turner, followed in 1926–8 by Banarsi Das Jain, attempted to solve the problem by accepting Pischel's accent for Māhārāṣṭrī and demonstrating its continued existence in Marāṭhī, whilst accepting Jacobi's accent for the other Prakrit dialects and their modern descendants.

[1] 1920, 50 ff. He ascribes the theories of the German scholars to a natural prejudice (based on their own language) and considers that the Felber (1912) phonograms contradict them.

[2] Banarsi Das Jain uses the term " syllabic prominence " as an alternative to stress accent in countering Bloch's rejection of stress in Indo-Aryan (1926–8, 315 ff.).

§ 75. In 1943 (129 ff.) Poucha published an article "Vom Vedischen zum Sanskrit-Akzent", on the origins of the penultimate stress, adducing accent-shifts already in Vedic tending towards the position of the Sanskrit penultimate accent (p. 148). He maintained that the Indo-European tone changed into a stress under the influence of the non-Aryan languages of India, and then conformed gradually to the penultimate rule governing its position in the word. He gives (p. 136) as the unanimous opinion of Indologists the statement that the decisive change took place between Pāṇini's time (the 4th century B.C.) and the 7th century A.D. (*Kāśikāvṛtti*), although the beginnings of the transition are to be found, as he shows, in the earliest Aryan records in India. Among the references he gives, however, Wackernagel (1896, p. 297) in fact remarks that the stress accent probably was widespread in Sanskrit speech already in Pāṇini's time, referring also to Leumann for the *Śatapathabrāhmaṇa* belonging to the period of transition. Jacobi's theory would seem to push the transition back before the 4th century B.C., since by that time Pali already possessed its characteristic accent system.[1]

§ 76. From Lin Li-Kouang's discussion (1949, p. 222) of certain traditions about the recitation of the texts, it appears that Early Buddhist recitation was very different from that of the contemporary Vedic tradition. The Vedic accent system is referred to, with the gestures accompanying the recitation, and rejected, the contemporary pronunciation and manner of recitation of the various Indian dialects being approved. Even the schools which used Sanskrit rejected the *chandas*, the Vedic manner of recitation, but this must refer to a somewhat later period. One source quoted by Lin, the *Vinayakṣudrakavastu*, allows that if the local usage of a country requires the musical accent (the Chinese text appears to be a translation of the term *āyatakagītasvara* frequently used for Vedic recitation) then it may be used. Perhaps this refers to the Buddhist

[1] We may note here the occurrence of non-etymological initial *h* in the Asokan inscriptions: *hevaṃ*, *hemeva*, called by Bloch (1934, p. 67) "*h* expressif", which is surely connected with the initial stress, and also *evaṃ* > *eṃ* resulting from a stress on the initial vowel.

practice in Mahārāṣṭra, or some other country in which, exceptionally we may infer, the old accent still survived.

§ 77. If we accept a penultimate stress accent in Pali, with a secondary initial stress, we next have to take up the question whether this new accent system played any part in versification. If the stress was sufficient to produce phonological changes, it might be felt by the poets and influence their fitting of words into the rhythm of the *pāda*, but presumably only if the metre possessed or developed an element, such as an ictus, which answered to the stress and tended to draw the words into positions in which stress and ictus would coincide. We must therefore refer to the ictus discussion in the Introduction (§§ 22–9).

It is significant that Westphal's ictus theory was applied first, by Cappeller in 1872, to the study of *gaṇacchandas*, the metre which is most closely connected with music. It is undeniable that in music the rhythmic periods are marked by a strong beat or ictus, and in a musical metre, if in any, we may therefore expect to find a " measure " defined by an ictus. (Cappeller's work will be discussed in Chapter VI.)

§ 78. Kühnau's *Die Triṣṭubh-Jagatī-Familie*, 1886, gives a full exposition of the ictus theory in relation to the " comparative metrics " of Indo-European. It then takes up Indian metrics and selects the *triṣṭubh* as the best subject for analysis on account of the great length of its history, although other metres, particularly *mātrāchandas*, are referred to for comparison. Kühnau seems to admit that in the fixed metres of Classical Sanskrit there would be no significance in an ictus (pp. v–vi), but he evidently regards this fixed or " uniform " type of metre as artificial (presumably as resulting from the supposed " external " schematic analysis of the Indian theorists who failed to penetrate to the inner nature of metre). What is important, in his view, is the evolution of metres and the changes of rhythm, from which standpoint the perfected array of Classical Sanskrit metres is merely a lifeless fossilization of some of the products of metrical development. He admits, however, that his attempt to differentiate the musical and metrical forms of rhythm is not entirely successful (p. vii). The reason for this is that he attempts to bring all metres under the purely musical laws of the *thésis* and *ársis*. In poetry, repetition is sufficient to constitute metrical form, and it may be repetition of a whole *pāda* of considerable length which is not analysable into smaller units. Stress may be added, marking the recurrence of a particular measure, but it is not essential in a metre where the rhythm is supplied by the opposition of quantities in the word-material, or perhaps only by variations of tone in a language dominated by a musical accent. The " conditions of rhythmical movement " laid down by the comparative metrologists are thus adequate for music but not broad enough for metrics. The Indian theory of the *cakravartana*, in Apabhraṃśa and Gujarātī metrics,[1] is much closer to an adequate theory of metrical structure.

§ 79. It is not necessary here to examine the methods of all the other workers in the field of metrics.[2] Some, like Oldenberg, whilst criticizing Kühnau's theory at some points, use ictus schemes in the study of Vedic and Sanskrit metre, and speak freely of " iambic ", " trochaic," " anapaestic," etc., rhythm in *anuṣṭubh* and *triṣṭubh pādas*. Others simply analyse the metres in *pādas* made up of long and short syllables variously arranged, with or without caesura, very much along the lines of the old Indian theory, sometimes using terms such as " diiambus ", but in a so to speak arhythmical sense implying only a certain arrangement of longs and shorts and not a true " measure ". We have seen that Arnold and Edgerton worked in this way. Others again, like Jacobi and Helmer Smith, do not seem to work consistently, so that it is difficult to tell whether they always mean a true " measure " when they write " foot " or whether the term is used arhythmically.

The tendency has been to revert gradually to the Indian system as a starting point for scientific research, as has happened in other fields of study, and thus to get free from traditional European preconceptions. In this way a new science

[1] Discussed by Dr. Dave in an article on " Gujerātī Prosody " circulated in typescript.

[2] See the Introduction, §§ 24–9, on methods of scanning the *triṣṭubh*.

of linguistics and related subjects is growing up on the basis of the highest achievements of both Indian and European science, but freed from the narrowness of both which had resulted from the absence of outside criticism.

§ 80. The modern attitude to the study of Indian metre has been best formulated by Belloni-Filippi (1912, pp. 5–6). Having rejected the *thésis—ársis* theory of Kühnau, he provisionally accepts Oldenberg's results for Vedic rhythm (pp. 18–20, on the rhythmic structure of the *triṣṭubh*), and looks to a future deeper understanding of Indian music for more light on the question of rhythm. Moreover he proposes a plan of experimental research and collection of material, accompanied by the study of the Indian metrologists, at the completion of which theoretical generalization about Indian metrics will become possible. Since 1912 Helmer Smith, probably, has done more than anyone else to carry out this plan. As for the music, the work of Dr. Bake, which it is to be hoped will soon be available in printed form, has cleared the way for the full utilization of the ancient musical tradition of India in theoretical research of this kind.

§ 81. In Apabhraṃśa and Hindī both stress and ictus play an essential part in the metrics. The latter was recognized in the theory as the *sam*, the concept being introduced from the musical theory (in which it is called *graha*) ; the former does not seem to have been recognized by the Indian theorists, its effect no doubt entering into the feeling for good versification known as *gati*. The musical theories were evidently introduced in connection with the *tāla vṛttas*, metres built up according to musical form from *pādas* of the *mātrā vṛttas* which were the direct descendants of the old *gaṇacchandas*. Clearly, however, the ictus was already present in the *mātrā vṛttas* : Sinha says in his Thesis on *The Historical Development of Medieval Hindī Prosody* (London, 1953, p. 102) : " For example [of the earlier metres, used for ' exclusively literary purposes ', which preceded the more popular and more musical *tāla vṛttas*], when one reads or sings a *pajjhaṭikā*, a metre frequently employed in Apabhraṃśa-Prakrit poetry, one unconsciously keeps time by stressing the first of every four *tāla mātrās*." The *pajjhaṭikā*, as Sinha points out (pp. 177–8), is directly descended from the *mātrāsamaka* of the ancient theory, which was a form of *gaṇacchandas* [1] or *mātrāchandas* unfortunately very rare in the extant ancient literature but very closely related to metres commonly used in Pali and elsewhere (see below in the Chapter on *gaṇacchandas*). In fact the *pajjhaṭikā* and the Pali *gīti* are remarkably similar in structure, both being formed of alternate *gaṇas* of ⏓⏓⏔ and ⏑,⏔⏑. The question is: how far back in Indian literature does the ictus or *sam* play a part in metres of this type? Was it present already in Pali?

§ 82. Although the ictus must have been present from the outset in the musical accompaniment to which the old *gaṇacchandas* metres were composed, it seems only gradually and much later to have come to play any part in the arrangement of the words. The new stress accent was in Pali apparently not sufficiently felt by the poets to impose a conscious, or even an unconscious, putting together of stress and ictus. We do not find in analysing Pali verses the regular coincidence of stress accent and presumed ictus which we see, for instance, in the strophe quoted by Sinha (1953, p. 178) from the *Mohamudgara* attributed to Śaṅkara:

nálinī-dála-gata-jálavat táralaṃ
tádvaj jívanam átiśaya-cápalaṃ
íti saṃsáre sphúṭatara-dóṣaḥ
kátham iha mánava táva santóṣaḥ

(metre: *pādākulaka*)

§ 83. In Pali it appears that any word can occupy any position in the *pāda* provided only that the succession of long and short syllables fits the metre. We have then to work on the assumption that the accent and ictus even in *gaṇacchandas* did not yet play the part they played later in Hindī and probably

[1] We have already noted Cappeller's application of the ictus theory to *gaṇacchandas*, and suggested that it was no accident that this metre should have been the first to be analysed in this way.

already in Apabhraṃśa.[1] Future research may perhaps determine how far any tendency for accent and ictus to coincide had gone in the latest Canonical texts, and when in the history of *gaṇacchandas* this coincidence became essential. In the non-*mattā* metres we cannot expect to find an ictus in Pali. It may be noted that as the musical metres evolved towards the Hindī system the other metres, except for those which were assimilated to the musical structure, such as the *varṇa vṛttas* of Hindī (Sinha, 44 ff.), fell into disuse except in Classical Sanskrit (and indeed in the Medieval Pali literature, where they led a still more artificial existence).

[1] The earliest *gaṇacchandas* rhythms, |⏑⏑—|⏑—⏑|, do not lend themselves to a coincidence of stress and ictus. The stress falls on a long syllable much more often than on a short, so that the stress in such poems as the *Upālisutta* or the *Mettasutta* falls much more often in the middle or at the end of a *gaṇa* than at the beginning : |⏑⏑—́|⏑—́⏑|. The early *gaṇa* rhythms are still based on the old type of metrical rhythm in that the alternation of quantities alone produces variation of rhythm, and we have not yet reached the stage where |⏑́⏑—|, |⏑́⏑⏑⏑| and |—́⏑⏑| are rhythmically equivalent. These points will be further developed in Chapter VI.

Chapter IV
FLUIDITY AND LICENCE

Introduction

§ 84. In *pādas* of more than eight syllables the earliest metres in Vedic, Avestan and Greek (and also the Latin saturnian) usually have a break consisting of an obligatory end of word at a defined place. This " caesura ", Meillet has suggested (1903/1949, p. 137), differs essentially from that of, for instance, the French classical alexandrine, which includes a certain suspension of sense.

The end of a word in the early Indo-European languages seems to have been marked by special pronunciation, giving the word its phonic individuality in the sentence. Thus a consonant in absolute final position was, according to the Indian grammarians, only imploded (*pīḍita*), which doubtless facilitated the loss of final consonants in Middle Indian.[1]

The syllable preceding the " caesura " would not have a fixed metrical quantity. Like the final note of a musical phrase, it could be prolonged (*pluta*) or followed by a pause (*cheda*) without any effect on the rhythm. We find in Vedic that the final syllables of words, which often occupy the position preceding a caesura or at the end of a *pāda*, are frequently indeterminate in quantity.[2]

§ 85. The crystallization of the rhythmical form of words in Vedic and other Indo-European languages appears to have been influenced by the cultivation of verse form for the earliest literature, as was pointed out by Zubatý (1888b, p. 133). A polysyllabic word tended to take a form having the maximum alternation of long and short syllables, so that it could be fitted easily into *anuṣṭubh* and *triṣṭubh* verses. In making this sort of description of the situation, however, we must avoid the falsification of separating " the language " or the " word material " from " the rhythm ", as though the words were

[1] The situation in Iranian is similar.

[2] cf. H. Smith, 1953, p. 138 : " L'autonomie du mot fléchi (et celle du membre de composé) qu'abolira la technique classique...".

fitted to the rhythm. The rhythm we are speaking of has no existence apart from the words, and it is also true to say that the rhythms found in the verses are derived from the nature of the word material, and we have already referred to a transformation of the metres apparently arising from changes in the language.[1] There is some deeper rhythm in a language, which expresses itself, which expresses perhaps the general meaningfulness, the life and purposefulness, of the language, in certain metrical rhythms. The forms of sentences and words express chips of meaning, of which the possibility of being related to other expressions of meaning, and thus " understood ", is proclaimed by their consonance with this deeper rhythm. It is to this rhythmic pulse in the living Vedic language that both the creation of the ***anuṣṭubh-triṣṭubh*** technique and the crystallization of the rhythms of particular words should be referred.

Nevertheless, once the metrical rhythms are well established they seem to exert a direct influence on word forms through the deliberate selection of suitable forms by the poets. If the " Law of de Saussure-Wackernagel " that tetrasyllabic words tend to take the form ⏑–⏑× rather than ⏑⏑⏑× illustrates the deeper rhythm working in the Vedic language and in Early Middle Indian, some of the phenomena noted by Kuryłowicz, such as the alternation of *jūjuvuḥ* and *juhve* according to metrical convenience (1949, p. 20), illustrate the direct influence of metrical rhythms on the choice of words and forms.

§ 86. In Pali we find a number of indeterminate endings, such as the feminines in *ī̆* and *ū̆* or the perfect *vidū̆*, some of them involving the penultimate vowel, such as *-ī̆su*, *-ū̆su*, *-ī̆hi*, etc. The fluidity in Pali, which is not found in Classical Sanskrit, is of a similar nature to that in Vedic, and shows the historical continuation of the old rhythmic situation to which we have just referred. The rich variety of forms from such a root as *dā*, or in the aorist, exemplifies the selection or preservation of forms by the metre. Sometimes there is a confusion of archaic forms with metrical licence, which led later, in Buddhist Hybrid Sanskrit, to a great extension of licence. As we shall

[1] See Introduction, § 30.

see below, licence is not fortuitous in origin, but is based on what may be called " morphological weaknesses ". The influence of the metre on the word material is based on the weak points left by the " deeper rhythm " during the growth of the language.

§ 87. In this chapter we have to define the limits within which fluidity and licence occur in ancient Pali verse. This is of particular importance for the study of *mattā-* and *gaṇa-cchandas*, where alteration of the quantity of a syllable affects not merely that syllable but frequently also the scansion of a whole *pāda*.

The situation in Pali is complicated by the fact that we find not simply the continuation of the old language-rhythm but the beginning of the transition to a new one: that of Apabhraṃśa. The " Law of de Saussure-Wackernagel " is in process of being reversed : instead of ⏑⏑⏑× > ⏑–⏑× we find the tendency ⏑–⏑× > ⏑⏑⏑× in some forms, notably in the future *karissati* > *karihiti* discussed by Smith (1952, p. 177). He describes such a quantitative reduction as difficult to admit in an epoch which still obeyed the Saussurian law, but surely his own distinction of a new *rhuthmizómenon*, P″, appearing already in Pali, must imply the beginning of this reduction, so appropriate for the new metres, and the rise of new rhythmic laws. It is this conflict between the two rhythms, the break-down of the heavy Old Indian language-rhythm and the first vigorous sallies of the new one, or in metrics the superseding of –/⏑ by –/⏑⏑ as the basis of rhythmic variations, which constitutes the special feature of Pali taken as the central topic in our study.

§ 88. *Na hi Bhagavā chandañ ca vuttiñ ca rakkhati nā pi sukhuccāraṇatthaṃ akkharalopādikaṃ karoti, yo hi sāsaṅko sabhayo, so aññesaṃ paṇḍitānaṃ saṅkāya uppajjanakanindā-bhayena chandañ ca vuttiñ ca rakkhati sukhuccāraṇatthañ ca akkharalopādikaṃ karoti, Bhagavā pana nirāsaṅko nibbhayo, Bhagavato pāvacane khalitaṃ natthi, so kathaṃ parappavādaṃ paṭicca chandañ ca vuttiñ ca rakkhissati sukhuccāraṇatthañ ca akkharalopādikaṃ karissati, vuttaṃ h' etaṃ Abhidhammaṭīkā-*

yaṃ : " *Bhagavā pana vacanānaṃ lahugarubhāvaṃ na gaṇeti, bodhaneyyānaṃ pana ajjhāsayānulomato dhammasabhāvaṃ avilomento va tathā tathā desanaṃ niyāmetī ti na kattha ci akkharānaṃ bahutā vā appatā vā codetabbā* " *ti*. (Aggavaṃsa, Sd p. 640.)

" The Bhagavant does not observe number and quantity nor make elisions, etc., of letters for the sake of euphony ; he who is anxious and fearful, he, when amongst other learned men, observes number and quantity and makes elisions, etc., of letters, for the sake of euphony, from anxiety and from fear of irrelevant (?) blame. The Bhagavant, however, being free from anxiety and fearless because there is nothing unsound in his teaching, why should he observe number and quantity and make elisions, etc., for the sake of euphony merely on account of the quibbling of others ? As it is said in a sub-commentary on the Abhidhamma : 'The Bhagavant does not consider short and long quantity in words ; he controls his speech so that it should not disagree with the nature of the doctrine whilst conforming to the mental dispositions of those who are capable of being enlightened. Thus the abundance or paucity of letters is nowhere to be questioned.' "

§ 89. Evidently the irregularities of the Canon had worried the Medieval Pali grammarians, who were not able to explain all of them by means of their linguistic science and metrical theory and therefore sought to evade the difficulty by invoking the Buddha's " fearlessness " in the use of the language. This attitude may partly explain the carelessness of the scribes in handing down the manuscripts on which we depend, such as the inclusion of obvious glosses in verses in defiance of the metre.

§ 90. On p. 843 of the *Saddanīti* Aggavaṃsa again refers to this difficulty, with the same quotation from an apparently lost sub-commentary, and refutes an objection as follows :

Yadi evaṃ, kasmā tattha tattha pubbācariyehi " gāthāsu chandamabhedattham akkharalopan " ti ca " vuttianurakkhaṇatthāya viparītatā pī " ti ca " chandānurakkhaṇatthāya sukhuccāraṇatthāya cā " ti ca vuttan ti. Saccaṃ, yattha chando ca vutti ca rakkhitabbā hoti, [*kiṃ*] *tattha Bhagavā chandañ ca vuttiñ ca rakkhati, yattha pana tadubhayaṃ rakkhitabbaṃ na hoti, na tattha Bhagavā chandañ ca vuttiñ ca rakkhati ; taṃ sandhāya vuttaṃ : " Bhagavā pana vacanānaṃ lahugarubhāvaṃ na gaṇetī " ti ādi. Chandañ ca vuttiñ ca rakkhanto pi hi Bhagavā na kabbakārakādayo viya savyāpāratāvasena rakkhati, atha kho aparimitakāle anekesu jātisatasahassesu bodhisattakāle akkhara-samayesu kataparicayavasena padāni nipphannān' eva hutvā sassirīkamukhapadumato niggacchanti, tesu kāni ci chando-vuttīnaṃ rakkhaṇasadisenākārena pavattanti, kāni ci tathā na pavattanti : yāni rakkhaṇasadisenākārena pavattanti, tāni sandhāya Bhagavā " chandañ ca vuttiñ ca rakkhatī " ti vattabbo, yāni tathā na pavattanti, tāni sandhāya Bhagavā " chandañ ca vuttiñ ca na rakkhatī " ti pi vattabbo, na hi Bhagavā paresaṃ codanāhetu sāsaṅko sappaṭibhayo, sāsaṅko yeva hi sappaṭibhayo chandañ ca vuttiñ ca rakkhatī ti daṭṭhabbaṃ.*

" If so, why did the old teachers say in various places : ' elision of letter to avoid spoiling the metre in verse,' ' change to observe the quantity,' and ' to observe the number and for euphony ' ?—Certainly where number and quantity ought to be observed the Bhagavant observes them, but where those two ought not to be observed the Bhagavant does not observe number and quantity. In this connection it is said : ' The Bhagavant does not consider short and long quantity in words . . . ' etc. The Bhagavant does not observe them professionally like writers of *kabbas* (*kāvyas*) and so on observing number and quantity. However, during the limitless time as Bodhisatta in many hundreds of thousands of existences, through acquaintance with spelling systems and becoming trained in words he came to have a glorious lotus-mouth. In some of these existences observation of number and quantity occurred and in some it did not : when it did occur it should be said that the Bhagavant ' observes number and quantity ' and when it did not it should be said that the Bhagavant ' does not observe number and quantity ', but the Bhagavant is not to be regarded as anxious and fearful on account of the criticism of others or as anxious and fearful in observing number and quantity."

§ 91. It has not been noticed that in those *Jātakas* where the Bodhisatta is presumably to be supposed to observe number and quantity the verses attributed to him are any freer from metrical difficulties than other Canonical verses. It might at first sight seem reasonable to suggest that the Bhagavant as Buddha, and the early Buddhists in general, were not concerned with perfection in the art of poetry but were content to use language in a less polished manner so long as they succeeded in making their teaching clear ; yet in fact the early Buddhists utilized the current arts of metrics and poetics to the full in their propaganda work, just as Aśvaghoṣa did after them. It is enough to refer to the elaborate techniques of the *Suttanipāta* to justify this view.

Still less can we accept the suggestion that the Buddha (or any of his followers) was above the rules and conventions of the language of the society in which he lived and used language in an arbitrary manner. We should continue Aggavaṃsa's own excellent research into Pali usage, *nīti sāsanassopakārāya yathābalaṃ amhehi ṭhapitā* (Sd p. 640),[1] in the hope of further reducing the area of uncertainty in the interpretation of the texts.

§ 92. In his chapter on *sandhi*, which we referred to in Chapter II, Aggavaṃsa calls *vuttasandhi* the alteration of sounds under the influence of metre or for the sake of smoothness or sonority. *Chandas* is defined as the determination of the number of syllables and *vutti* as the determination of the quantity of syllables. Letters may be elided to observe the *chandas* or changed to observe the *vutti*. In prose elision and change are made " for euphony ". This in practice refers to certain ancient usages, and particularly to certain dialectal variants such as fragments of Māgadhī. Exceptional forms not otherwise understood by Aggavaṃsa are generally explained away as " for euphony ". It will be useful to compare Aggavaṃsa's research in *vuttasandhi* (Sd pp. 632–40) with the observations of modern scholars, and to compare this Pali usage with that of other languages closely related to it.

§ 93. The quantitative variations in Vedic have been the subject of extensive research, notably by Benfey (1874–80),

[1] " rules established by us, according to our ability, for the benefit of the teaching."

Zubatý (1888b–90 [1]), Arnold (1905, especially Chapter VI), Meillet (1920, pp. 194–5, etc.; 1903/1949, p. 139) and Kuryłowicz (1949, 8 f., etc.). General agreement does not seem to have been reached as to the exact nature of these phenomena, mainly on account of the uncertainty about the traditions of the *Saṃhitā* and *Pada* texts as we now have them. Whether the alternatives represent an indeterminate or fluid stage of the language or artificial poetic licence, or, as seems probable, a combination of the two, must be left to Vedic scholars to determine. Arnold's objections (1905, xi–xii) to the second view surely exaggerate the opposition between the two phenomena. We should expect to find rather a limited use of licence sanctioned by at least the memory of indeterminate quantity in certain syllables. These changes in Vedic are clearly akin to those in Early Middle Indian and we shall examine some parallels, the Vedic examples being taken mainly from Zubatý.

For Epic and Classical Sanskrit parallels we rely on Zubatý (1889, 619 ff.) and Ballini (1912, part 2, pp. 7–8, 34, 60).

§ 94. Edgerton has made a very thorough study of the Buddhist Hybrid Sanskrit usage, as a result of which we are now well informed on the immediate post-Pali stage. The main outlines are given in an article in the JAOS (1946) which has been subjected to careful criticism by Smith (1950a, 1 ff.), to which Edgerton has replied in his *Buddhist Hybrid Sanskrit Grammar* (1953, pp. 5–6) where he adds many more examples. Further examples may be found in Smith's article, in Régamey (1938, 15 ff.) and in Lin (1949, Chapter IV).

For Ardhamāgadhī we have only Jacobi (1884, p. 596; cf. 1883, p. 320) and Banarsi Das Jain (1923, p. x) and for the Prakrit Inscriptions of the period 3rd century B.C.–2nd century A.D. Mehendale's remarks (1948, xxii, etc.). For Classical Prakrit there are a few notes in Pischel's Grammar (1900), to which we might add those in Pṛthvīdhara's commentary on the *Mṛcchakaṭika* (1936).

[1] Publication not completed on account of Arnold's work being forthcoming.

Let us examine first the types of variation which result from the fluidity of Pali in its grammar and lexicon, and afterwards consider, and endeavour to classify, the types of "pure" licence which are not directly justified by such fluidity. There are of course many border line or transitional cases, through which we can see how from a pair of variants, that is originally from an ambiguous form, arose a normal form and a rare by-form kept alive by poetic licence.

Phonological variants

§ 95. In Chapter I we have discussed metrical variants arising from epenthesis and contraction. Aggavaṃsa lists some examples of this kind of *vuttasandhi*, such as :

sāmī/suvāmī
macco/mātiyo
padmāni/padumāni (same in BHS—Edgerton § 3.114)
āceraṃ/ācariyaṃ (!—these are metrically equivalent in the Canon : ---, but in Medieval Pali they are used as metrical variants : -⏑⏑-, e.g. by Aggavaṃsa himself, Sd p. 928).

We have also the futures noted by Smith, 1952, p. 169 :

hessati/bhavissati (Bv 2.66)
jessati/jayissati (Vv 312)
(in both cases the two variants occur within a single strophe).

Alternative Sandhis

§ 96. These have been discussed in Chapter II. *Sandhi* is more frequent in verse, under stress of metre, than in prose. Often it has to be made in verse where the manuscripts leave the words uncombined.

Morphological Variants

§ 97. These are the indeterminate endings, apparently derived from the Vedic period of the language, which we mentioned at the beginning of this chapter. Geiger gives a number of examples in his Pali Grammar :

-ī̆naṃ
-ū̆naṃ [1]
-ī̆hi
-ū̆hi
-ī̆su
-ū̆su
-ī̆to (abl. sing.)

—the last of these sometimes takes the long form in verse but the short in the commentary on it. The others are usually short in verse but long in prose. In Geiger §§ 86–7 we see the confusion between feminine nouns in *i* and *ī* and in *u* and *ū* in the nominative and also in the genitive (*rattiyā/ratyā*, etc.), and in § 90 we have the variations in *satthā̆-* perhaps on the analogy of these. The *-in* declension was absorbed into this *ī̆* system: *hatthī̆-*.

In the conjugation system we may note the verbs of (Sanskrit: which Geiger follows) classes IX (*jānā̆ti, jinā̆ti* (= Aggavaṃsa's class 5); *gaṇhā̆ti* (= Aggavaṃsa's class 6); etc.), V (= Aggavaṃsa's class 4 *suṇo-/suṇā̆-* and 7 (part of) *sakka-/sakkuṇā̆-*) (frequently transferred to class IX and similarly variable: *o/ā̆*), VIII (= Aggavaṃsa's class 7) (extraordinary variety of forms from √*kar*). We have also the *-is* aorist (*pakkā̆mi, acā̆ri, atā̆rī̆*, etc.) and the two causatives, (*p*)*aya/e*, in which the quantity of the radical vowel also may vary: *jā̆leti, nikkhā̆meti, ṭhā̆peti*, etc. Aggavaṃsa has noted (p. 635) *-iṃsu/-isuṃ* in the aorist.

Professor H. Smith has collected many examples of variants of this type in the article just quoted: " Le futur moyen indien et ses rythmes " (1952, 169 ff.), e.g.:

dassaṃ/dassāmi (J IV 405, etc.)
padissanti/padissare (Bv 2, 83)
disvā/daṭṭhu (Sn 424)
pakāsesi/pakāsayi (Bv 4, 3–5)
plurals in *ā/āyo*.

He notes similar variants in Ardhamāgadhī.

[1] In feminines with the suffix *-nī* from stems in *-i* and *-u* there is the same uncertainty. In some of the manuscripts of Th II, for instance, we find *bhikkhūnī* in several places instead of the usual *bhikkhunī*.

Syntactic Variants

§ 98. Under this heading we may note the metrical expedient called by Smith the " split-compound ", e.g. *amatatala-* > *amataṃ tala-* (see CPD Epilegomena to Vol. I, p. 32). Further studies along the lines of Hendriksen's *Syntax of the Infinite Verb-Forms of Pali* (1944) would enable us to describe other variations in sentence > *pāda* construction.

Lexicographical Variants

§ 99. A long list of these is given by Aggavaṃsa (Sd pp. 921–2). Some of them do not seem to have been found in the Canon and may be merely Medieval usage. It is probable, however, that a good many such variants have been ignored or " corrected " by modern editors, and excluded from the PED. Some of Aggavaṃsa's examples belong to our category of phonological variants (epenthesis/contraction), but others may conveniently be listed here. Of metrical importance are :

ā̆gāraṃ
nimeso/nimiso
ī̆riṇaṃ
elamūgo/elamukho

—many cases with or without suffixes such as *-ka*, *-na*, and of variations of gender, are noted. An interesting case is :

upayānaṃ/upāyanaṃ, " approach "

—the first is from *upa-√yā*, the second from *upa-√i*. The second has normally the special sense " offering ", " present ". A few examples may be culled from the PED, such as :

mahī̆sa/mahiṃsa
virava/virāva
viliva/vilīva
vuḷha/vūḷha
vyadhati/vedhati

Variations of Usage (*rūḷhibheda*)

§ 100. To complete this survey we might add Aggavaṃsa's category *rūḷhibheda*, " variation of usage " (Sd pp. 923 and 261–3), which overlaps the preceding three categories and includes the coining of new words and the use of alternative cases or numbers in declension to express the same relationship. The study of this vast field belongs to the future, although a start has been made by Hendriksen (1944) and by Smith, in his examination of style and rhythm in Sanskrit *sūtras*, and in Pali treatises belonging to the same tradition, at the end (pp. 31–7) of the remarkable article: "Retractationes Rhythmicae" (1951).

Licence

§ 101. Positio debilis, which is a form of licence in some of the other languages,[1] has been disposed of in Chapter I, section vi, since in Pali it is a regular phonological phenomenon in certain words.

Helmer Smith has observed (1950a, p. 36, with reference to pp. 6–8) that Pali orthography is very little sensible of metrical exigencies [2] (licence is indicated by the orthography in a much smaller percentage of its occurrences than in the Buddhist Hybrid Sanskrit manuscripts). We have to assume licence in some cases of apparent irregularity, without the support of any manuscript. The cases quoted below where the quantity required by the metre is not absolutely certain, but only highly probable, have been indicated by a question mark.

Licence is rare in Pali, compared with the usage in Buddhist Hybrid Sanskrit, and where it occurs it is limited to certain "weak points" (even Buddhist Hybrid Sanskrit resisted licence in internal or root syllables: Smith, 1950a, pp. 32–3). It is likely that in the earliest verses we possess there was least licence and on the other hand the greatest freedom in the structure of the metres: thus a short syllable might have been permitted before the caesura at the fifth of the *tuṭṭhubha* in early times,[3] but later we can be sure that the long was established,

[1] Epic Sanskrit (see Zubatý, 1889, Jacobi, 1893a, Hopkins, 1902, Ballini, 1912, part 2, pp. 7, 34 and 60); Classical Sanskrit (Bollensen, 1859, 291; Ballini, 1912, 7–8; Dāmodara, *Vāṇībhūṣaṇa*, I, verse 6—before *pr* and *hr*); Hindī (Sinha, 1953, p. 10).

[2] The emendations of some of the Burmese scribes (for instance in MSS. of Sn: adopted and extended by Fausbøll, and to a lesser extent by Andersen and Smith) are not likely to have been based on any ancient tradition. Their lack of authenticity is clearly shown by such cases as the omission of *ca* (Sn second edition, p. 47, notes 1 and 5) to compensate the number of syllables after the medieval misreading of *-cariyā* as three syllables.

[3] But not before that at the fourth, unless early Pali was freer than Vedic.

preparing the resolution allowed in Buddhist Hybrid Sanskrit.[1]

In the remainder of this Chapter about one hundred cases of metrical licence in Pali are classified. They are taken from Aggavaṃsa (A), Geiger (G), the PED and CPD, Simon (RS),[2] Mayrhofer (M), Smith (HS), Fausbøll (F) and Dhammapāla, supplemented by the present writer's collections (not marked).

The Final Syllable

§ 102. The plasticity of final syllables was a legacy from Old Indo-Aryan metrics. Zubatý in a series of articles (WZKM 1888–90) quotes many Vedic examples showing the variation of quantity in such cases as:

conjugation: *-tī̆* (*rákṣatī̆*, etc.)
-thā̆ (*jīváyathā̆*, etc.)
-hī̆
-ā̆ (perfect: *ā̆́hā̆* 3s., *vidā̆́* 2p.)
-svā̆

declension: *-enā̆*
-asyā̆
-ā̆ (vocative)
-an stems > *ā̆*
sá > *sā́*

adverbs and particles (here Zubatý finds a correlation with the position of the accent;[3] the long ending is generalized when oxytone as in *purutrā́*):

-trā̆ (*átrā̆*, *tátrā̆*, etc.)
-thā̆
-dhā̆ (*ádhā̆*)
ca > *cā* (twice only in ṚVS)
ná > *nā́* (once only in ṚVS)
caná > *canā́* (once only in ṚVS)
ácchā̆
smā̆
adyā̆
kílā̆

[1] See Ch. VIII on the evolution *tuṭṭhubha* > *upajāti*.
[2] ZDMG, 1890.
[3] cf. § 73 above.

yádī̆
tū̆́
sū̆

These variants were not generated " metri causa ", and according to Zubatý (WZKM 1888, p. 139) the long final appeared originally before a single consonant or in absolute final position [1] and the short final before a double consonant or at the close of a grammatical or metrical unit (≏ " nexus ") : " am Schlusse eines grammatischen (. . . metrischen) Ganzen." The anticipation of the " Law of morae " is interesting.

In Pali we find the following alterations of the normal quantity in order to satisfy the metre :

§ 103. Lengthened final :

nadatī (Th I 832) (G)
bhāvayatī (Dh 350) (RS)
ravatī (J I 77) (RS)
saratī (J II 127) (RS)
passatī (Dh 119) (RS)
bajjhatī (Sn 508)
ramatī (Sn 985)
yajatī ? (Sn 509) (F)
passathā ? (Sn 177)
vadā ? (Sn 383)
pānudī ? (Sn 476)
sambhontī (Th II 329) (RS)
patthayasī (M) (Sn 18 ff. and Th I 51 ff. in *opacchandasaka* cadence)
munī ? (Sn 838)
tayī ? (Sn 382) (F)
cā [2] (Sn 41, 67 ?, 82 ?, 481 ?)
nā (Pv 28) (Dhammapāla)
sū (Sn 181, 885, 970)

—the same result is in one case indicated by writing a doubled consonant after the final vowel :

[1] It seems likely that in all Indo-Aryan metres the *pāda*-final, if short, was lengthened, cf. §§ 225–6 below.
[2] On this see H. Smith, 1950a, p. 7 " 3.4 ".

sarati bbayo (J III 95) (G)
(= *vayo*)

—one case of nasalization has been found (but not for the purpose of lengthening):

idham (Sn 151) (HS) (*sandhi* consonant ?)

§ 104. Shortened final:

akaramhasa (for *-se*) (J III 26) } (A)
okkantāmasi (for *-se*) (J VI 555) } (A)
siñcitva (Sn 771) } (HS)
chetva ? (Sn 66) } (HS)
(*chetva* Sn 29 in *opacchandasaka* cadence)
puggala (Vv 617c) (Dhammapāla) [1]
nimmakkhŏ ? (Sn 56)
okamokata (for *-to*) (Dh 34) (G)
sīlavatātŏ (Sn 899)
kāmĕ ? (Sn 464)
va (" or ") (Sn 222) (G)

—the same result is also obtained by denasalization:

pāpuṇi (Th II 91) (G)
phassetŭṃ ? (Sn 393) (F)
addhāna (Dh 207) (G)
jātĭṃ ? (Sn 462)
pañcannăṃ ? (Sn 964)
paṭhamasmĭṃ (Sn 233)
ayăṃ (Sn 594)

—" in *sandhi* ": *samatimaññi 'haṃ* (Th II 72) (G)

—several other examples of denasalization of final are given by A (Sd 630), who evidently regards it as a possible result of ordinary *sandhi*, not as *vuttasandhi* or metrical licence.[2] We noted in Chapter II, however, that the cases he quotes are mostly under stress of metre. In Chapter III we have discussed

[1] Followed by Aggavaṃsa. Hardy, however, in the PTS edition with the Commentary, 1901, prints as compound with the following word. Aggavaṃsa says (Sd pp. 15 and 634) that the inflections, especially *-o*, may be left off nouns (*avibhattikaniddeso*), giving this illustration and *thera vādānam* (Dīp.), but remarking that others read *theravādānam* !

[2] cf. § 64 above on (exceptional) simplification of a following conjunct when a vowel is elided after *niggahīta*: does this indicate that a short syllable results ?

the possibility that such cases indicate not denasalization but the existence of short nasal vowels in Pali, the prototypes of those in Apabhraṃśa.

§ 105. The final syllable was occasionally elided altogether under stress of metre :

chamā (for *chamāya*, loc. s ?) [1] (J VI 89)
somana- (for *somanassa-*) (Sn 67) } (A)

acchodi (for *acchodaka*) (D II 135)
aḍḍhake (for *-esu*) (Ap 75, 77, 439)
anussāvane (for *-ena*) (Vin V 203)
avijjā (for *-āya*) (Sn 1033) } (HS in CPD)

§ 106. In Buddhist Hybrid Sanskrit, as Edgerton has shown, alteration of the ends of words under stress of metre is very common. The licence already practised in Pali was greatly extended. The verb ending *-ti* is frequently lengthened to *-tī* and also *-te* and all other verb endings may similarly be lengthened or shortened. Any word, including indeclinables, ending in *-a* may be lengthened to *-ā* (*cā*, etc.) but much more often to *-o* (*tena* > *teno*, *pañca* > *pañco*, etc.). The final vowels *i* and *e*, *a* and *o*, are generally interchangeable, and not only denasalization, but nasalization of the final, which is practically unknown in Pali, is common.

In Ardhamāgadhī, according to Jacobi, we find denasalization of finals m.c. throughout the declension (1884, p. 596). According to Banarsi Das Jain (1923, p. x) the *anusvāra* is quite generally variable for metrical convenience. Jacobi further states that *e* and *o* may be long or short ; in the manuscripts *i*, *u*, *a*, are often written for them.

The Seam

§ 107. The " seam ", whether between stem and suffix (in cases where the suffix was still felt to be something added to the stem), between words in a compound, or between prefix and root, was another weak point where the quantity of the syllable could be altered without offence to the ear. In Vedic Kuryłowicz (1949) has noted a certain fluidity in the length of antesuffixal

[1] According to the PED, however, this is the instrumental used adverbially, cf. Vedic : *kṣamā*.

vowels, sometimes utilized for metrical purposes, whilst Zubatý in the articles already quoted has shown that the indeclinables *ádhī̆, abhī̆, párī̆, atī̆, pratī̆, vī̆, ánū̆*, which normally end in a short vowel, may sometimes, but especially in compounds (in the case of the last four, only in compounds), end in a long vowel. Between two prefixes Meillet has noted from Wackernagel (1905, p. 71) *anānukṛtyá-* m.c.,[1] and he has also noted nasalization in the seam, m.c., in *dadhanti* and *dadhantu*.

In Pali we find :

§ 108. Lengthened seam :

satīmant- (S I 81, Dh 91, 181, Sn 45, Th II 35) (A, G, PED)
jutīmant- } (RS)
dhitīmant- } (RS)
matīmant- (HS)
therīke (Th II 1) (G) [2]
mutīyā (Sn 846)
sarabhāmiga (J VI 537)
kimādhikaraṇaṃ (J IV 4)

(but cf. *-ā-* in compounds : many similar cases are not metrica lengthening, and these too are doubtful. See G § 33)

anūdake (J VI 499) (G)
anūpama (Ap 319, Bv VI 1)
anūpaya (Sn 786, 897)
anītiha (Sn 934, 1053, 1066, Th I 331, etc.)
anānugiddha (Sn 86, 778)
anānupassi ? (U 74)
anānupuṭṭha ? (Sn 782)
anānuyāyi (Sn 1071–3)
anānuruddha (S IV 71)
anānuloma (D II 273)
anānuvajja (Vin I 359)
anāpara (Sn 1094)
anāvara (I 76)
} (CPD)

[1] But cf. *anu-* > *ānu-* in the next section (§ 111).
[2] This, however, may be a recent Burmese emendation.

(these and a number of others like them are clearly facilitated by the " Law of de Saussure—Wackernagel ". Some do not occur with the short seam ; they had become fixed in the language with the long form suited to the " old language-rhythm ").

In the words *vitarāsi* (J II 14), *garahāsi* (J IV 248), (G) we may have lengthened seams, or they may be genuine subjunctives.

—the same by doubling the following consonant :

paribbasāno (for *-v-*) (Sn 796) (G)
suggatiṃ (J IV 496) }
na ppajjahe (J III 14) } (A)

no doubt *parijjanā* at A III 38 is m.c. for *parijanā*.

§ 109. Shortened seam :

paccanĭkā (G)
purăṇo ? (Sn 312)
gimhisu (for *-esu*) (Dh 286) (A and G)

—by simplifying the following conjunct :

ākiñcăñaṃ ? (Sn 1070–2)
dakkhĭsaṃ ? (Th II 84) (G)
sikkhĭsāmase ? (Sn 814) (F)
apaccĭsaṃ (J VI 16) (A)
nĭdoso (Sn 476)
ăñāṇā ? (Sn 839) (F)
dŭkhaṃ (very frequent—by analogy with *sukhaṃ*, J VI 552, Th I 734, etc.) (A and G)

—by both :

padīpeyyaṃ > *padīpĭyaṃ* (Vv XXII 5—but this may be a by-form ; cf. § 52)

—by denasalization :

jīvăto (J III 539) (G)
dīyănte (Th II 475)

§ 110. In Buddhist Hybrid Sanskrit we again find this form of licence much extended, e.g. *śonīta, sūrata* (but cf. Smith, 1950a, pp. 12–13), *Sūdhana, cajjino, mīḍhaggirī, Sarvajjagābhimukharūpa* (Smith, 1950a, p. 9 quotes this incorrectly), *śīlaṃśrutajñāna-, bībhatsa.*

Lengthened Initial Syllable (especially Initial Vowel)

§ 111. Meillet has noted after Wackernagel (1905, p. 71) that in Vedic *anu-* sometimes becomes *ānu-* before -⏑, e.g. *ānuṣūka-*. In Pali we find a few similar cases of lengthened initial vowel:

ānubodhiṃ (A V 46) (HS)
ūpanissaya (Sn 867, 901?)
ūbhayaṃ (S I 134, A III 311)

There was a definite tendency to lengthen initial syllables in Pali and in Buddhist Hybrid Sanskrit, not so much for metrical convenience but as part of the phonology of the languages. If in the "old language-rhythm" there was, besides the Saussurian ⏑–⏑– law, a "law" which we might name after Meillet: ⏑⏑–⏑ > –⏑–⏑ (although clearly it had much less force than the other law), in the "new language-rhythm" its place was taken by the more effective initial stress discovered by Jacobi (see Chapter III).[1]

In BHS Edgerton notes "presumably m.c." (*Grammar*, § 3.11) *ānubhāva, ātireka, pāripūrṇa, bhāvāmi,* and others: clearly this form of licence too was much extended.

Licence Apparently Based on Historical and Dialectal Variation

§ 112. If the Vedic, Ardhamāgadhī or Apabhraṃśa cognate had a rhythm different from that of the normal form of a Pali word we need not be surprised to find that a poet occasionally lapsed into this alternative form under stress of metre.

[1] Edgerton, 1953, *Grammar*, § 3.9, questions this accent-theory, which he finds in Geiger, § 24, without stating his reasons (he questions the whole theory, including the penultimate accent—see § 2.77 n.). It seems, however, that sufficient evidence has been adduced to prove it (see the discussion in Ch. III), at any rate for Pali and Ardhamāgadhī. It would be surprising to find that it did not apply in BHS, and the onus is surely on Edgerton to disprove it if he can.

Alteration to the Vedic rhythm :

dutiyena > *dutīyena* (Sn 49, 450, 884)
tatiyaṃ > *tatīyaṃ* (Dh 309) (G)

Alteration to later Prakrit rhythms :

evam > *em* (J II 40) (A) (cf. AM *em*)
-jĭviṃ ? (Sn 181–2) (this is in any case uncertain, but cf. Apabhraṃśa *jiya*, Alsdorf : *Der Kumārapālapratibodha* (1928), p. 54 ; his glossary suggests that *jīva* is, however, still the more usual form in Apabhraṃśa).

Metrical Haplology

§ 113. *accupatati* > *accupati* (J IV 250) (HS in CPD)

Other Types of Licence and General Conclusions on Licence

§ 114. Other types of metrical licence are very rare in Pali.[1] The root vowel appears to be shortened in the following cases (cf. *-jĭviṃ* ? above) :

mĕdassa ? (Sn 196) (cf. p. 35 above : √*mĭd*)
ñăṇena (Sn 839 = 1078) (written long)
ĕso ? ? (Sn 61 twice)

Finally we have to read *anusāyitaṃ* for *anusayitaṃ* in Sn 355 (pp. of *anuseti*).

The above lists could be considerably extended, but they are sufficient to indicate the types of licence which were accepted in ancient Pali verse. Here they are as far as possible limited to examples which are clear from our knowledge that the *vatta* and *tuṭṭhubha-jagatī* cadences were fixed well before the Pali period (otherwise they are marked as doubtful). In the light of a fuller understanding of the metres it will be possible to detect many other metrical alterations. The present chapter, however, is intended as a preliminary to the study of the metres, independent of that study and serving as part of the basis for it.

We may formulate a general rule for licence in Pali (if not in all languages) : that the poets sought to disguise licence and to

[1] Even in BHS metrical alterations are much less common " in the interior of a word "—Edgerton, 1946, p. 205.

make the altered forms pass as regular ones. In this way, of course, they assisted in the establishment of new forms in the language and in later dialects. Smith (1950a, p. 4) has noted that *iha* > *ihaṃ* in BHS is not pure metrical licence, but may be justified morphologically by comparison with *kahaṃ*, *tahaṃ*, etc. The same applies to *idha* > *idham* in Pali.

The fluidity of the language, persisting from ancient times, justified the majority of the alterations. Although in most cases we can say that one alternative was normal in Pali, the other evidently passed without offence to the ear. In some of these cases an archaic form perhaps enhanced the effectiveness of the poetry, in others, where the fluidity was a new development in Middle Indian resulting from the confusion of declensions, etc., the form passed by analogy.

Chapter V
MATTĀCHANDAS

Citram āmnāyād anyo nūtanacchandasām avatāraḥ

—Bhavabhūti

General—The Musical Metres

§ 115. The *mattāchandas* were the first new metres to appear in the post-Vedic period. Although some changes took place in the *anuṭṭhubha* and *tuṭṭhubha* during their long history preceding the appearance of *mattāchandas*, there was no decisive break but only a gradual tendency towards more fixed forms of *pāda*. With *mattāchandas*, however, even if its origins can be traced in the Vedic techniques of verse making, we find a radical departure, the establishment of a completely new principle of verse building, which led on the one hand to the countless new metres of Classical Sanskrit and on the other to the musical metres of Apabhraṃśa and the modern vernaculars. The establishment of the principle of *mattā* measurement was decisive for the whole subsequent history of Indian poetry, and this extraordinary event took place during the period we are studying, its first manifestations being found in ancient Pali verse.

§ 116. In Indian music a two-fold division is recognized: *mārga* and *deśī*.[1] The former is generally regarded as limited to the Vedic tradition, although there has been a tendency in recent times to define all music which is said to be able to lead the soul to liberation as *mārga*. As opposed to the *sāman* chant, all secular music, whether actual folk music or the " classical " tradition of the professional city and court musicians (which was based on the folk music) appears in the medieval period, and perhaps earlier, to have been called *deśī*. This interesting term indicates the folk music origin of all the secular, non-Vedic, music. Thus Mātaṅga, writing perhaps in the 9th or 10th century A.D., called his treatise on music the *Bṛhaddeśī*. More modern writers such as Dāmodara (*Saṅgītadarpana*, *c.* 1620 A.D.) have

[1] It is convenient to use the Sanskrit terms, although the Pali equivalents exist in both the ancient and the medieval literature and are sometimes of special interest, e.g. *tāḷa* for *tāla*.

unfortunately obscured the matter by calling all classical music *mārga* and using *deśi* as a derogatory term for popular music.[1]

§ 117. The classical secular music was distinguished from the liturgical music of the Veda not only by its new scales and modes probably derived from folk music but also by its rhythms, or *tālas*. The Vedic chant had no *tāla*, since it followed the verse and derived its rhythm from the metre. As we have just said, the new metres, which we are going to study in this chapter and the next, are fundamentally different in structure from Vedic verse, and they differ precisely in that they are related to *tāla*. It is probably no accident that the earliest extant poems in the new metres are in a vernacular dialect and not in the learned language of the Vedic schools. The *vetālīya* [2]—perhaps the most important of the new metres—was also known as the *māgadhikā*, which probably indicates its origin amongst the poets and singers of Magadha.[3] The metre thus appears in Pali, at one stage removed from its native dialect, along with the literature and philosophy of Buddhism radiating westwards from the same country. The Ardhamāgadhī literature which is extant does not appear to be as ancient as the earliest Pali literature in which the new metres are represented (see § 191 below on the *vetālīya* in the *Sūyagaḍaṃ*), but a pun in the *Veyāliyajjhayaṇa* (Sūy. 1.2.1, last verse) shows how close this dialect was to the original Māgadhī of the new metrical techniques :

veyāliyamaggamāgao = " he who has entered the road { leading to destruction (of *karman*) ".
described in *veyāliya* (*vetālīya*) metre ". }

—*veyāliya* means either the metre or Sanskrit *vaidālika*, " destruction ". This old Jaina literature seems to be directly descended from the original Māgadhī literature of perhaps the

[1] The usual Pali term however (Cy. trad.) is *gandhabba-sippa* (*gāndharva-śilpa*).

[2] We follow the conventional spelling of later times. *Vetālīya* however was probably the original pronunciation.

[3] See the references given by Velankar, 1949, p. 28. (This book is useful, especially for the texts and references, but the introductory matter is highly erratic.)

6th or 5th century B.C., in which the new techniques were developed, a point we shall come upon again in discussing *gaṇacchandas* (the "hypermetre" of the *Varṇakas*). Very probably the Ājīvikas were the first sect to use these techniques in the verses used in their ritual song and dance, which appear to have played such an important part in their cult,[1] and the other sects such as the Buddhists and Jainas merely emulated and tried to outshine their rivals.

§ 118. The name *vetālīya* suggests some connection with music, although its exact significance has been forgotten. *Vetāla* at D I 6 is "some magic art, probably connected with music (*ghana-tāḷaṃ*, cymbal beating) such as raising the dead by *mantras*" (PED based on the Commentary). At *Sūyagaḍaṃ* 2.2.15 (p. 87, Vaidya's edn.) *veyāli* is probably the same magic art (Jacobi suggests punishment by spells, following the Commentary). *Vetālika* in Pali means some office at court conected with music, etc.—a "bard"; hence *vetālīya* would be a metre to be used in such singing or chanting. The name *gīti* of the earliest *gaṇacchandas* suggests a completely musical metre.

§ 119. If we look at the first few syllables of a *mattāchandas pāda* (*opacchandasaka* or *vetālīya*) and compare them with those of several other *pādas* in the same metre, we see at once that besides the difference between the prior and posterior members of each *pādayuga* a number of variant structures are current, such as --⏑⏑, ⏑⏑--⏑⏑, ---, -⏑-⏑, -⏑⏑- and so on (prior *pāda*). These are followed by a cadence which appears to be fixed: -⏑-⏑-× (*opacchandasaka*) or -⏑-⏑× (*vetālīya*). The first part of the *pāda* may contain any number from three to six syllables, but it seems to be constant (possible exceptions will be discussed below) in containing six *mattā*, or eight *mattā* in the case of the posterior *pāda*. Such a variation is quite incompatible with Vedic recitation, which depends on the number of syllables, but is entirely compatible with *tāla*, since the length of the whole group of syllables remains constant. This is the new principle, referred to in the Introduction, of the exact

[1] See Basham, 1951, 116–7, etc.

equivalence of two short syllables to one long one.[1] Whereas in the old metrics ⏑⏑-- may be equivalent to ---- and even ⏑⏑⏑- to ----, in the new metrics we find ⏑⏑--=----=⏑⏑⏑⏑⏑⏑ etc.

§ 120. The new metres are further distinguished by being *aḍḍhasamavutta* (*ardhasamavṛtta*), having the two components of the *pādayuga* of different structures. This feature greatly complicates their study, in that we do not find a simple repeating musical rhythm as in, for instance, the Apabhraṃśa *pajjhaṭikā*, which is what we might have expected on the first introduction of musical rhythms into the poetry. What we find resembles rather the result of an attempt to combine musical and metrical rhythms, which on further reflection we might expect as the first step in introducing a new or unfamiliar technique into the metrical tradition : a combination of new and old may be understood and accepted where a totally new form of versification may not. This observation applies particularly to the cadence, which resembles those of the old *tuṭṭhubha* and *anuṭṭhubha*, but the combination of *pādas* of different lengths also was not unknown to the old metrics, being in fact an important feature of Vedic versification in the so-called " lyric metres ". These points will be studied in detail below, but we may make the general observation here that the history of Indian literature shows the successive appearance of more and more fully musically articulated metres—*mattāchandas*—*gaṇacchandas*—*mattāvutta* (*mātrāvṛtta*, not the same as *mattāchandas* !) [2]—*tālavutta*.

[1] It is worth noting in this connection that the tendency to exact oppositions of long and short syllables seems to develop especially when a number of people recite or sing in unison. Dr. Allen has obtained a remarkable recording of Vedic chanting in unison in which this exact opposition of quantities is maintained, giving a striking quasi-*tāla* effect. It appears to have been most unusual in the Vedic tradition for the brahmans to sing in this way, only solo recitation being required in the performance of the ritual. In the non-Vedic traditions such as Buddhism, Ājīvikism and Jainism, on the other hand, recitation of the Canonical texts by large gatherings (*saṅgīti*), in unison, is an essential feature of the life of the communities. This practice may well have been a contributory cause, or " catalyst ", in the development of the new metres in the period of the rise of these communities.

[2] The term *mātrāvṛtta* was applied to the Apabhraṃśa and Hindī musical metres derived from *gaṇacchandas* after the true *mattāchandas* had long been extinct in India. The same word is also used generically to cover all metres in which the *mattā* count is an essential feature of the structure, including all four classes mentioned here.

§ 121. This process of musical infiltration of Indo-Aryan metrics began at a definite stage in the evolution of the Indo-Aryan languages. The interconnection of language and metrics has been noted in the Introduction (§ 31) and at the beginning of Chapter IV. The appearance of musical metres in Pali should not be interpreted as indicating that the *deśī* music (as opposed to " Vedic music ", if such a term has any meaning outside its application to the chanting of sacred texts) originated in about the 5th century B.C., although the nature of those metres may be expected to throw some light on the history of the music by establishing the existence of a particular *tāla* in that early period.[1] It is probable that the Vedic chant itself was derived from the *deśī* music of a very ancient period, but that owing to the nature of the language the *tālas* of that music could not be reflected. With the beginning of the transition to Apabhraṃśa, however, the language and metrics became susceptible of penetration by musical *tālas*, and Canonical Pali shows Indo-Aryan in that critical stage. As the language became more supple (> Apabhraṃśa) its metres became more musical.[2]

§ 122. The two main *mattāchandas* metres are *opacchandasaka* (*aupacchandasika*) and *vetālīya* (*vaitālīya*). It should be noted that the classical metres which bear these names are not *mattāchandas* but have fixed schemes, although they are evidently descended from *mattāchandas* and retain the same numbers of *mattā* per *pāda*. Like *pupphitaggā* (*puṣpitāgrā*) and *aparavatta* (*aparavaktra*) they are merely particular cases of *mattāchandas pāda* structures. We can identify other *mattāchandas* and metres of *mattāchandas* origin by their being

[1] It is possible that this *deśī* music was that of the pre-Aryan population of the Ganges region : it imposed its rhythms, etc., on the Aryan literature (and music ?) just at the time when other presumed pre-Aryan features were imprinted on the religion, etc., of the region (asceticism and Vaiṣṇavism with temple cults, etc., and transmigration).

[2] The primary cause of this evolution Old Indo-Aryan (in fact Indo-Iranian) > Apabhraṃśa, etc., was perhaps the impact of the non-Aryan languages of India. First we get the distinction of dentals and cerebrals, later we get (gradually) a rhythmical assimilation of the Aryan language to its new Indian environment. The Dravidian metres have the exact opposition of quantities ; Munda metrics awaits clarification, but cf. Khmer metrics (exact opposition).

aḍḍhasamavutta. Besides those mentioned, we find in our texts *svāgatā* (still in the *mattāchandas* stage, but not so fluid in structure as the main metres) and *vegavatī* (also approaching its classical fixed structure). In addition to all these we find *samavuttas* which appear to be of *mattāchandas* origin, being particular cases of *mattāchandas* (including *vegavatī*) *pādas* generalized: *rathoddhatā*, *dodhaka* (*meghavitāna* does not seem to occur in the Canon). Finally we may note that the *visamavutta upaṭṭhitappacupita* (*upasthitapracupita*) with its variant structures appears to be derived from *mattāchandas*. This wonderful invention of the old Buddhist poets, which was perhaps the first *tāḷavutta* in Indian literary history, is analysed in Chapter IX on *akkharacchandas*. In their fixed forms all the metres considered here belong to that chapter, where they are accordingly reclassified, but their origins are discussed in the present chapter, since they help to illustrate the nature of *mattāchandas* structure.

§ 123. Some particular *pāda* structures of *opacchandasaka* and *vetālīya* have names, such as *bhaddavirāja*, *pavattaka*, and others (see the tables below), but it does not seem necessary to discuss them as separate metres since they are found only in conjunction with the two main metres. The two main metres occur either independently or in mixed strophes. In the latter case the mixing is normally not haphazard as in *tuṭṭhubha-jagatī* but is a regular alternation of *vetālīya* and *opacchandasaka pādas*. We should perhaps regard this mixed strophe as a third main metre, but its structure does not differ in any respect, other than the cadence, from the first two.[1] In the tables its *pādas* have been counted under *opacchandasaka* and *vetālīya*.

Tables of Mattāchandas *Structure*

§ 124. No detailed discussion can be given in this and the following chapters on the metrical interpretation of particular *pādas* according to the rules given in Chapters I–IV, and no account is given of the hundreds of emendations which had to be made to the printed texts (usually with manuscript support)

[1] See §§ 183 ff. below on strophe structure for an account of the mixed strophe.

in order to scan them, except in isolated cases of special interest. It is hoped to publish a new edition of a typical text (the *Therīgāthā*) in illustration of the metrical interpretations.

§ 125. The present piece of research is of a preliminary nature, and aims at understanding the main usages as a basis (itself liable to modification as our knowledge of ancient Pali increases) for further detailed and more accurate investigations. The extent of the uncertainty in scanning old Pali verses which results from the fluidity of the language and a certain use of licence, as we have already seen, makes it impossible to arrive at precise figures—quite apart from textual corruption. There is thus some scope for the exercise of subjective judgment, the amount of which, and the resulting amount of possible distortion, has been approximately estimated. The figures arrived at indicated that the general picture of *mattāchandas*, for instance, given here, might be about 3 per cent in error, whilst in some of the details, particularly the permissibility of certain *pāda* structures, a much greater local error might be made. After some years of studying these metres and trying to acquire a " feeling " for them, the analysis offered here seems nearest to the truth and can apparently be justified, in its main outlines but probably not in all details, by the study of ancient Pali metrics as a phase in the history of Indian metre. Many doubtful structures have here been recorded and considered, although the eventual conclusion is that all forms defective in quantity (*mattā* count) should be emended. This conclusion cannot be assumed in these preliminary tables.

§ 126. The following tables show the structure of the great majority of the *opacchandasaka* and *vetālīya pādas* in the Pali Canon (a few stray strophes in the *Vinaya* and other predominantly prose texts are not noted here ; however, the aim was to scan everything that could be found in these metres in the Canon, although no doubt a few verses have been overlooked). The schemes show the first part of each *pāda*, consisting of six *mattā* in the prior and eight in the posterior, the cadence being assumed to be fixed : –⏑–⏑–⏓ (*opacchandasaka*) or –⏑–⏓ (*vetālīya*). This is the form of the cadence as given by the Indian theory (e.g. Piṅgala IV 32), and the deviations from it are so rare as to be almost certainly corruptions. It must be noted, however, that some *mattāchandases*, or metres of *mattāchandas* origin, had a different cadence, which we must attempt to explain, and that a certain amount of rhythmic interplay between the free and fixed parts of the *pāda* sometimes seems to involve an overlap in which the first syllable of the cadence belongs to both parts, or even to the free part and not to the cadence at all. It is possible that in these exceptional cases, which have here been called " syncopated ", this syllable could be altered, as long as the *mattā* count of the *pāda* was maintained, and therefore the few examples found where such an alteration appears have been recorded.

§ 127. A number of *pādas* which could not be scanned satisfactorily owing to extensive corruption, have been omitted. Prior *pādas* were more liable to corruption than posterior *pādas* : whereas posterior *pādas* were protected by the prior *pādas* preceding them, prior *pādas* were sometimes remoulded into other metres which were presumably more familiar to the reciters and copyists. The same thing happened in the *gaṇacchandas* verses. These missing *pādas* belong mainly to Sn (twenty-six cases), which was studied first : in working afterwards on the other texts greater efforts were made to obtain some kind of probable scansion, except in the most desperate cases, or when the substituted *pāda* in some other metre left no indication at all of what originally stood there. It will be noticed that owing to this corruption of prior *pādas* the total number of posterior *pādas* scanned in the tables is 5½ per cent greater than that of the prior *pādas*. Owing to the greater length of the posterior *pāda* and the consequent larger number of possible structures, the discrepancy is no doubt partly due to the accepting of corrupted posterior *pādas* merely because they chanced to fit the *mattā* count. A third cause which increased the proportion of posterior *pādas*—especially in Sn—is the occurrence of large numbers of repeated *pādas* as refrains in the fourth *pāda* of the strophe. These were less liable to corruption than the multiform prior *pādas* which accompanied them. All figures should be taken as approximations or estimates only.

§ 132. There are nearly 400 verses in *opacchandasaka* and *vetālīya* in the Canon. The other metres we have mentioned occur much less frequently. *Vegavatī* is represented by twenty-five verses, or thirty-four if we count those which appear in both S I and Th I each time they appear. There are twelve verses predominantly of *pupphitaggā* (which have been included in the tables of *opacchandasaka*) and two of *aparavatta*. *Svāgatā* appears in at least nine verses. Of the *samavuttas*, *dodhaka* seems to be limited to three verses in Vv, but *rathoddhatā* is fairly common; forty-six verses were counted.[1] There are fifteen strophes of *upaṭṭhitappacupita*. Some of these metres are still fluid in the Canon, the alternation –/⏑⏑ being apparently allowed in certain positions, and sometimes ⏑⏑–/⏑–⏑ and other variations. On account of the small numbers of examples, however, one can hardly formulate exact rules. The normal schemes of these metres are as follows:

pupphitaggā ⏑⏑⏑⏑⏑⏑–⏑–⏑–⏓ | ⏑⏑⏑⏑–⏑⏑–⏑–⏑–⏓ × 2
aparavatta ⏑⏑⏑⏑⏑⏑–⏑–⏑⏓ | ⏑⏑⏑⏑–⏑⏑–⏑–⏑⏓ × 2
vegavatī ⏑⏑–⏑⏑–⏑⏑–⏓ | –⏑⏑–⏑⏑–⏑⏑–⏓ × 2
svāgatā –{⏑–⏑/⏑⏑–}– –{⏑⏑/—} ⏓ | –{⏑–⏑/⏑⏑–}– – ⏑⏑–⏓ × 2
dodhaka –⏑⏑–⏑⏑–⏑⏑–⏓ × 4
rathoddhatā –⏑–⏑ ⏑⏑–⏑–⏓ × 4
upaṭṭhitappacupita – – –⏑⏑–⏑–⏑⏑⏑– – | ⏑⏑–⏑⏑⏑⏑–⏑–⏑– – |
⏑⏑⏑⏑⏑⏑⏑⏑–(⏑⏑⏑⏑⏑⏑⏑⏑–) | ⏑⏑⏑⏑⏑⏑⏑⏑⏑⏑⏑–⏑⏑–⏓ × 1
or – – ⏑⏑–⏑–⏑– |

The Mattāchandas *Texts*

§ 133. Before proceeding with our analysis of *mattāchandas* structure and taking up the question of the origin and history of these metres, we may make some general observations about the texts in which they occur. It is part of the purpose of this study to deduce a chronology for some of the Canonical texts on metrical grounds, and little weight is attached here to any of the speculations on Canonical chronology which are based on

[1] *Pādas* of *rathoddhatā* also occur in *vetālīya* verse as a regular variation (at least 20 examples).

such criteria as the development of the doctrine. It has been suggested, for instance, that texts containing " highly systematized " doctrine such as the " eightfold path ", and even the " four truths ", are later in origin than texts of a more poetic nature. The strongest argument in favour of this criterion is that the *Abhidhamma* texts, which are pure systematization, are indisputably later compilations than the *Dhamma-Vinaya* in all the Schools of Early Buddhists, and are largely recognized as such by the traditions. This argument, however, cannot be extended to the analysis of the *Dhamma-Vinaya* texts, and in any case the *Abhidhamma* compilations are almost certainly based not on, or not directly on, surveys of *Dhamma* (*Sutta*) texts but on old lists or *Mātikā* (*Mātṛkā*) of topics, elements, and phenomena, which cannot be proved to be later than the *Dhamma-Vinaya* and may well have formed part of the earliest collection of *Dhamma*.

§ 134. As for the subjective argument that a religious movement necessarily starts on its career with beautiful and inspiring poetry, and afterwards loses its creative élan and produces only dry manuals of doctrine, one can equally convincingly argue the other way round : that Buddhism, for instance, began as one of the countless sects of early philosophical inquirers in India, each with its own system of elements and so on (much of it held in common by many of them), and afterwards grew into a great popular movement with poets and preachers using all the literary arts to arouse and persuade the lay people on whom the success of the movement depended. The History of Buddhism was clearly much more complex than any such over-simplified scheme can indicate. The chronological arguments in this study are advanced on purely metrical grounds, although interesting correspondences with some of the speculations referred to have been found. Some of these may provisionally be indicated here, subject to detailed confirmation in the analysis which follows.

§ 135. The pre-Pali literature possessed a very small number of metres, whilst the post-Pali literature used a very large number of metres, the new ones being constructed on principles quite different from those of the old metres. We may therefore expect to find Pali texts standing at different stages in this development in their use of metres, unless all the texts were composed at the same time and show only one stage. An extreme case is the *Lakkhaṇa Sutta* in D III, which contains a greater variety of metres than any other Canonical text, all of them, moreover, being either new " Classical " type metres or Classical forms of old metres. In the latter category we find *rucirā* and *vaṃsaṭṭhā* (*vaṃśasthā*), in the former *rathoddhatā, upaṭṭhitappacupita, uggatā* and *pamitakkharā* (*pramitākṣarā*). Besides these six metres we find verses which are predominantly *pupphitaggā*, sprinkled with *pādas* of the more common forms of *opacchandasaka*, some or all of which may be corruptions. These metrical considerations justify the conclusion that this is a late text standing on the threshold of Classical Sanskrit metrics. It is therefore of great interest to note that in content this *sutta* is an elaborate piece of " Buddhology " describing in minute detail the thirty-two physical characteristics of the Buddha. In the histories of the religion this iconographic development has often been supposed to be a late development in Early Buddhism, tending to Mahāyāna, and this more or less subjective argument can now be supported by the objective evidence of the metre. Finally, on turning to the commentary on this *sutta*, we discover that the orthodox tradition records that the verses are not so ancient and authentic as the bulk of the Canon by attributing them to Ānanda : *etā pana gāthā porāṇakatherā Ānandatherassa ṭhapitā vaṇṇagāthā ti vatvā gatā* (DA p. 922).

§ 136. The earliest stratum of Pali verse is not so easy to locate, since the use of only one or two metres is not in itself proof that the others were unknown. There are, for instance, such uninspired compositions as the *Cariyāpiṭaka* and the *Apadāna*, which may be shown to be derivative from the *Jātaka* and *Theratherīgāthā* and entirely devoid of originality or poetic interest.[1] Apart from three garbled verses copied from *ariyā* verses of Th II, the metrical outlook of these two texts is limited to pedestrian *vatta* composition with a very few

[1] On Cp cf. § 6 above.

tuṭṭhubha strophes. In these cases we may safely conclude that the pious monks who compiled the texts had no knowledge of metrics beyond the two commonest metres and no poetic aspirations. These texts tacked on to the end of the last *Nikāya* of the Canon may represent a final decadent phase of Pali composition, later than the great period of innovation and creation of new techniques which culminated in the *Lakkhaṇa Sutta*, when the Theravāda Pali poets were left behind by those of newer schools with new ideas to express (see e.g. the *Mahāvastu*).

§ 137. The *Suttanipāta* contains a high proportion of *mattāchandas*, fairly homogeneous in structure and not characterized by successions of short syllables or other techniques of classical metrics. The collection as a whole, however, is far from homogeneous, as we shall see when we analyse the *vatta* poems in it (cf. also § 20 above), and whilst it may contain some of the earliest Pali verses we possess, its composition extended over a long period. Its metrical techniques do not include those of the latest phases, although they do include *gaṇacchandas* and *vegavatī*, so it would appear that it represents an early, or at least an intermediate, period preceding that which ended with the *Lakkhaṇa Sutta*. An inscription of Asoka appears to refer either to the whole collection at some stage in its growth or to the *Muni Sutta* (*tuṭṭhubha*) which concludes its first *vagga*.

§ 138. A large part of the *Therīgāthā*, and part of the *Theragāthā*, seems to be especially characteristic of the later creative period leading up to the *Lakkhaṇa Sutta*. Here we find the tendency to successions of short syllables and certan other " classical " techniques. We are fortunate in possessing the *Subhā Jīvakambavanikā* poem in *vetālīya*, which is an excellent example of proto-classical *kabba* composition, not only in its metrics but also in its vocabulary and *alaṅkāras* :

madhurañ ca pavanti sabbaso,
kusumarajena samuddhatā dumā |
paṭhamavasanto sukho utu,
ehi ramāmasi pupphite vane ||

kusumitasikharā va pādapā,
  abhigajjanti va māluteritā |
˘ ⟨-⟩
kā tuyhaṃ rati bhavissati,
[-]
  yadi ekā vanam ogahissasi ||
vāḷā[1]*migasaṅghasevitaṃ,*
  kuñjaramattakareṇulolitaṃ |
asahāyika gantum icchasi,
  rahitaṃ bhiṃsanakaṃ mahāvanaṃ ||
tapanīyakatā va dhītikā,
  vicarasi cittarathe va accharā |
kāsikasukhumehi vagguhi,
  sobhasi vasan⟨avar⟩ehi 'nūpame ||
ahaṃ tava vasānugo siyaṃ,
  yadi viharemasi kānanantare |
⟨-⟩
na hi m' atthi tayā piyataro,
  pāṇo kinnarimandalocane || Th II 371–5

§ 139. The *Sagātha Vagga* of the *Saṃyutta* (S I) is another collection which is rich in metrical innovation and in poetic content. The *vegavatī* verses [2] ascribed to the famous poet Vaṅgīsa or Vāgīsa Thera occur in both this collection and the *Theragāthā*.[3] Other *mattāchandas* verses in S I attributed to Vaṅgīsa include the *vetālīya* strophe (*Pavāraṇā*) and the remarkable " unpremeditated " verses of the *Parosahassa* section in which Helmer Smith (Sd 1171) sees the fusion of old rhythms from which will develop the *caupāī* of Apabhraṃśa and later vernacular poetry. Elsewhere in S I we find the *svāgatā* metre. Both the advanced nature of these metres and the tradition that some of the poems were composed by a disciple and not by the Buddha (cf. the *Lakkhaṇa Sutta*) point to a late period : indeed a large part of the *Sagātha* poetry is assigned to persons and beings other than the Buddha, although

[1] Or perhaps *viyāḷa-* (*udiccavutti*), cf. Sanskrit *vyāḍa*.
[2] *Arati* and *Pesalā-atimaññanā*.
[3] Note also the connection between S I and the *Therīgāthā* (*Bhikkhunī-saṃyutta*).

as is usual in such cases in the Canon he is supposed to have been present to approve the verses. In folklore this is perhaps the richest part of the Canon, and we seem to have a glimpse of the Early Buddhists working to spread their teachings in a popular milieu through the medium of a popular style of composition akin to folk music and dancing. The name *geyya* for this type of composition (tradition of the commentaries, referring to S I) may indicate some kind of performance of these short dramatic scenes with musical accompaniment. The study of this *geyya* literature should help us to understand the *deśī* (folk music) origin of the new metres in the vernacular languages, to which we referred in the first section of this chapter. Indian folk music and popular poetry, defying systematization, continuously created new techniques, which re-fertilized the more artificial " classical " literature from the time of Vaṅgīsa down to that of Puṣpadanta and Jayadeva.

§ 140. The *Jātaka* used folk stories to popularize the teaching in a way similar to the use of folklore by the *Sagātha*. A large part of it, like most of the *Sagātha*, may tentatively be associated with our " later creative period ", but other parts of this vast collection may be at least as old as anything in the *Suttanipāta*, since they exhibit similar styles of composition to the latter. The bulk of the *Jātaka mattāchandas* resembles that of Sn in structure, whilst we shall see that the *gaṇacchandas* resembles that of Th II ; this apparent discrepancy is due to there being no connection between these *Jātakas* in different metres other than their inclusion in the same collection, which probably took place at different periods.

§ 141. The *Vimānapetavatthu* may be entirely late in composition. It has been pointed out that it includes a reference to events which took place about two centuries after the Nibbāna,[1] and its level of literary inspiration is well on the downward path to the piety of the *Apadāna* and the *Cariyāpiṭaka*. Only rarely

[1] Piṅgalaka being king of Suraṭṭha : see PvA, p. 244. The *Theragāthā* includes verses ascribed to at least six *theras* who are recorded by the Commentary to have been ordained after the Nibbāna, three of them in the Moriyan period (Tekicchakāni, Vītasoka and Ekavihāriya). Vv and Pv are probably still later than this, i.e. considerably later than the traditional date of Piṅgalaka.

do we come across anything of interest, such as a story which is told in a different version but with some of the same verses (*mattāchandas*) in the *Jātaka*.

The remaining *mattāchandas* verses are scattered strophes about which we can say very little as yet, since the anthologies (*Udāna*, *Dhammapada*) and prose texts (D II, *Vinaya*, *Udāna*) in which they appear have not yet been subjected to serious historical analysis.[1] There seems to be no reason to suppose that any of these verses are very early, with the possible exception of one or two *udānas*.

§ 142. Although there are no hard and fast boundaries between the periods or phases of Pali literature to which we have referred, and most of the Canonical collections overlap at least two of them, it is worth noting here that this tentative survey of some of our material would suggest, when placed against the historical background (see our Introduction and the stray references in the texts mentioned above), that it might be useful to assume three phases :

(i) An earlier period, during which *mattāchandas* and *gaṇacchandas* first appeared, represented by most of the *Suttanipāta*. This is a pre-Moriyan period, but we have not found evidence to indicate whether it includes anything as early as the 5th century B.C., and, if not, whether any extant Pali literature belongs to a still earlier period.

(ii) A later period, during which both new classes of metre became markedly transformed in structure in accordance with the tendency to Apabhraṃśa rhythms, and new metres of the fixed classical type appeared in increasing numbers ; represented by a large part of the *Therīgāthā*, part of the *Theragāthā* and the *Lakkhaṇa Sutta*. This approximately coincides with the period of the Moriyan Empire.

(iii) A period of decline in literary creation, represented by most or all of the *Petavatthu* and the whole of the *Cariyāpiṭaka*. This decline may have begun under the Moriyan Empire, at the

[1] On Dh see Senart, *Les Inscriptions de Piyadasi*, II, Paris, 1886, pp. 314–22, who points out the resemblance between the doctrine of Dh and that of Asoka's inscriptions.

end of the 3rd century B.C., but coincides roughly with the 2nd century B.C.

The Origin of Mattāchandas

§ 143. In the ZDMG of 1884 (vol. 38), pp. 591–5, Jacobi outlined his conceptions of the origin of *vetālīya* (i.e. of *mattāchandas* generally), its further development giving rise to *aparavatta* (through what he calls the " victory of the quantitative principle "), and the evolution of *gaṇacchandas*.[1] Hopkins (1902, p. 337, etc.) gives a different theory contradicting Jacobi's (although he does not seem to have known Jacobi's work), on the basis of his study of the Epics.

Hopkins bases his theory on the fact that *opacchandasaka* and *vetālīya* are almost unknown in the *Mahābhārata* (except for what he calls a " sporadic approach to *vaitālīya* . . . in a late passage of *Vana* and in *Śānti* ") whilst *pupphitaggā* and *aparavatta* occur more than ninety times (" chiefly in later part of the epic "—also in *Harivaṃśa*, where *pupphitaggā* is sometimes mixed with *upajāti*, 3, 6, 10). If Hopkins is right in assigning the main composition of the present *Mahābhārata* to about the 2nd century B.C. with additions until the 4th century A.D. (1902, p. 398, etc.), then it is later than the Pali Canon, which we saw in our Introduction to have been composed between the 5th and the 2nd centuries B.C. Oldenberg's researches on the *vatta*, which led to the conclusions we have stated in § 20 (see Chapter VII for more details), are in complete agreement with these deductions on the relative ages of the Canon and the Epic.

§ 144. Some verses in the Epic may be earlier than the 2nd century B.C., being taken literally, or perhaps with linguistic adaptations (Sanskritization ?) not always affecting the metre, from the old *Itihāsa* mentioned in the Pali Canon, but probably none of the *pupphitaggā* or *aparavatta*, which Hopkins associates

[1] See also Kühnau, 1886, pp. 178 ff. and 206, etc., on apparent correspondences between *mattāchandas* and *tuṭṭhubha* and *virāja* (*virāj*) and the probable origin of *mattāchandas*. These researches seem to have been quite independent of those of Jacobi, although they were published two years later. Ballini, 1912, part 2, 73 ff. simply reports the conclusions of Jacobi and Hopkins without adding new arguments.

with the later parts of the Epic, are so old. We can therefore refute Hopkin's theory that *opacchandasaka—vetālīya* evolved out of *pupphitaggā—aparavatta* simply by placing the Pali evidence beside that of the *Mahābhārata*, whatever the reason for the preference for the latter metres in the Epic.

Hopkins is apparently on stronger ground with the *Rāmāyaṇa*, where he finds *pupphitaggā-aparavatta* tags in Books I–VI but *opacchandasaka–vetālīya* tags in Book VII. Unfortunately he overlooked the fact that these *opacchandasaka–vetālīya* verses are in the fixed classical form of the metres, not in the true *mattāchandas* form of the Pali Canon. In any case it is certain that the *Rāmāyaṇa* in its present form is not only later than the Canon but, on the average, later than the *Mahābhārata*, although the latter probably had some additions made to it down to a still later date. The argument deriving *pupphitaggā* directly from *tuṭṭhubha-jagatī* (Hopkins, p. 337) by the resolution of two long syllables to give a posterior *pupphitaggā* (the derivation of the prior *pāda* along similar lines would be still more arbitrary) is thus entirely fanciful, and Hopkins was completely mistaken in supposing that the fully fledged *pupphitaggā* (with its long successions of short syllables) appeared first and was followed by a reversion to a metre much closer in structure to the *tuṭṭhubha*.

§ 145. Jacobi regards *pupphitaggā* as a development from a "pure" *mattāchandas* (early *opacchandasaka*), and derives *vetālīya* (which he takes as the basic type—Hopkins takes *opacchandasaka* as the type and describes *vetālīya* as "catalectic") from the Vedic *satobṛhatī* (2 × 12 + 8 syllables). This is plausible in that the appearance of successions of short syllables can be followed stage by stage through the transition to classical metrics. In our earliest *opacchandasaka–vetālīya* the principle of *mattā* measurement was perhaps not yet fully established (this is Jacobi's view), so that only the unevenness of the prior and posterior *pādas* is the essential characteristic which distinguishes metres belonging to the *mattāchandas* family. The derivation of *vetālīya* from *satobṛhatī*, however, is unconvincing owing to the great gap in time between the Vedic and Pali periods of Indian poetry. Jacobi's idea of ritual tampering with Vedic metres leading to metrical experiments which resulted in *vetālīya* is even less happy than Hopkins' forced derivation of *pupphitaggā*.

§ 146. The theory that the new metres were a continuation of the Vedic "lyric metre" tradition of the combination of unequal *pādas* (which otherwise has to be regarded as having disappeared completely without being replaced by any new technique) can in fact be improved. It is not necessary to divide the first "foot" of the *satobṛhatī* and to transfer three of its syllables to the posterior *pāda* as "anacrusis", for in the *Suttanipāta* we find two poems having a strophe structure closely paralleling the Vedic lyrics. This is the mixed *vetālīya-opacchandasaka*, in which the *vetālīya* always takes the prior position and the *opacchandasaka* the posterior :

baddhā hi bhisī susaṅkhatā,
tiṇṇo pāragato vineyya oghaṃ |
attho bhisiyā na vijjati,
atha ce patthayasī pavassa deva || Sn 21

—let us compare this not with the *satobṛhatī* but with what Arnold calls the "uneven lyric" : *anuṣṭubh* + *triṣṭubh* (instead of *anuṣṭubh* + *jagatī*) :

ágne tvám no ántama,
utá trātā́ śivó bhavā varūthyàḥ |
vásur agnír vásuśravā,
áchā nakṣi dyumáttamaṃ rayíṃ dāḥ |
sá no bodhi śrudhī́ hávam,
uruṣyā́ ṇo aghāyatáḥ samasmāt |
táṃ tvā śociṣṭha dīdivaḥ,
sumnā́ya nūnám īmahe sákhibhyaḥ || ṚVS V 24

– – ˘˘– ˘ – ˘ –, – – – ˘ ˘ – ˘ – ˘ – –|
– – ˘˘– ˘ – ˘ ˘, ˘˘– – ˘ ˘ – ˘ – ˘ – ˘ || Sn 21
– – ˘ – ˘[1] – ˘ ˘, ˘ – – – ˘ – ˘ – ˘ – [˘][2] – |
˘ ˘ – – ˘ – ˘ –, – – – – ˘ – ˘ – ˘ – –|
˘ – – – ˘ – ˘ ˘, ˘ – – – ˘ – ˘ – ˘ – –|
– – – – ˘ – ˘ –, – – ˘ – ˘ – ˘ – ˘ – – || ṚVS V 24

[1] *nŏ* short metrically when followed by a vowel : Arnold, 1905, pp. 6 and 7.
[2] The accent would indicate that this *y* counts as a separate syllable : Arnold, 1905, p. 83. But exceptions are possible.

—the general similarity here is at once apparent. Other *pādas* in the Pali poem appear to coincide exactly with individual Vedic *pādas* : compare *puttā ca me samāniyā arogā* (Sn 24b) with the final Vedic *pāda*, or *sutvā devassa vassato* (Sn 30c) with the penultimate Vedic *pāda*.

§ 147. Although this bringing together of texts so widely separated in time and in manner of recitation cannot show a direct correspondence, it does seem possible that both groups of metres belong to the same class (a class of specifically "lyric" metres having special connections with music ?) at different stages of development, and that the coincidence is not accidental. We may suggest that the combining of the Vedic lyric metres with a musical accompaniment (including *tāla*) led to changes in rhythm (groupings of syllables) within the framework of the ancient *pāda* structure (number of syllables and quantity of each syllable, where this was fixed, especially in the cadence). Eventually, with a firm musical basis established of $14 + 18 \times 2$ *mattā* corresponding to the average duration of the old syllabic strophe, the number and quantity of the syllables may be varied without disturbing the flow of the verses. The new metre would then be not a curious and apparently arbitrary combination of 14 and 18 *mattā pādas*, but the result of a natural historical development : the supplanting of an old metre by a new one on a new basis but conditioned by its origin within characteristic limits.[1] We shall have more to say on the relationship between *mattāchandas* and the older metres in the following sections, since, whatever their past interconnections may have been, they certainly seem to have interacted on one another during the Pali period.

§ 148. To summarize the discussion in this section on the origin of *mattāchandas* we should first stress the importance of its special connections with music and the musical organization of its rhythmic structure.[2] There is no proof of any connection with the metres of the Vedic tradition, and the new metre may

[1] Assimilation of Indo-Aryan lyric metres to the pre-Aryan ?

[2] The alternation ⏑⏑/–. The structure will be discussed in detail below, and its musical affinities will then be seen more clearly.

have had its origin in *deśī* (Māgadhī) [1] folk song : its rhythms may even be non-Indo-Aryan in origin, coming perhaps from some Munda tradition in Eastern India. The arguments for a Vedic origin are the unevenness of the *pāda* structure, the use of *vetālīya* prior *pādas* and *opacchandasaka* posterior *pādas*, and not vice versa, in the mixed strophes, and the apparent similarity between the shortest *pāda* and *anuṭṭhubha* and between the longest *pāda* and *tuṭṭhubha*. These three points suggest a connection with the Vedic lyric metres, which Arnold believed to have special musical affinities when he so named them. The internal chronology of the *Veda*, and the development of its metres, is still uncertain (apart from such obviously later developments in speculation as a large part of the Tenth Book). Arnold assigns the majority of the lyric verses to the earliest period, but one of his arguments for this is their " being practically unknown in later literature " (1905, p. 9). He also says that in several cases of apparent lyric metre occurring " in the late Rigveda the metre seems to be confused rather than lyric " (p. 50). It may be suggested that in this confusion we might seek the beginning of the transition to *mattāchandas*, and that if they are connected with *mattāchandas* the argument for their great antiquity is reversed, and they may represent a late development in Vedic metrics.

Relationships with other Metres

§ 149. The poem in mixed *vetālīya-opacchandasaka* quoted above in comparison with the " lyric " metres commences with a *tuṭṭhubha pāda* :

pakkodano duddhakhiro 'ham asmi Sn 18a

—this is almost certainly a substitution for or corruption of the original *vetālīya pāda*, but it is not altogether accidental, for as we have seen the two metres may be related through the *opacchandasaka*, which sometimes is very similar to the *tuṭṭhubha* in its posterior *pāda*. There is some metrical evidence in the Canon which suggests that poems have been altered slightly, perhaps to adapt them to Theravāda doctrine, and

[1] Note the alternative name *māgadhikā* for *vetālīya*.

plenty of evidence of substitutions by careless repeaters or scribes : in any case we have good reason to suppose that some of the ancient *theras* responsible for the formation and preservation of the Canon had very little knowledge of metrics and were quite capable of mistaking a *mattāchandas* poem for *tuṭṭhubha*, or a *gaṇacchandas* for *vatta*, even before the partial interruption of the tradition in the 1st century B.C. Similar substituted *pādas* occur elsewhere in Sn, especially in the *Sabhiya Sutta* (510–40), which includes *jagatī pādas*.

§ 150. We have noted the resemblance between the posterior *opacchandasaka pāda* and the *tuṭṭhubha*, particularly in the case where the latter forms the posterior *pāda* of an " uneven lyric " metre : in the case quoted it is interesting to observe that the whole *mattāchandas* cadence is regularly paralleled in the older metre (–⏑–⏑– –) although only the last four syllables are normally reckoned as cadence in the *tuṭṭhubha*. Of still greater interest, however, is the structure of the " break ", the middle part of the *tuṭṭhubha pāda*, in its more regular forms in both Vedic and post-Vedic metrics. In the early form of the metre with caesura after the fourth syllable (Oldenberg, 1915, p. 490 = Arnold's " primitive trimeter verse ") we have × – × –, ⏑ ⏑ – – ⏑ – ×. Less often, but increasing in frequency until it displaces this form altogether in the post-Vedic period, we find × – × –, – ⏑ ⏑ – ⏑ – ×, which is very close to the alternative early form with caesura after the fifth syllable × – × – (×), ⏑ ⏑ – ⏑ – ×, and eventually coalesced with it to form the classical *upajāti* which has no caesura. In these forms the break always contains a pair of short syllables which gives the metre its characteristic ring : a kind of syncopation cutting across the rhythm of the opening, the tension thus created being released in the cadence. Although such a *pāda* is a single integrated rhythmic unit, and cannot be subdivided into " feet " (cf. the discussion on the " ictus " in the Introduction), we see that in the Vedic metre the conflict of rhythms which gives life to the *pāda* may be produced in different ways by the different forms of the break : . . . ⏑ –|⏑ ⏑ – ×| – ⏑ . . . or . . . ⏑ – ×| – ⏑ ⏑|– ⏑ . . . or . . . ⏑ – –|⏑ ⏑|– ⏑ . . . The pair of short syllables seems to oppose itself to the single short syllables of the opening and the cadence, but it also opposes itself, one feels, to the long syllable which precedes or follows it : ⏑ | ⏑ ⏑ but also - | ⏑ ⏑. In other words we seem to find in the *tuṭṭhubha* break an anticipation of the new technique of variation of rhythm by the opposition of two short syllables to one long one, and even a kind of proto *gaṇa* ⏑ ⏑ - or - ⏑ ⏑ anticipating the 4 *mattā gaṇa* of *gaṇacchandas*. This gives us a further indication of the way in which the musical technique could penetrate into the old metrics and find there an element with which it could combine to form the basis of the new metrical technique, once the other conditions (linguistic changes, etc.) were favourable for such a development.

The Pali *tuṭṭhubha* seems never to have a *pāda* structure which coincides even superficially (i.e. in the mere succession of longs and shorts) with any *mattāchandas pāda* structure. Such ambiguous forms were probably disliked, and we may surmise that there was a direct connection between the development of the new metres and the limitation of the old ones. The Vedic *triṣṭubh* could take almost any form, although some forms were more popular than others, and could even coincide superficially with the *opacchandasaka*, as we have seen. The successive limitations of its structure until in the later parts of the *Mahābhārata*, in the *Rāmāyaṇa* and in the Classical Sanskrit literature we find only the fixed forms *upajāti* and *vaṃśasthā*, together with fixed derivatives such as *rucirā*, would be very difficult to account for except by noting the appearance and development of new metres, in ever increasing numbers, many of which tended to coincide with it. The *triṣṭubh* was thus narrowed down to its most characteristic form ⏓ - ⏑ - - ⏑ ⏑ - ⏑ - ⏓, which is least like any other metre.

§ 151. In the case of the *vatta* a similar process of restriction of the Vedic *anuṣṭubh pāda* took place, although it did not go so far. The *anuṣṭubh* itself was not broken up into a series of fixed forms, and very few of the new metres had a *pāda* of as few as eight syllables which might coincide with it. The " invention " of the *vatta*, or epic *siloka* (*śloka*), and its adoption as the epic narrative metre in which it was practicable to compose poems of epic length, prevented the process from going any further. The epic metre had to be variable in structure to avoid monotony and also to satisfy the need for a flexible *siloka* into which a simple straightforward narrative would fit easily and naturally.

We have noted that the Vedic *anuṣṭubh* could coincide with a prior *vetālīya*. In Pali the form - - - - ⏑ - ⏑ ⏓ may occur in either metre, and, as we shall see in the Chapter on the *vatta*, the form with initial resolution ⏑ ⏑ - - - - ⏑ - ⏑ ⏓ may also occur in either. These forms, however, are not of frequent occurrence in either metre, except in the posterior *pāda* of the *vatta*, where of course there is no coincidence since the posterior *vetālīya* is longer. ⏓⏓ - - - - ⏑ - ⏑ ⏓ is fairly common in the prior *vetālīya*, although it disappeared in Classical metrics, whilst . . . ⏑ - ⏑ ⏓ in prior position, as *vipulā*, although common in the earlier Canonical verse, died out rapidly in the later phase of composition, very probably under the impact of *vetālīya*, and afterwards gave place to the classical *vatta* with only the *pathyā* and four *vipulā* forms excluding . . . ⏑ - ⏑ ⏓ from the prior *pāda*.

§ 152. The relationship between *mattāchandas* and *gaṇacchandas* is of a much closer nature, and is best considered as part of our study of the origins of *gaṇacchandas* in the next chapter. When *gaṇacchandas* had developed fully and produced the flexible *ariyā*, it appears that *mattāchandas* rapidly lost favour. True *mattāchandas* does not seem to have been used at all after the period of the early Buddhist and Jaina literature, and its fixed derivatives became part of the general classical stock of metres, not specifically restricted to musical performances as *gaṇacchandas* was (apart from certain technical treatises).

We now proceed to a detailed study of the structure of the *mattāchandas pāda* and strophe.

The Mattāchandas Pāda

§ 153. We have noted that the *pāda* falls into two parts, the cadence, which is fixed (apart from the alternation of *vetālīya* and *opacchandasaka*), and the variable opening part.[1] European

[1] There is no caesura in the *mattāchandas pāda*.

scholars (e.g. Fausbøll, Jacobi, Smith) have for some reason (comparison of *vetālīya* with *vatta* ?) generally described only the last four (or five in *opacchandasaka*) syllables as the cadence, and treated the preceding syllable as part of the opening. They have then divided this opening into two or even three " feet " or *gaṇas* in various arbitrary fashions. If the *pāda* is to be subdivided for convenience of analysis, and in order to understand the mechanism of its variations, we must make more careful tests on the basis of our statistics concerning the usage. In regard to the cadence, we find in practice, as in the Indian theory (noted by Jacobi, 1884, p. 594),[1] that the fifth (sixth in *opacchandasaka*) syllable from the end is regularly long, the exceptions amounting to less than 2% of our collection. We may assume, then, that the fixed cadence was normally –⏑–⏑$\overset{(\smile)}{-}$(×), although it remains possible that our exceptions, or some of them, are not mere corruptions but a rather rare form of variation of the *pāda* (see the discussion of " syncopated " structures below).

§ 154. Since the cadence appears to resemble that of the *tuṭṭhubha* we may now make a closer comparison of the two metres than we did in studying the origins of *mattāchandas*. This may help us to understand the articulations of the *pāda* :

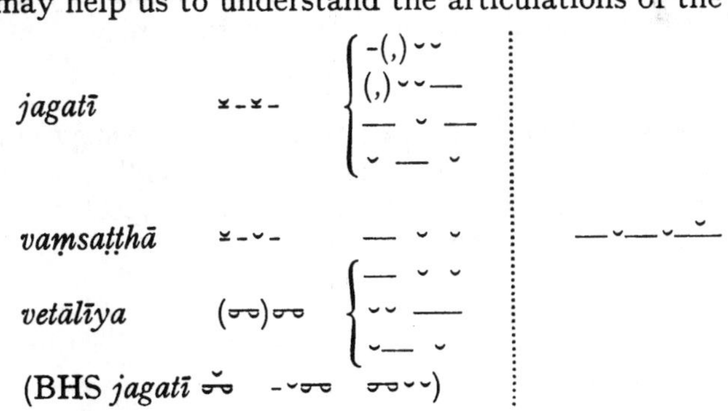

<table>
<tr><td>jagatī</td><td>×–×–</td><td>–(,)⏑⏑
(,)⏑⏑—
— ⏑ —
⏑ — ⏑</td><td rowspan="4"></td></tr>
<tr><td>vaṃsaṭṭhā</td><td>×–⏑–</td><td>— ⏑ ⏑</td></tr>
<tr><td>vetālīya</td><td>(⏕)⏕</td><td>— ⏑ ⏑
⏑⏑ —
⏑— ⏑</td></tr>
<tr><td>(BHS jagatī ⏕̆</td><td>–⏑⏕</td><td>⏕⏑⏑)</td></tr>
</table>

—⏑—⏑$\overset{\smile}{—}$

[1] The Indian scheme for *vetālīya* when classified as a *jāti* metre is 6/8 *mattā* + *ra la ga* (when classified as a *vutta* metre the fixed scheme is *sa sa ja ga*| *sa bha ra la ga* × 2 ; it is then sometimes termed *viyoginī*). In fact this *jāti* form of the metre does not seem to have been found in the extant classical literature, and it is probably merely a scheme taken over by the classical metrists from earlier treatises or traditions relating to the pre-classical period. This of course gives it greater authority for us (Piṅgala IV 32).

(whereas *tuṭṭhubha* and *upajāti* drop the last syllable of this cadence, *opacchandasaka* adds a syllable :

tuṭṭhubha : *jag.-vet.* : *opacchandasaka* :

- ᵕ - ⨯ / - ᵕ - ᵕ ⨯/ - ᵕ - ᵕ - ⨯ .)

—the apparent anticipation of *mattāchandas* rhythms in the " break " of the *jagatī* is striking.

§ 155. For the free part of the *pāda* we obtain the following statistics from the tables given in §§ 128–31. It might appear at first sight that there would be no difference between *opacchandasaka* and *vetālīya* except in the cadence, and that to obtain larger samples as a basis for statistical discussion we should simply combine the tables. Although it is useful to do this, and it does indeed give a sharper outline to our statistical charts, the usage in the two metres differs in some important details. Thus the form of *vetālīya* posterior *pāda* used also as the *samavutta rathoddhatā* is very rarely paralleled in *opacchandasaka*. Evidently there is a close union of the two parts of the *pāda*, which was always felt as a unity despite its contradictory rhythms. In our analysis we must never lose sight of this unity.

§ 158. The variations in the free part of the *pāda* suggest a kind of articulation into groups, or " proto-*gaṇas* ", normally of 2 + 4 *mattās* in the prior and 4 + 4 in the posterior. The normal variations are then as follows :

Prior *Pāda* :

	2	4		
commonest form	-	—ᵕᵕ 42%	83%	88·5% of the sample (probably 93–94% if we could restore all the corrupted *pādas*)
substitutions	ᵕᵕ	ᵕᵕ—		
.....		ᵕ- ᵕ		

Posterior *Pāda* :

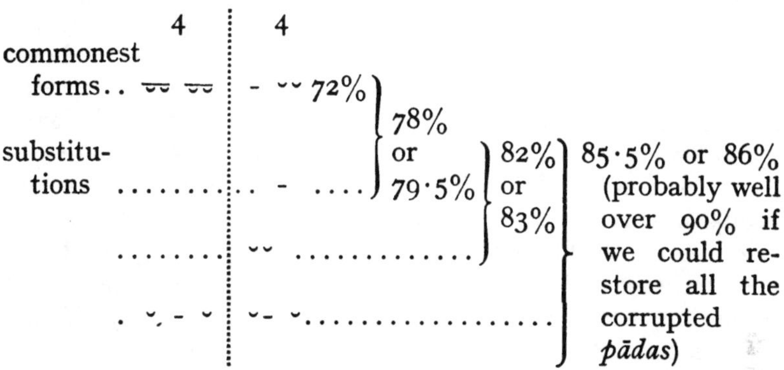

§ 159. Quite regularly, although very infrequently, we find what appears to be a syncopation of these articulations identifiable through the shifting of the last substitute shown above in the four *mattā* groups (⏑- ⏑) into a position overlapping the usual groups, and even overlapping the first syllable of the cadence, which is sometimes resolved :

Prior *Pāda* :

4 ⋮ 4? ⋮
2?.

⏑ -⏑ ⋮ ⏑⏑(- ⋮ ⏑-⏑ ⏑̲ (×)) } just over 4% (probably over 5%)
- - ⋮ ⏑-⏑ ⋮(⏑-⏑ ⏑̲ (×))
(etc.)

Posterior *Pāda* :

2 ⋮ 4 ⋮ 4? ⋮
2?.

— ⋮ ⏑- ⏑ ⋮ - (- ⋮ ⏑-⏑̲ (×)) } 4·5–5% (perhaps more than 6–7%)
⏑⏑ ⋮ ⋮ ⏑⏑
- - ⋮ ⏑- ⏑ ⋮ (⏑-⏑ ⏑̲ (×))
⋮ (etc.) ⋮

This alternative grouping, which in the above cases so strikingly anticipates the cadence rhythm (⏑-⏑ | - -), may have been felt also in *pādas* which appear "normal", e.g. -⏑⏑| - -|⏑-⏑- -, -|-⏑⏑|- -|⏑-⏑- -, or even --|⏑⏑-|⏑-⏑--, where we cannot identify it with certainty. No doubt some sort of usage was current whereby perhaps 10–15% were sung with "syncopation", reflected in the musical setting but only apparent in the actual text in the 5% which have the forms shown above. No doubt also this usage was fairly freely interpreted in practice by the singers, and the same *pāda* might be sung in both ways if its structure permitted. The *ekarūpā*, - -|-⏑⏑| ⏑-⏑- - × 4 (two *pādas* in Sn seem to have this form, but they are probably corruptions), may be another syncopated form, the resolution of the first syllable of the cadence implying that it has been transferred to the free part of the *pāda*. Other cases of this resolution, however, such as - -|⏑-⏑|⏑⏑ ⏑-⏑- - (Sn)—if this is not a corruption—would contradict this theory.

§ 160. We shall trace below the tendency to a more restricted technique with groups of two *mattā* each only: 2|2|2| cadence |2|2|2|2| cadence ||, and the relationship between these *mattāchandas* variations and the early *gaṇacchandas* rhythms. It should be noted that boundaries between these groups could occur only after even numbers of *mattā*, i.e. groups containing odd numbers of *mattā* were not allowed. This rule is in fact given by the Indian theory (of later redaction but probably based on usages more ancient than the extant treatises) as reported by Jacobi (1884, p. 594).

The overall scheme for *mattāchandas* is thus:

```
        :  ⏑-  ⏑  :  ⏑-  ⏑  :
(-)     :    -| - :  ⏑⏑|- :  ⏑-⏑ (⏑)/- (×) × 4
(⏑⏑)    :  ⏑⏑|⏑⏑  :   - |  :
(⏑ - ⏑)   | ⏑ - ⏑    |
```

Using the musical terminology we may say that the *pādayuga* begins *atīta* (i.e. before the beat, or *graha*),[1] whilst the posterior *pāda* follows through *sama* (i.e. it begins with the *graha*). E.g.:

yo upatitaṃ vineti kodhaṃ,
visataṃ sappavisaṃ va osadhehi |
so bhikkhu jahāti orapāraṃ,
urago jiṇṇam iva tacaṃ purāṇaṃ Sn 1

[1] Or perhaps *anāgata* (after the *graha*), but in any case *viṣama*.

§ 161. It would be possible to put forward other schemes to account for *mattāchandas* structure. For example, it could be suggested that, in opposition to the *caturasra tāla* of *gaṇacchandas*,[1] *mattāchandas* was based on the other fundamental *tāla* of the ancient music, the *tryasra* (SIIS or -˘˘-). We could scan in *gaṇas* of 6 *mattās* each :

-́/˘˘ -˘˘|-́˘-˘|-́(-),⏓⏓|-́ -˘˘|-́˘-˘|-́(-) × 2

—the whole strophe consisting of twelve *gaṇas* organized in four groups of three marked off by the cadence-rhythm -́˘-˘. Such a description would avoid the difficulties we experience in dealing with mixed *pādas* in binary (the free part) and ternary (?—the fixed cadence) rhythms. There is no justification, however, for thus assimilating *mattāchandas* to *gaṇacchandas* by scanning it in *gaṇas* throughout with the same alternation of a *gaṇa* of special (fixed) rhythm to mark off the " bars " or " phrases " of a fully musical structure. Had the distinction between the two metres been simply the difference of *tāla*, not merely the theoretical descriptions but the whole subsequent history of the musical metres would surely have been quite different from what we actually find. It seems most natural (and in all science we have to prefer a simpler description to a more complicated one, provided that it accounts for all the facts) to regard *mattāchandas* as the semi-musical forerunner of the fully musical *gaṇacchandas*.[2] We can then account satisfactorily for the disappearance of true *mattāchandas* after the development of *gaṇacchandas*, without having to explain the absence of *tryasra tāla* from the musical metres of later times. *Mattāchandas* and *gaṇacchandas* are indeed very closely related, but in a much more organic way than they would be if they were merely the reflection of two different musical *tālas*, one having twelve 6 *mattā gaṇas* and the other sixteen 4 *mattā* (or eight 8 *mattā*) *gaṇas*. The strongest argument for the explanation of *mattāchandas pāda* structure adopted in this section lies in the analysis of the origins of *gaṇacchandas* which is set forth in Chapter VI and partly anticipated at the end of this section.

§ 162. With reference to §§ 133–148 of this chapter, we may make a comparison of earlier and later *mattāchandas* texts in

[1] See the following chapter for an explanation of this description.
[2] cf. §§ 120–1.

the Canon with a view to tracing the tendencies in the development of the metre. We have suggested that the *Suttanipāta* verses belong to an earlier period (i) whilst those in the *Therīgāthā* belong to a later period (ii). Let us compare the techniques used in these two texts :

§ 163. TABLE 7a

Prior *Pāda*

	Sn	Th II	Sn %	Th II %
– – ⏑⏑	93 (109)	15 or 16	53 (55)	23 or 25 (23 or 24)
⏑⏑– ⏑⏑	31	15 (16)	17·5 (16)	23 (24)
– ⏑⏑–	10	5	5·5 (5)	7·5
⏑⏑⏑⏑⏑⏑	1	1	0·5	1·5
– ⏑– ⏑	10	0	5·5 (5)	—
– ⏑⏑⏑⏑	4	9	2·25 (2)	14
– – –	8	3	4·5 (4)	4·5
⏑⏑– –	1	2	0·5	3
⏑– ⏑⏑⏑	0	2 or 3	—	3 or 4·5
⏑– ⏑–	2 or 3	1	1 or 1·5	1·5
– – ⏑–/⏑	1 (6)	1	0·5 (3)	1·5
> – – ⏑⏑ ? ⏑ – ⏑⏑	2	0	1	—
– ⏑– ⏑– ⏑	2	0	1	—
> – – ⏑⏑ ? – ⏑ ⏑⏑	1	2	0·5	3
> – – – ? – – ⏑	2	0	1	—
⏑⏑– ⏑⏑⏑/⏑ ?	0	1	—	1·5
– – – ⏑/⏑	0	1	—	1·5
⏑⏑⏑⏑–	0	1	—	1·5
> – – – ? ⏑ – –	0	1	—	1·5
⏑– ⏑⏑–	0	1	—	1·5
–⏑– ⏑⏑	0	1	—	1·5
defective	7	2	4 (3·5)	3
Total	176 (197)	65 (66)		

§ 164.

TABLE 7b

Posterior *Pāda*

	Sn	Th II	Sn %	Th II %
– – – ⏑⏑	45 (49) or 47 (51)	23 (25) or 24 (26)	28 or 29 (23 or 24)	37 or 38 (38 or 39·5)
⏑⏑– – ⏑⏑	47 (75)	23	29 (35)	37 (35)
– ⏑⏑– ⏑⏑	6	8 (9)	3·5 (3)	13 (14)
⏑⏑⏑⏑– ⏑⏑	0	4	—	6·5 (6)
– – – –	5 (21)	1 or 2	3 (10)	1·5 or 3 (1·5 or 3)
⏑⏑– – –	7	0	4·5 (3·25)	—
–⏑– ⏑⏑⏑	1?	0	0·5	
– – ⏑⏑–	6 (8)	0	3·5 (3·75)	
– – ⏑⏑⏑⏑	7	0	4·5 (3·25)	
– – ⏑– ⏑	3	0	2 (1·5)	
⏑⏑– ⏑⏑–	2	0	1 (1)	
⏑⏑– ⏑– ⏑	2	0	1	
– ⏑⏑⏑– ⏑	1 (2)	0	0·5 (1)	
– – – ⏑–/⏑	1 (2)	0	0·5 (1)	
– – ⏑– ⏑⏑/⏑	1	0	0·5	
– ⏑⏑⏑⏑⏑⏑	0	1	—	1·5 (1·5)
defective	28 (29)	2	17 (13·5)	3 (3)
Total .	162 (215)	63 (66)		

§ 165. It is clear that a considerable change has taken place. Whereas in the older text – –⏑⏑ in the prior *pāda* accounts for more than half the verses and ⏑⏑–⏑⏑ for only about one-sixth, in the younger text this ratio of 3 to 1 between the two commonest forms has changed to one of approximate equality. In the posterior *pāda* the corresponding commonest forms do not show this change, presumably because apparently for reasons of balance and contrast the form ⏑⏑– –⏑⏑ is already at least as common there as – – –⏑⏑. The contrast between the prior and posterior *pāda* has given place to a closer parallelism between them, certain forms being regularly associated with one another no doubt as a prerequisite for the formation of new metres such as *aparavatta.* This point will be further developed below in considering the strophe structure.

The historical tendency to resolve the longs into pairs of shorts and so to produce successions of short syllables can also be seen in some of the other forms. Thus -˘˘˘˘ increases from about 2% to 14% and four cases of posterior ˘˘˘˘-˘˘ (*aparavatta*) appear which are not paralleled at all in the older text (one *pāda* only of the associated prior form ˘˘˘˘˘˘ appears in each text). In single examples only several other new forms appear showing the same tendency: ˘˘-˘˘˘/˘, ˘˘ ˘˘-, -˘˘ ˘˘˘˘. We may note also in the *udiccavutti pādas* the tendency ˘-˘˘- > ˘-˘ ˘˘. A curious counter example is the disappearance of - -˘˘˘˘ (about 4% in Sn). If we count the actual number of syllables in the tables above we find in Sn 657 (849) longs against 791 (966) shorts and in Th II 243 (252) longs against 371 (387) shorts, a change from 55 (53)% shorts to 60·5% shorts.

§ 166. The complete disappearance of -˘-˘ prior, which accounts for at least 5% in the Sn cases, is very striking, although there is a slight increase in the forms of the *udiccavutti*, which also contains ˘-˘, but in the initial position (from about 1·5% to about 5 or 6%). This change probably reflects the tendency to group the *mattās* in pairs referred to above (2|2|2(|2)). In the posterior *pāda* likewise the 4 or 5% of forms 2|2|˘-˘ have disappeared. *Paccavutti* proper does not appear in either text except for one doubtful *rathoddhatā pāda* in Sn;[1] we find - - - ˘-|˘ once (twice) in Sn. Finally the form - -˘-|˘, which may be taken to be a variety of *udiccavutti*, occurs in one *pāda* in either text, but is in Sn a refrain which appears six times (3%).

The Th II *vetālīya*, we conclude, shows a definite development in the direction of the classical metre which has the fixed scheme ˘˘-˘˘-˘-˘×|˘˘- -˘˘-˘-˘× × 2.[2] It also shows the

[1] Note that in Th II *rathoddhatā* is an independent metre which has separated off from *mattāchandas* (*Ambapālīgāthā*).

[2] The proportion of longs to shorts in the formerly free parts of the *pādas* is three to eight, i.e. 73% shorts.

proto *pādas* of *aparavatta* in the period immediately preceding the separating out of *aparavatta* as an independent metre.

§ 167. Glancing at the other later texts, we see in the *Lakkhaṇa-sutta* (D III) the stage following Th II, in which *pupphitaggā* (cf. *aparavatta*) appears as an independent metre. A dozen *pādas* of *pupphitaggā* are found in the *Vimānavatthu*. This is about one-fifth of the *pādas* found in that text, so that these verses may perhaps be reckoned as showing an intermediate stage between Th II and the *Lakkhaṇa*. The *vetālīya* verses in Vv are borrowed from the *Jātaka*. The few verses in the *Petavatthu* are similar in structure to those of Th II. In the *Theragāthā*, although again it contains only a few *mattāchandas* verses, there seems to be a clear distinction between the *opacchandasaka* verses and the *vetālīya*. In the former we find the initial long in a higher proportion of *pādas* than in any other text, not only in the prior but in the posterior *pādas* also. These *opacchandasaka* verses therefore appear to be very old. In the *vetālīya*, on the other hand, the initial long in both *pādas* is more frequent than the shorts, but only as 10 : 8 (or 15 : 12 including all structures, not merely the two commonest) in the prior and as 13 : 7 (8) (or 17 : 9 (10) ?) in the posterior. This arrangement is very different from that of Sn, since in Th I the shorts are most frequent in the prior *pāda*, whereas in Sn they are as common as the long in the posterior *pāda* but less than one-third as common in the prior. The high proportion of shorts in the prior *pādas* of the Th I *vetālīya* is surely the most significant feature here, and we may conclude that these verses are a good deal younger than those of Sn and only a little, if at all, older than those of Th II. This conclusion seems to be confirmed by the occurrence of three *aparavatta* prior *pādas* in Th I, against only one in Th II in more than twice as many verses, Th I having also one posterior *aparavatta* against four in Th II. Finally, the *Sagātha Saṃyutta* has a great preponderance of shorts in the prior *pāda* but approximate equality in the posterior. In this collection, as in Th II, all the verses are *vetālīya*, and in structure they appear more advanced than the Th I *vetālīya*, although there are no *aparavatta pādas*.

We still have to consider the verses in the *Dhammapada*, the *Udāna* and the *Jātaka*:

§ 168. TABLE 8a

Prior *Pāda*

	Dh	U	J	Dh %	U %	J %
– – ⏑⏑	25 (28)	9 (10)	86 (87) or 87 (88)	45	35 (36)	48–9 (47)
⏑⏑– ⏑⏑	15 (17)	5	20	27	19 (18)	11
– ⏑⏑–	4	3	11 (16) or 12 (17)	7 (6·5)	11·5 (9·5)	6·5 (9)
⏑⏑⏑⏑⏑⏑			5			3
– ⏑– ⏑	7 (8)	5 (6)?	11	12·5 (13)	19 (21)	6
– ⏑⏑⏑⏑		2?	7 (8)		8 (7)	4 (4·5)
– – –	2	1	14	3·5(3·25)	4 (3·5)	8 (7·5)
⏑⏑– –		1	5 or 6		4 (3·5)	3
⏑– ⏑⏑⏑	2?	1	2	3·5 (3·25)	4	1
⏑– ⏑–			4?			2
– – ⏑–/⏑			4 or 5			2·5
⏑– ⏑⏑–/⏑			1?			0·5
–⏑– ⏑⏑			1			0·5
⏑– ⏑⏑–			1			0·5
defective	1		about 5	2 (1·5)		3
Total .	56 (62)	26 (28)	178 (185)			

§ 169. TABLE 8b

Posterior *Pāda*

	Dh	U	J	Dh %	U %	J %
– – – ⏑⏑	24 (25)	9	56 (61) or 58 (63)	40 (37)	33 (31)	33–4
⏑⏑– – ⏑⏑	19 (25)	9 (10)	29 (33) or 30 (34)	32 (37)	33 (34·5)	17–17·5 (18)
– ⏑⏑– ⏑⏑	1	4 (5)	23 (24) or 27 (28)	1·75 (1·5)	15 (17)	14–6 (13–5)

	Dh	U	J	Dh %	U %	J %
⏑⏑⏑⏑– ⏑⏑	2			3·5 (3)		
– – – –		1	6		4 (3·5)	3·5
⏑⏑– – –	1		4	1·75 (1·5)		2·5 (2)
– ⏑– ⏑⏑⏑	2		11 (12)	3·5 (3)		6·5
⏑⏑⏑– ⏑–	1		1	1·75 (1·5)		0·5
– ⏑– ⏑–		1?	2		4 (3·5)	1
– – ⏑⏑⏑⏑			1?			0·5
– – ⏑– ⏑			4			2·5 (2)
⏑⏑– ⏑⏑–			1			0·5
⏑⏑– ⏑– ⏑			1?			0·5
⏑⏑– ⏑⏑⏑⏑			2?			1
⏑⏑– – ⏑–/⏑			1 (4)			0·5 (2)
– ⏑⏑⏑⏑–	1?		1	1·75 (1·5)		0·5
– ⏑– ⏑⏑			3			2 (1·5)
–⏑– – ⏑⏑	2 or 4		3?	6·5 (6)		2 (1·5)
– ⏑⏑⏑⏑⏑⏑			1			0·5
⏑ – – ⏑⏑ >– – – ⏑⏑?	1			1·75 (1·5)		
⏑– ⏑– –			1			0·5
⏑⏑– ⏑– ⏑–	1					
– – ⏑– ⏑–	1					
– ⏑– ⏑– ⏑	1		1			
⏑– ⏑– ⏑⏑		1	1		4 (3·5)	
– ⏑⏑– –		1	2 (3)			1 (1·5)
⏑– ⏑⏑⏑⏑⏑		1				
⏑⏑⏑⏑– –			1			
defective	1		4			
Total .	60 (67)	27 (29)	170 (185)			

§ 170. In the prior *pāda* the frequencies in J are very close to those in Sn, but in the posterior *pāda* the long opening syllable is twice as common as the two shorts, whereas in Sn these alternatives are about equally common. Other differences in the posterior *pāda* include the much greater frequency of -⏑⏑-⏑⏑ in J and also of the various *paccavutti* forms. These discrepancies may be due to the considerably higher proportion of *vetālīya* in J (nearly twice as frequent as *opacchandasaka*) as compared with Sn (only about one-quarter as frequent). We must conclude that the great majority of the *Jātaka mattāchandas* texts belong to the earlier period, but we must also note a tendency in the direction of the later style: in the posterior *pāda* -⏑⏑-⏑⏑ is as common in J as it is in Th II (although ⏑⏑⏑⏑-⏑⏑ is absent in J). The large proportion of *rathoddhatā pādas* in J may also be reckoned as a tendency leading into the later period when *rathoddhatā* became an independent metre. This is the kind of evolutionary process which tends to confuse our picture of the metres based on our preliminary rough distinction of earlier and later styles: between the periods of the Sn verses and those of the Th II we now have to postulate an intermediate stage in which *rathoddhatā pādas* had become very popular, leading to the formation of a new metre and the subsequent avoidance of *rathoddhatā pādas* in *mattāchandas*. In J these three periods are all represented, since the independent *rathoddhatā* appears in the *Kuṇālajātaka* (No. 536).

The *Dhammapada* verses may belong largely to this intermediate period, although -⏑⏑-⏑⏑ appears only once. This structure has a high frequency in the *Udāna*, although since there are only some fifteen *mattāchandas* strophes in that collection it is not a satisfactory sample for our calculations. Probably the U verses too belong to the intermediate period between (i) and (ii).

§ 171. We must now study the differences between *opacchandasaka* and *vetālīya pāda* structure which have come to our notice several times in the preceding discussions. Tables 5 and 6 (§§ 156–7) show the total occurrences of each form of prior and posterior *pāda* as *opacchandasaka* and as *vetālīya*.

In the prior *pāda* and the posterior *pāda* the *bhaddavirāja* (*suddhavirāja*) type is about equally common in both metres.

This type appears to be the fundamental rhythm of *mattāchandas* from which the others had been derived by resolution. In the second most important type there is already a sharp distinction between the two metres, which seems too great to be mere chance : in the prior *pāda* the *opacchandasaka* shows only 12% of the *vasantamālikā* type against the *vetālīya's* over 20% ; in the posterior *pāda* if we count the repetitions there is very little difference (28/30%), otherwise without repetitions only 22% of *opacchandasaka* but 29% of *vetālīya*. In the third type (-˘˘-/-˘˘-˘˘ —if it is correct to bracket these prior and posterior forms) there is little difference in the prior frequencies, but in the posterior there is a great increase in the frequency in *vetālīya* (*opacchandasaka* : 5%/*vetālīya* : 12%). The greater frequency of *pupphitaggā* as against *aparavatta* is due to the inclusion of the *Lakkhaṇa* verses which are almost pure *pupphitaggā* and should perhaps have been excluded along with the poems in *rathoddhatā*. In the other *opacchandasaka* texts the frequency of *pupphitaggā* is no higher than that of *aparavatta* in the *vetālīya* texts. The inclusion of the *Lakkhaṇa* verses lowers the percentages of the other *opacchandasaka* types very slightly as compared with those of the *vetālīya* (the *bhaddavirāja* type would in fact increase by 5% in the prior *pāda*, the *vasantamālikā* type by 1·5%, the others by not more than 1% : the present discussion is not appreciably affected by this correction). The other prior types do not show any marked difference between the two metres. In the posterior *pāda* the fifth type (- - - -), which appears in only about 1·5% of the *vetālīya* sample, rises to more than 7% in the *opacchandasaka*, if we include repetitions. The *rathoddhatā*, which is extremely rare as an *opacchandasaka pāda* (only one clear case, some cases of -˘- -˘˘ may be corrupted *rathoddhatā* or intended to be given the *rathoddhatā* rhythm by licence), accounts for nearly 5% (perhaps considerably more if we are right in correcting all cases of apparent -˘- -˘˘) of the *vetālīya*. In this connection we may note that the other *udiccavutti* types, though rare everywhere, show a slightly higher frequency in *vetālīya*. - - ˘˘˘˘ is twice as frequent in *opacchandasaka* as in *vetālīya*, and - -˘˘-, which accounts for 2·5% of the *opacchandasaka*, does not appear at all in the *vetālīya* sample. - -˘-˘, which may be compared with these two forms (and they may all be compared with - - - -), is likewise much commoner in *opacchandasaka* (2%/0·25%). The other types are too rare to be compared, except perhaps in the light of conclusions drawn on the basis of those we have already examined.

§ 172. Our findings may be summarized as follows :

Prior *Pāda* :

Little difference except that ⏑⏑- ⏑⏑-⏑-⏑- is considerably more frequent than ⏑⏑- ⏑⏑-⏑-⏑- - and that if we disregard the *Lakkhaṇa* - - ⏑⏑-⏑-⏑- - is more frequent than - - ⏑⏑-⏑-⏑-.

Posterior *Pāda* :

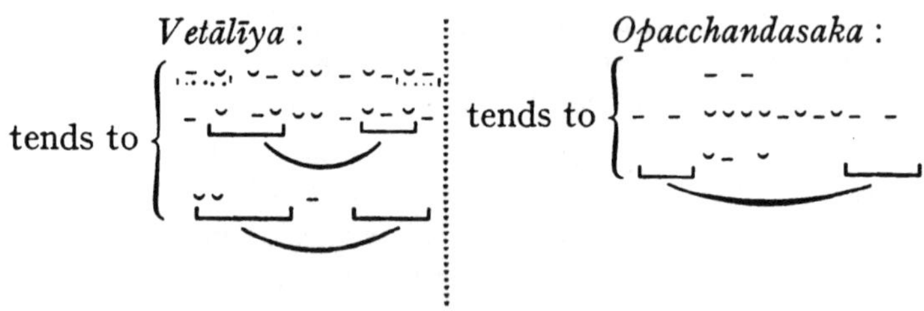

§ 173. The only explanation, unless we suppose simply that *opacchandasaka* is more archaic than *vetālīya*, which seems able to account for these differences in the handling of the two metres is the apparent parallelism between the cadences and the favoured openings : *opacchandasaka* - - · · · - - and *vetālīya* -⏑-⏑ · · · ⏑-⏑- (when not "syncopated" we might suggest that -⏑(⏑) · · · ⏑- is the nearest approach possible to such parallelism or interplay between opening and cadence). It seems that there was a strong tendency of this type in the posterior *pāda* because the cadence of the *pādayuga* was prominent, compared with that of the prior *pāda*, and also, we may suggest, because, according to the proto *gaṇa*-division implied by other features of the versification, the complete 4 *mattā* group at the beginning of the normal posterior *pāda* was felt as a unity which, in *opacchandasaka*, could answer to the final group of the cadence : - -|4|-⏑:-⏑:- - (compare :

2|⏑-⏑|4|⏑-⏑|- *rathoddhatā—udiccavutti*). In the prior *pāda* there is a weaker tendency to - | - · · · - - which perhaps checked the rise of the initial resolution in *opacchandasaka* (but not in *vetālīya*) to some extent. In the next section we shall develop this discussion further in connection with the interplay of the *pādas* in the strophe.

§ 174. To conclude this section we have to say something about the development of the other metres and clarify one or two other points concerning the *pāda* structure which bear on this development.

Jacobi suggests (1884, p. 592) that the first syllable in *mattāchandas* is anceps just like the last. This is his reason for accepting the opening -⏑-(|- . . .), which if included in our scheme would constitute a kind of 5 *mattā* " *gaṇa* ". In the earlier research on *mattāchandas* for this study this 5 *mattā gaṇa* was accepted and incorporated in the schemes as a kind of " cyclic dactyl " or at any rate as being equivalent to a 4 *mattā gaṇa*. The " anceps " idea was rejected and |-⏑-| was accepted medially as well as in the initial position. In the light of further study of metrical licence and of the origins of the *rathoddhatā* it seems we may now abandon the " 5 *mattā gaṇa* " and consider it more satisfactory to regard any *pāda* opening with -⏑- - . . . as being in fact an original -⏑-⏑ . . ., ⏑⏑- - . . . or -⏑⏑- . . . . Practically all the examples of this in the *Jātaka* contain syllables which elsewhere are regularly shortened by metrical licence, so that the *pādas* can be scanned in the alternative ways quite naturally. Other cases (which are recorded in the tables) are probably corruptions, and in some cases inferior readings accepted by editors such as Fausbøll himself and others who like him and Jacobi regarded -⏑- - . . . as a normal *mattāchandas* opening.

It should be noted that the anceps initial syllable was essential for Jacobi's theory of the origin of the posterior *vetālīya* through the dropping of the first syllable of a *jagatī pāda* :

(×)-⏑- . . .
↓
becomes anceps

—having rejected this theory we do not need to assume the anceps syllable. However, in common with all Vedic period verse we may assume that the pre-Pali metre from which *mattāchandas* evolved had the anceps initial. In this case there may be traces of such a usage in the earlier Pali verses, or at least the initial syllable of a *pāda* may be more liable to metrical alteration than the other syllables, that is, a syllable of a Pali word which is not normally liable to metrical lengthening or shortening may be altered if it happens to occupy this position in the *pāda*.[1] This would of course apply to such cases as ⏑|–⏑⏑ . . . > –|–⏑⏑ . . . and others, besides –⏑– > ⏑⏑–.

§ 175. In discussing the origin of *gaṇacchandas* Jacobi again makes use of the posterior opening –⏑–:

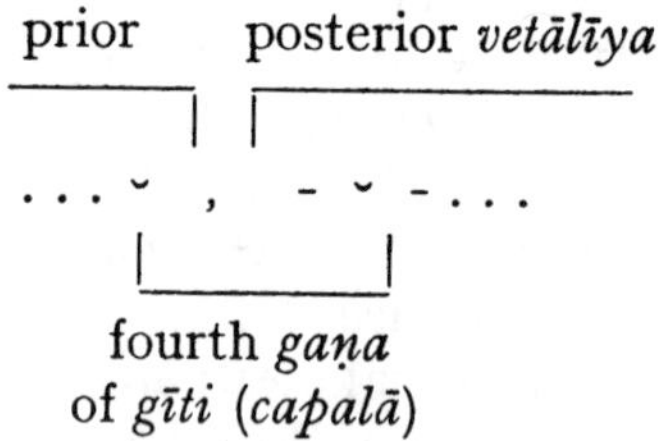

—it is true that the *gīti* seems to have appeared in the earlier period (a fact not known to Jacobi) and may have owed its origin partly to this anceps syllable, but it should be noted that the last syllable of the prior *pāda* (like the last syllable of any *pāda* in Indian metrics, which normally may be lengthened) is much more certainly anceps and that we find . . .|–, ⏑⏑| . . . also as the fourth *gaṇa* in some of our earliest *gīti* verses. This junction *gaṇa* linking the *pādayuga* may therefore have been more flexible than Jacobi supposed, so that his scheme of derivation may be too artificial, or may be only a special case.[2] It is easy to see why ⏑––⏑ was the favourite form for the fourth

[1] There appear to be similar cases of exceptional licence in the initial syllable in the oldest *gaṇacchandas* verses (cf. § 226).

[2] In the following chapter we present an improved theory of the origin of *gaṇacchandas* including intermediate stages, or perhaps parallel lines of development, not noted by Jacobi, which, besides accounting for the displacement of the "cadence" rhythm, allows us to see the possibilities of variation in the fourth *gaṇa*.

gaṇa in early *gaṇacchandas*, without insisting on this exact correspondence with a *mattāchandas* prototype.

§ 176. We now come to the following statement by Professor Smith (1949, p. 1155) : " Devant cette ligne impaire... on place aux endroits pair... une ' base ' : normalement ⏑⏑ ou -, anciennement aussi -⏑ ou ⏑-, base, qui, nonobstant l'autonomie des *gaṇa*, formera plus tard, avec la mesure suivante, une unité à six mores..."—He instances the *samavutta* forms *aparantikā*, *rathoddhatā*, and also *svāgatā* and the fused types resembling it : -⏑-⏑(⏑-⏑-). Now in his study of *mattāchandas* Smith employs as far as possible the *gaṇa*-division : ⏑⏑-|⏑⏑-|⏑-⏑-||⏑⏑|- -|⏑⏑-|
" base "
⏑-⏑-||. We reject this, except for the rare *pādas* which we have termed " syncopated ", and give as the normal form : ⏑⏑|-⏑⏑|-⏑-⏑-(-)||⏑⏑-|-⏑⏑|-⏑-⏑-(-)||. The " base " here appears in the prior *pāda* (" ligne impaire ").[1]

§ 177. In the syncopated *pādas* (according to our analysis) the " base " in the prior *pāda* is absorbed into an opening *gaṇa* and a second *gaṇa* overlaps the cadence as in Professor Smith's scheme : ⏑-⏑|⏑⏑-|⏑-⏑-. This perhaps originated through beginning *sama* with the musical accompaniment, the first syllable coinciding with the *graha* instead of anticipating or following it (cf. § 160). In the posterior *pāda* the same shift takes place : -|⏑-⏑|⏑⏑-|⏑-⏑-. This *pāda* now begins *viṣama* with the musical accompaniment, instead of *sama*, and a " base " appears. As before the cadence is overlapped. In the *pavattaka* of the metrical theory both *pādas* of the *yuga* are syncopated

⏑-⏑|⏑⏑-|⏑-⏑⁝- , -|⏑-⏑|⏑⏑-|⏑-⏑⁝-

—notice how the *gaṇa* division may here be carried right through the *pādayuga*, which is impossible in the normal form. This point will be developed in the following chapter, in discussing the origins of *gaṇacchandas*.

[1] cf. Fausbøll, followed by Jacobi : ⏑⏑|-⏑⏑-|⏑-⏑-||⏑⏑-|-⏑⏑-|⏑-⏑-|| with the tetrasyllabic " feet " supposedly inherited from Vedic metrics : it may be seen from the schemes given above (§§ 150 and 154) that the tetrasyllabic " foot " is not the rule even in Vedic *triṣṭubh*.

The " unité à six mores ", if it is of any significance, is normally a feature of the prior *pāda* and not the posterior, both in the texts and in the Indian theory. It would appear in the posterior *pāda* in the syncopated forms. It is correct to say that the openings –⏑ and ⏑– are early, but already, and not merely at a later stage, they would show a probable 6 *mattā* unity with the following syllables, as in the common Sn prior *pāda* –⏑–⏑ . . . (⏑–⏑– . . . occurs once in Sn). On our analysis, of course, these forms are regarded not as 6 *mattā gaṇas* but as respectively normal and syncopated openings involving a proto *gaṇa*-division : –|⏑–⏑ or ⏑–⏑|–.

§ 178. In the light of this discussion we may consider briefly the ways in which the other metres belonging to the *mattāchandas* family appear to have originated.

In the first place we have seen how the tendency to successions of short syllables gave rise to *pupphitaggā* and *aparavatta* and to the fixed classical forms of *opacchandasaka* and *vetālīya* (§§ 166–7).

In the second place we find the *samavuttas* produced by the repetition of a single *pāda*-structure in place of the *aḍḍhasama pādayugas*. Of those formed directly from the two main metres the *rathoddhatā* is the only one which occurs in the Canon : as we have seen it originated from the syncopated form of the posterior *pāda* of *vetālīya* known as *paccavutti* :

⏖ ⏖ | ⏖ x̲x̲ | – ⏑–⏑– . . . posterior *vetālīya*
⏖ | ⏑–⏑ | x̲x̲ – | ⏑–⏑– . . . *paccavutti*
– | ⏑–⏑ | ⏑⏑ – | ⏑–⏑– × 4 . . . *rathoddhatā*

—it is possible that the alternative forms of the *paccavutti* were still allowed in the Canonical *rathoddhatā* :

– | ⏑–⏑ | – – | ⏑–⏑–

sā jarāya bhaggā vināsitā Th II 262c
but there are no examples of this in the other texts, J V 452–4 (*Kuṇālajātaka*) and D III (*Lakkhaṇasutta*).[1]

[1] A score of useful examples of metrical licence may be adduced from these texts in a fixed metre.

§ 179. The *dodhaka* (and the *meghavitāna*, which does not occur as an independent metre in the Canon and is merely anticipated in J III (VIIth *nipāta*, 149a) and possibly in a corrupt *vetālīya* strophe in Dh) is formed by repeating a *vegavatī pāda* (*dodhaka* = posterior *vegavatī* × 4, *meghavitāna* = prior *vegavatī* × 4).

The *vegavatī* and *svāgatā* appear to have resulted from an attempt to simplify the structure of *mattāchandas* by bringing the cadence into line with the opening of the *pāda*. They doubtless originated in the same period as the *gīti* (both are found in the Th I verses ascribed to Vaṅgīsa), when various ways of making *mattāchandas* more singable were being tried :

⏓⏓:- .˘˘:- .˘-˘.- ,⏓⏓.⏓⏓:- .˘˘:- .˘-˘.- *vetālīya*
˘-:˘ .˘˘:- .˘-˘.- ,- .˘-:˘ .˘˘:- .˘-˘.- *pavattaka*
- :˘˘.- :- .-:˘˘.-,- .˘-˘ .-:- .˘˘-.- *svāgatā*
˘˘:- .˘˘:- .˘˘:-.-,- .˘˘:- .˘˘:- .˘˘:-.- *vegavatī*
˘˘:- .˘-:˘ .- -. ˘-˘,- .- :- .˘-:˘ .˘˘-.- *gīti*

—it should be noted that these three metres all have the cadence ˘˘- - to the *pādayuga*. The *vegavatī* may have been the earliest, being based on a normal *vetālīya pādayuga* :

˘˘|-˘˘|-˘-˘-||-˘˘|-˘˘|-˘-˘-
>-˘˘|-- >-˘˘|--

The *svāgatā* is based on the *paccavutti*, i.e. it has the posterior *pāda* syncopated. It is thus related to the *rathoddhatā*. In the *svāgatā* the *pādas* thus all open in the same way and the *aḍḍhasama* form is maintained only by an additional long syllable at the end of the posterior *pāda* : -|˘-˘|- -|˘˘-(-). Later, the classical fixed *svāgatā* has the form -|˘-˘|- -|˘˘-|- × 4 derived from the posterior *pāda*. Its structure should be compared with that of the *gīti* :

. . . . . .,- :˘-˘:- -:˘˘-:- *svāgatā*
: : : : :
: : : : :
. . . :˘,-˘ :- -:˘-˘:˘˘-:- *gīti*
: : : : :
⟷
└───┘ └──┘

§ 180. The *vegavatī* (as well as the *svāgatā*) may not be a completely fixed metre in the Canon, i.e. it may still be a *mattāchandas* in the proper sense of the term :

-| - ⏑ ⏑ | - ⏑ ⏑| - -
yo lobhaguṇe anuyutto,

- ⏑ ⏑|- ⏑ ⏑|- ⏑ ⏑|- -
so vacasā paribhāsati aññe | Sn 663 ab

⏑ ⏑|- ⏑ ⏑| - ⏑ ⏑|- ×
mukhadugga vibhūtamanar'ya,

- ⏑⏑| - ⏑ ⏑| - ⏑⏑| - ×
bhūnahu pāpaka dukkatakāri | Sn 664 ab

(the initial long occurs several times in Sn 663–678)

⏑ ⏑| - ⏑ ⏑|- ⏑ ⏑|- -
atha saṭṭhisitā savitakkā,

⏑ ⏑ ⏑ ⏑|- ⏑ ⏑| - ⏑ ⏑|- -
puthujanatāya adhammaniviṭṭhā | S I 187
= Th I 1217 ab

§ 181. The *svāgatā*, whose posterior *pāda* resembles that of the *gīti* (as we have just seen), originally opened in a very similar manner to the *vegavatī*. It may perhaps be regarded as a modified form of a proto *vegavatī mattāchandas* :

⏑⏑|⏑⏑⏑⏑|- ⏑⏑|- -, ⏑⏑⏑⏑|- ⏑⏑|- ⏑⏑|- - proto *vegavatī*

- |⏑⏑⏑⏑|- - |⏑⏑-, - |⏑⏑⏑⏑|- - |⏑⏑- |- *svāgatā*

—the cadence although apparently similar in the posterior *pāda* probably had a different rhythm : - ⏑⏑|- - > ⏑⏑- |-. The Pali *svāgatā* is a true *mattāchandas* in the sense that it is to some extent variable within the *mattā* count. Unfortunately there are so few verses in this metre in the Canon that their analysis is extremely precarious and it is hardly possible to go beyond Smith's description (1949, p. 1169) which is supplemented by, if it was not originally based on, his analysis of the *svāgatā* verses in BHS (1950a, p. 26). Smith has pointed out the significant affinities between the ancient *svāgatā* as represented in S I (together with the metres of Th I 382–4, 1242–5, and the *vegavatī* and *ariyā*) and the Apabhraṃśa > Hindī techniques which culminated in the *caupāī* (1949, 1171, 1950a, 40). His demonstrations are not invalidated by his assumption of a 6 *mattā gaṇa*, although there does not seem to be any good reason to postulate such a *gaṇa* in either Pali or Hindī metrics (cf. Sinha, 1953, p. 180). We should merely alter his scheme for the *svāgatā* (1949, 1169) to :

— / (⏑ ⏑ ?) | ⏑ – ⏑ / ⏑ ⏑ – | – – | ⏓ ⏓ – || – / (⏑ ⏑ ?) | ⏑ – ⏑ / ⏑ ⏑ – | – – | ⏑ ⏑ – | – × 2

§ 182. The last of these metres belonging to the *mattāchandas* family which are found in the Canon, the *visamavutta upaṭṭhitappacupita*, should be considered with *svāgatā* and the other associated metres mentioned by Professor Smith in tracing in the later ancient Pali metrical techniques the origins of the Apabhraṃśa—Hindī system. The analysis of this metre must be deferred until after we have studied the rhythms of *gaṇacchandas*, since there are striking parallels between these two and our study of the latter will enable us to dissect the complicated *upaṭṭhitappacupita* strophe. It will therefore be convenient to consider the metre in Chapter IX, which is in any case appropriate since already in Pali it shows its three fixed forms as classified in the Indian theory and is not a true *mattāchandas*. We may anticipate here, however, by saying that this complex metre appears to have been based originally on the mixed *vetālīya—opacchandasaka* strophe structure as exemplified in the *Suttanipāta*.

The Mattāchandas *Strophe*

§ 183. In the last section we reached the conclusion that the prior and posterior *pādas* unite in a *pādayuga* which normally opens *viṣama*, with an incomplete proto-*gaṇa*, and follows through *sama* with the presumed *tāla* accompaniment in the posterior *pāda*, which has a complete initial proto-*gaṇa*. We do not seem to be justified in speaking here of *gaṇas* in the strict sense, since such an articulation of the *pādas* has not yet fully crystallized, especially in the cadence, and *mattāchandas* may loosely be described as a " semi-musical " metre.[1] Two *pāda*-

[1] See the discussion at the beginning of this chapter (§ 120). All Indian metres are of course " musical " in the broad sense that they are usually sung, but these metres are further " musical " in a stricter sense to the extent that they are organized on the musical basis of *tāla*. According to the old Indian theory (reported by Weber, 1863, 281, etc.) the distinction between *gaṇacchandas* and *mattāchandas* is that in the latter the *mattā* are not divided in a fixed number of *gaṇas*.

yugas form the *mattāchandas* strophe [1] (the strophe of three *yugas* does not seem to have been used in our texts, but it was probably known and very likely used in these metres, since it appears in *gaṇacchandas*) :

```
—:—;⏑⏑:-⏑;-⏑:-(-)|—;—:—;⏑⏑:-⏑;-⏑:-(-)|| × 2
⏑⏑:⏑⏑;—:  ;  :     ⏑⏑;⏑⏑:⏑⏑;—:  ;  :

(2) 2  2  2 3  3  2(2) 2  2  2  2   3  3 2(2)
└─────┘└────┘└────────┘└───┘└───┘  └────────┘
 (4)    4    cadence    4    4      cadence

  └──────┘(-;⏒⏒:⏓⏓;-)└────────┘(-;⏑⏑:-;-)
     6                   8
           └──────────┘           └────────┘
(└───────┘) alternative           alternative
     8        cadence               cadence
```

—the grouping of the cadence in three-*mattā* segments is suggested by Smith's characterization of the rhythm of the metre as " binaire — ternaire " (1949, 1155), but he would presumably divide the cadence differently : (-):⏑-;⏑-:(-). The structure indicated for the free part of the *pāda* is not absolute and may be syncopated. Moreover its rhythms interact with those of the cadence not only in that they may overlap but also in that they tend to reflect or compensate one another (*opacchandasaka*/*vetālīya*/*vegavatī*/*svāgatā*). The extra syllable at the end of the *opacchandasaka* was perhaps felt to be awkward in the prior *pāda*, especially as the desire for a more fully musical metre developed, hence the extensive use of the mixed *vetālīya*—*opacchandasaka pādayuga*. In the *vetālīya* the final syllable may have been *pluta* or followed by a *cheda*, making three *mattā* as in the preceding segments of the cadence.

§ 184. The use of the different structures of the free parts of the *pādas* in the composition of strophes does not appear to have been governed by chance. The various prior and posterior *pāda*

[1] The term " strophe " seems most convenient in place of *gāthā*, which is a vague general term often meaning a whole poem. " Stanza " is not a good name for the Indian unit, which is usually a quatrain and is sometimes built up into larger *pādas*. " Strophe ", with its strong implication of a completed unit or division (a " turn " in a dance), seems happiest for musical metres which were probably closely connected with dancing.

structures are related to one another by the similarities and oppositions of their rhythms, and a strong feeling for imitation, contrast and balance in the interplay of these rhythms manifests itself in the structures of the *pādayuga* and especially of the strophe as a whole which are found in our texts.

§ 185. Turning first to the *Suttanipāta*, we notice at once in the first poem [1] (in *opacchandasaka*) a regular strophe structure A2A2 [2] unbroken throughout verses 1–6, with the resulting contrast between the openings -/⏑⏑. Verses 7–15 then show many different structures (apart from the refrain *pādayuga* A2 continuing from the opening verses), which, however, resemble one another in that all the *pādas* open with a long syllable. The concluding two strophes (verses 16–17) then revert to the structure A2A2.

§ 186. The next poem (Sn 18–34, *Dhaniyasutta*) is in the mixed *vetālīya-opacchandasaka* metre (strophe : VOVO normally, with a number of irregularities probably due to corruption) with three " tag " verses in pure *vetālīya*. The *sutta* is a dialogue in which the two speakers utter alternate strophes (strophes 1–12), followed by a narrative strophe (13), two strophes (14–15) in which Dhaniya makes known his resolve to become a disciple of the Sugata, and an altercation (strophes 16–17) between

[1] The *Uragasutta*.

[2] It may be convenient to repeat here the letters and numerals used as shorthand for the more important *pāda* structures :

Prior			Posterior	
A	— —⏑⏑		1	— — —⏑⏑
B	⏑⏑ —⏑⏑		2	⏑⏑ — —⏑⏑
C	— ⏑⏑—		3	— ⏑⏑ —⏑⏑
D	⏑⏑ ⏑⏑⏑⏑		4	⏑⏑ ⏑⏑ —⏑⏑
E	— ⏑—⏑		5	— — ⏑—⏑
F	— ⏑⏑⏑⏑		6	— — ⏑⏑⏑⏑
G	— ——		7	— — ——
H	⏑⏑ ——		8	⏑⏑ — ——
			9	— — ⏑⏑—
X	⏑-⏑ ⏑⏑		10	- ⏑- —⏑⏑
Y	⏑-⏑ —		11	- ⏑—⏑ ⏑⏑
Z	—— ⏑—/⏑		12	⏑⏑ ⏑—⏑ —
			13	— ⏑—⏑ —
			14	⏑⏑ —— ⏑—/⏑
			15	— —— ⏑—/⏑

Māra and the Bhagavant. It is possible that the last three strophes in *vetālīya* (15–17) were added later to make up the same total as in the *Uragasutta*. The first twelve strophes—the dialogue—have a constant refrain *pāda : atha ce patthayasī pavassa deva*, which appears also in Th I 51–4. The poem is apparently not so well preserved as the preceding one : besides some *opacchandasaka pādas* where we expect *vetālīya*, spoiling the mixed metre, we find two *tuṭṭhubha pādas* (1a and 2a). The last two strophes seem to have been borrowed from S I 6 (para 2), where they also occur, or from a source common to both collections. Strophes 3–8 are of the same type as those of the middle section of the *Uragasutta* ; 9–11 (or 12) form a separate group, united by their subject matter, in which the first *pādayuga* resembles the type of strophes 3–8 whilst the second *pādayuga* has the structure B2. It is possible that in both these poems the middle sections (Sn 7–15 and Sn 20–5) were the original kernels to which other verses were later added.

The next two *mattāchandas* poems in Sn (83–90 and 359–375) are in *opacchandasaka*. No particular strophe structure repeats over any number of these verses, but the second poem, the *Sammāparibbājaniyasutta*, has a refrain *pāda* of structure 7 throughout : *sammā so loke paribbajeyya*.

§ 187. The *Sabhiyasutta* (Sn 510–540) is in the mixed metre with seven *vattas* tagged on (541–7). There is a prose introduction and conclusion, together with a few explanatory sentences amongst the verses. The forms A, B, 1 and 2 predominate, especially with the opening long, A and 1 (but these are not as prominent as in the previous poems), with an occasional E and one *pupphitaggā pāda*. This poem and the *Jarāsutta* (Sn 804–813), which although in *vetālīya* otherwise resembles the *Sabhiyasutta* in its forms, appear to be of later composition than the others analysed above, tending towards the style of the later period (Th II, etc.).

§ 188. The following is the structure of the *Subhājīvakambavanikāgāthā* (Th II 367–399 ; 366 is an introductory *vatta*) :

A1B2 (367)
B1B1

C2A1	
B7C3	(370)
B4D'3	(D' = ⏑⏑⏑⏑⏑-)
D2A2	
X3B2	(a may be A instead of X)
B4F6'	(6' = -⏑⏑⏑⏑⏑⏑⏑)
X6B1	(375)
B2A2	
F2F2	
X3D3	
(379 very uncertain)	
A4C1	(380)
A1B1	
F2B1	
B3B2	
B1G1	
C1H2	(385)
A2H2	
C?1A7?	
C2F1	
A1C1	
A1A2	(390)
A1?G1	(or first *yuga* : Y ⏑-⏑⏑⏑- . . .)
Y2A1	
X?3B1	(or . . . F1)
A2B2	
F1B2	(395)
A2C?3	(or . . . H3)
F1C2	
C1Z?2	(or . . . G2 by *sandhi*)
A2F1	(399)

§ 189. The *mattāchandas* strophes in the *Dhammapada* are constructed as follows:

B11A1	(15)	a group of verses very similar in content. B . . . 1 constant with interplay of rhythms 11, A, 2, E in between.
B2A1		
B11E1		
B2E1	(18)	

A2E10	(24)	
A2A2	(44)	
A2A2	(45)	
B2A1	(80)	cf. 15–18 above, especially 16.
B11?B1	(95)	
(B2A1	145)	(= 80)
C8?A2	(179)	A2 is refrain
E1A2	(180)	
A1B2	(184)	
C4A1	(235)	
E1A1		
B11A1		
E1A2	(238)	
B1?A2	(240)	
A2B1	(284)	
A2E1	(285)	
B12A4	(324)	
B1C?2	(334)	
B2?A1	(341)	
B2A3		
B2A1		
A2A1	(344)	
C1A2	(348)	
X?10G11		(or X11 . . .—can gen. in *-assa* be shortened to *-asa* m.c. ?)
X2E1	(350)	
F?6?A1	(362)	(? cf. *lalitā*)
. . . 1A6	(371)	(cf. S I 200, Th I 119 and J III 412, line 6, for the corrupt first *pāda*)
C2A1	(388)	

(note frequency of a strophe or a group of strophes opening with C)

An interesting group of strophes in the *Jātaka* is the following (*Udayajātaka* : vol. IV, 111–2) :

D1B14	(54)	(the syncopated *pāda* " 14 " is a refrain)
B1A14		
A1A14		
A1C14	(57)	

§ 190. Most of the texts show some feeling for strophe structure, for the grouping of strophes and for the agreeable variation and interplay of rhythms in longer poems. We may have a regular strophe A2A2 (Sn) or a basic form B2A1 more or less freely varied (Dh 15–18 and many other Dh verses); A1 is favoured as the concluding *pādayuga* of a strophe or a group of strophes (Dh, J IV 99–105: *Maṭṭakuṇḍalijātaka*, U III 7–8 and VIII 5–7). Sometimes the form C is used only to begin *mattāchandas* poems and not in the interior of a poem (Dh and U). Elsewhere we find complete freedom of structure (e.g. Sn 83–90, 510–540), sometimes with excellent craftsmanship in the association and contrast of the various *pāda* forms: this more refined art was probably a later development in *mattāchandas* composition, it is well illustrated in the *Subhājīvakambavanikāgāthā*. Not only are the normal variations used frequently (as in the *vatta*, but without the great preponderance of one form found there and with a larger number of common *vipulās*), but extremely rare variations may be introduced, probably with a conscious feeling for the special effect produced. Thus we have the refrain " 14 " in the *Udayajātaka*, Z in Sn, and others. The rare *udiccavutti* and *paccavutti* (including the *rathoddhatā* " 11 ", which sometimes is quite common) are used in this way, and apparently occasional *pādas* of metres other than forms of the *opacchandasaka* and *vetālīya*: *meghavitāna* (Dh 371a ? and parallels cited above), *lalitā* (? Dh 362), *vijayanandinī* and perhaps others, but in such isolated cases it is very hard to tell whether we have true mixing or mere corruption. Unfortunately it was impossible to make a thorough investigation of such mixing/corruption of metres within the limits of the present study. This is an interesting problem awaiting research.

The composer in *mattāchandas* had great resources at his disposal for shaping and varying his style and for rousing the attention of his hearers by an unexpected turn. Perhaps the name *opacchandasaka* was adopted on account of the flexible structure and sinuous *pāda*-rhythm of the metre (*upa*-$\sqrt{}$*chand* = " coax ", " entice ", " persuade ").

§ 191. It is interesting to compare the technique of Ardhamāgadhī *mattāchandas* with that of the Pali Canon. The first section of the *Veyāliyajjhayaṇa* in the *Sūyagaḍaṃ* (Sū 1. 2. 1) scans as follows (*vetālīya*) :

A1A3
H1A1
A3A1
B7B7
G2A1
A3'A1 (3' = -ᵕᵕ-- . . .)
A3B7
B2C7
D4C7
B2A1
B8B7
H1?A1
B7A8
B2H2
B4A6
F2B2
B2H1
D'2B1 (D' = ᵕᵕᵕᵕ- . . .)
A3A3
G1B1
A1B3'
A4'G1 (4' = ᵕᵕᵕᵕ-- . . .)

—this style is reminiscent of the Th II poem : it contains *aparavatta pādas* and *pādayugas* (D4) and other forms having successions of short syllables (F, D', 6, 4'). The *pādayuga* B7 is strikingly frequent, however, and on the whole this style appears to represent a period a little earlier than that of Th II. There are no syncopated forms.

§ 192. We may distinguish phases in the development of strophe structure corresponding to those already noted for *pāda* structure and further clarifying the history of *mattāchandas*. In the earlier period we find the long-opening *pādas* tending to form regular strophes A1A1, but frequently combining with the resolved-opening *pādas* to form the very popular strophes A2A2 and B2A1. This inaugurates the transition to the later period through the further increase in the use of short syllables and the rejection of the tendency to rigid strophe structures found in the earlier period. The poets now seem to delight in the interplay of the numerous *pāda* structures which have become familiar. This transition is well under way in the *Sabhiyasutta* (Sn 510–540) and with the *Sūyagaḍaṃ* we seem to have entered the later period, which is seen at the peak of its development in Th II. In the preceding section we postulated an intermediate phase of development represented by parts of J but especially by Dh and U. This seems to be confirmed by our analysis here, in which we have been led to describe the strophe structures A2A2 and especially B2A1 as showing the beginning of the transition to the later period. B2A1 is characteristic of Dh and . . . A1 of U and parts of J. Dh and U are also related in their use of the opening C. Finally a new development puts an end to the free style of the later period : rigidity in the *pāda* appears in place of the old tendency to rigid strophe structures, and the more popular forms become separate metres. *Gaṇacchandas* has taken the place of *mattāchandas* as the flexible musical metre, and the fixed *vetālīya* and *opacchandasaka* B2B2, together with the *aparavatta* and *pupphitaggā* D4D4, take their places as *aḍḍhasamavuttas* amid the galaxy of classical metres deriving their beauty from the exact quantitative opposition of long and short syllables in fixed *pādas*.

§ 193. In the Pali Canon we have thus distinguished five phases of *mattāchandas*, represented by the texts as follows :

(i) Earlier period characterized by A1A1 (Sn 1–34) but more generally by the predominance of long syllables (Sn 83–90, 359–375, parts of J).

(ia) Intermediate period of transition B2A1, etc. > increasing successions of shorts ; origin of *rathoddhatā* (Dh, U, parts of J).

(ii) Later period of free style characterized by the predominance of short syllables (Th II, parts of Th I, S I).

(iia) Further development towards classical metrics with fixed *pādas* (*Lakkhaṇasutta*, with Vv showing the transition from (ii) to (iia) in a few verses).

(iii) Period of decline in Theravāda literature ; borrowings from (Vv *vetālīya*) and imitations of (Pv *vetālīya*) earlier literature leading to the complete abandonment of the new metres and pedestrian compilation of edifying legends, seldom rising to epic narrative, in the familiar epic *vatta* with occasional *tuṭṭhubhas* (Vv, Pv, Ap, Cp).

(The *Sūyagaḍaṃ* may belong to (ia) or (ii).)

§ 194. The feeling for strophe structure which we have observed in our texts indicates that the Pali *mattāchandas* was a " lyric " or " strophic " metre (as opposed to an " epic " metre), as we should expect from its connection with music.[1] In Classical Sanskrit, *vaitālīya* and *aupacchandasika* were used as canto metres in the *mahākāvyas*, unlike *gaṇacchandas* which was not so used, but their musical origin had then long been forgotten and they were simply fixed metres having certain structures like any other classical fixed metres. In apparently epic type literature such as the longer *Jātakas* and the Th II " ballad ", the *mattāchandas* strophes are still " lyric " or " strophic ". They are usually dramatized dialogue, not narrative, often organized in groups with refrains, as when in J No. 458 the four *opacchandasaka* strophes constitute the moral *ovāda* delivered by the Bodhisatta at the end of the episode (with a refrain common to all four). In the *Subhājīvakambavanikā* ballad, although the whole story is in *vetālīya* (with the significant exception of a preliminary narrative *vatta* which sets the scene and introduces the speakers), refrains are frequent and—as often in Pali ballads—the episode tends towards drama rather than epic: it consists almost entirely of dialogue and the speakers sing rather than declaim their parts. A " performance " would resemble that of a Classical Sanskrit drama, in which the verses are sung, but without the prose speeches since everything necessary to the action is included in the verses, which are not more or less adjuncts to the action (however relevant), as in the Classical, but integral parts of it despite the

[1] In §§ 227 ff. of the next chapter we shall suggest that the adoption of the *aḍḍhasama* structure was the first stage in the transition to fully musical metrics which was consummated by the invention of the *visama* structure in the *ariyā* : the strophe thus became a clear metrical unit, satisfying the feeling for its unity observed already in *mattāchandas*.

elaborate descriptions in which they anticipate the descriptive verses in the Classical drama.

In the early texts the strophes sometimes seem to be associated in groups or *pădas* by the use of structural patterns linking the series or of actual verbal refrain. In any case the technique of building up larger structures more complex than the mere succession of *pādas* is well established, even if we are not justified in describing it as the prototype of the Apabhraṃśa *pada*. The *mattāchandas* strophe, the mixed strophe, the complex *upaṭṭhitappacupita* with its sometimes doubled third *pāda*, and above all the system of chaining verses through verbal and rhythmic repetitions and patterns: these are so many techniques of Middle Indian lyric poetry which were well known in the ancient Pali literature and lived on to produce new blossoms in the scintillating strophes and *padas* and the supremely musical *tāḷavuttas* of Apabhraṃśa literature.

Chapter VI

GAṆACCHANDAS

Further Development of the Musical Metres

§ 195. During the period which we are studying, all the arts (and sciences) experienced a rapid development in India, and acquired the main forms which remained their basis throughout the " classical " period. By the end of our " pre-classical " period the *Nāṭyaśāstra* had systematized the conventions of the drama, music, dancing, poetics, and other related arts. At about the same time the *Piṅgalasūtra* had probably received its present form, incorporating the fixed syllabic metres characteristic of the " classical " *kāvya*. In the course of this development new combinations of the different media of expression were tried and all the arts interacted on one another, the drama, it seems, being the unifying goal in which successful experiments found their consummation, with an appreciative audience. In the popular arts, folk music and vernacular poetry, in which this classical art had its ultimate source, the different means of expression, such as rhythm, mode, versification, mime, costume, banners, combined naturally and were never really separated.

§ 196. As we saw in the last chapter (§§ 115–121), the new musical metres were closely related to instrumental music, which had developed in India prior to our period and no doubt continued to evolve its complex system of *tālas* and scales, through experiments on the *vīṇā*, throughout the " pre-classical " period until its fundamental conventions were codified in the *Nāṭyaśāstra*. We know, from the history of Indian science and technology, that mathematics was highly developed by the Moriyan period (e.g. in astronomy and architecture). It is against this sort of intellectual background that we have to chart the rise of the musical mathematics of rhythms and scales, and of the metrical mathematics of *gaṇacchandas* and of metre in general which we see worked out " astronomically " in

Piṅgala.[1] When Varāhamihira selected the *āryā* as his medium he was perhaps inspired not only by the flexibility of its structure, into which any technical term could be fitted without difficulty (Professor H. Smith, 1950a, p. 14), but also by a sense of the fitness of a metre which could be governed by mathematical principles.

§ 197. The principle of exact quantitative opposition (⏑–⏑) having been established with the development of *mattāchandas*, the next step in the adaptation of *deśī* verse for songs with instrumental accompaniment was to make the entire strophe subordinate to the new quantitative principle. We saw in the last chapter that this was tried within the framework of *mattāchandas* by means of a new cadence (*vegavatī*, *svāgatā*), but at the same time, or perhaps even earlier, experiments had been made involving the reorganization of the whole strophe. Whereas the simple reduction of the cadence to the prevailing rhythm, as in *vegavatī*, produces a rather monotonous metre, the flash of genius which invented the division of the strophe into equal *gaṇas* (perhaps suggested by the *vegavatī*) realized also the possibility of varying the rhythms of these *gaṇas* : every second *gaṇa* has a rhythm opposed to its neighbours, which appears in fact to have been derived from the old *mattāchandas* cadence (-⏑-⏑-(-)). Thus originated the earliest recorded *gaṇacchandas* metre, called appropriately the *gīti*, " song ". We shall examine this transformation of the *mattāchandas* strophe in detail below (§§ 230 ff.). It may be noted here that the *svāgatā* was a kind of compromise between *mattāchandas* and *gaṇacchandas* in which, the cadence having been assimilated to the prevailing rhythm, as in *vegavatī*, the old cadence-element (-)⏑--⏑ was introduced in the opening part of the *pāda* by way of diversifying the rhythm, without, however, reorganizing the strophe in a system of *gaṇas*.

§ 198. By the end of the period we are studying the old *gīti*,

[1] See e.g. IV 53, on calculating the number of long syllables in a strophe (given the length in *mattā* of the strophe and the total number of syllables it contains), and the end of VIII for calculating the number of permutations possible in any metre.

with its rigid *capalā* alternation of the two *gaṇa*-rhythms, had been superseded by an *ariyā* in which almost endless variation of rhythm, within the limits of exact quantitative opposition and the *gaṇa* organization, was practised, as a glance at the tables will show. The new technique of versification thus evolved did not remain limited to the musical metres, however, for the entire repertoire of Indian metrics, with the single exception of the epic *vatta*, was assimilated to the new principles. Not only is exact quantitative opposition the very basis of all the classical fixed syllabic (*vṛtta*) metres as well as of the musical (*jāti*) metres, but phrases or segments of rhythm clearly taken from the *gaṇacchandas* system, and familiar in the Pali *ariyā*, abound in the fixed syllabic metres, and probably the majority of them will be found to have favourite *gaṇacchandas* phrases, rather than modifications of the *tuṭṭhubha*, as their basis, just as in our period it was *mattāchandas* which gave rise to the majority of the early fixed syllabic metres.[1] The *tuṭṭhubha* was assimilated to exact quantitative opposition, as we shall see in Chapter VIII, before taking up its special duties as sophisticated narrative metre in the classical repertoire (tradition represented by Aśvaghoṣa) with the alternative forms *upajāti* and *vaṃsaṭṭhā*.

§ 199. We have already mentioned the two forms of *gaṇacchandas* which predominate in the Pali Canon, the *gīti* and the *ariyā*, which appear to represent successive stages in the evolution of the metre rather than alternative structures used contemporaneously. A few strophes of *uggīti* (*udgīti*) (inverted *ariyā*) and *upagīti* (the two short *pādayugas*) are found, which presumably belong to the later stage. The *samavutta pamitakkharā* (*pramitākṣarā*), the *visamavutta uggatā* (*udgatā*) and other fixed syllabic metres derived from *gaṇacchandas* will be studied in Chapter IX, although some references to their origin will be made here. The discussions in Chapter IX are in

[1] It may be suggested that the mysterious *dhruvā* metres of the drama, which are "syllabic" but apparently derived from music (being opening strophes of songs), have the same origin, and may illustrate the formation of the classical syllabic metres, but these have not yet been studied (see Nitti-Dolci, 1938, pp. 84 ff.).

fact a continuation of the present Chapter, since we have to regard the formation of the classical fixed metres as an extension of *gaṇacchandas* technique. The more direct continuation of the musical metres which led to the Medieval *mattāvutta* (cf. § 120) is not discussed in this study. The *gaṇacchandas* form of musical metre, especially the *ariyā*, remained in use for some centuries (Māhārāṣṭrī lyric, for instance) before the transition to *mattāvutta* took place when the Apabhraṃśa stage of the language had been reached.

§ 200. Besides the distinctions based on the lengths of the *pādayugas*, *gaṇacchandas* is classified in other ways: according to the position of the caesura at the end of the prior *pāda* (*pathyā*/*vipulā*) and according to the presence (*capalā*) or absence of the rhythm ⏑–⏑ in every even *gaṇa*. These distinctions are of very great importance in Pali *gaṇacchandas*, whereas in the classical literature they are secondary refinements, whose significance is not very clear. The ancient theory which describes them is thus more closely related to the Pali metre (although the rules do not apply exactly to the Pali examples, and are evidently based on the literature of a somewhat later period) than to the classical metre, which rarely deviates from the standard *ariyā pathyā* and merely adheres to the rules without fully exploiting the resources they offer, the rhythmic variations which they reflect having no doubt disappeared from the living practice. The traditional total of eighty forms of *gaṇacchandas* (see § 202) represents the possible combinations and permutations of *pathyā*, *vipulā* and *capalā* in the two *pādayugas* of *gīti*, *ariyā*, *uggīti*, *upagīti* and *ariyāgīti* (this last has not been found in the Pali literature). Finally we have to examine the *gurviṇī* (= **gubbinī* in Pali ? [1]) metre, which possibly occurs in the Canon (or the apparent examples may be mere corruption), in which the rhythms of the odd and even *gaṇas* are simply interchanged. The early *gaṇacchandas* was in fact a single metre which underwent gradual modification and was capable of various alternative structures, the most important of which were named.

[1] cf. *gubbiṇī* in the *Prākṛtapaiṅgala*, p. 120.

Before examining Pali *gaṇacchandas* in detail and discussing the evolution of the metre it is desirable to give a fuller account of the traditional theory and its terminology.

The Traditional Theory of Gaṇacchandas—*Terminology*

§ 201. We have already remarked that the Indian theory seems to have been based on a stage of *gaṇacchandas* a little later than that represented in our texts, but nevertheless closely akin to our stage and following many of the same rules. We may therefore adopt this terminology, bearing in mind, however, that it is not the original terminology and views the metre from a different standpoint : the *ariyā pathyā* non-*capalā* is taken as the norm, whereas in our texts the *capalā* is everywhere the predominant structure, the *gīti vipulā capalā* is the original form of the metre, and the *vipulā* is as important as the so-called *pathyā*. In fact the whole theory is standing on its head as far as we are concerned, but it represents the perfected metre for which our poets were preparing the ground. Sometimes our verses seem tentative and experimental in character (this is a purely subjective judgment hard to substantiate with the badly preserved material at our disposal), as if new rhythms were being tried out in various combinations and a classical norm of usage had not yet been arrived at. We must therefore beware of imposing the later rules throughout the Pali verses in attempting to restore them out of the chaos of the manuscripts copied for two millennia by scribes who did not understand the metre. One is constantly in danger of " over-restoring "—as we might call it when freer verses or a more fluid language is forced into some classical norm. We should remember Professor H. Smith's remarks (1950a, p. 9) concerning the reduction of Pali and BHS *tuṭṭhubha* verses to the " banale " *upajāti* rhythm by the classicalists :

> " On renchérit donc sur les licences prosodiques en faisant scander (Mv)... **arthadasī matīnāṃ** au lieu de... *v⟨i⟩yākare arthadarśī matīmāṃ* ~ *sevetha naṃ atthadassī mutīmā* Sn 385d (ici la v.l. *atthadasso*, comme *atthadassā* J VI 260.4 au même endroit du vers, remonte peut-être à un **atthadasa-*, bâti comme *duddasa-. . . durdṛśa*, et introduit ici par quelqu'un qui affectionnait la *triṣṭubh* banale et classique)."

§ 202. The terms used by the Sanskrit writers on *gaṇacchandas* are as follows :

the five metres described by the early writers from Piṅgala onwards	*gīti* (30 + 30 *mattā*) *āryā* (30 + 27 : the short sixth *gaṇa* in the second half) *udgīti* (27 + 30) *upagīti* (27 + 27) *āryāgīti* (32 + 32 : full eighth *gaṇa*)

From these five with *vipulā* and/or *capalā* in both *pādayugas*, in either, or in neither (= *pathyā*) we obtain the traditional eighty kinds of *gaṇacchandas*. The later theoretical writers worked out and labelled all possible combinations of two *pāda-yugas* of 30, 27, 32, or 29 (short sixth and full eighth *gaṇas*) *mattā*, making altogether sixteen metres and 256 kinds of *gaṇacchandas*. Cappeller decided (1872, p. 25) that the 29 *mattā* form is quite artificial and never existed in the literature, which would rule out the seven metres which are said to use it : *saṅgīti*, *cārugīti*, *vigīti*, *mañjugīti*, *pramadā*, *pragīti*, *candrikā*. This leaves the above five with four others making a total of nine, which is also a traditional figure in connection with varieties of *gaṇacchandas*. The four are all metres with the full eighth *gaṇa* in one *pādayuga* :

sugīti	(32 + 27)
anugīti	(27 + 32)
vallarī	(32 + 30)
lalitā [1]	(30 + 32)

§ 203. In the extant Classical literature, Sanskrit and Prakrit, only the *āryā* is common, as we have already noted, whilst in Early Middle Indian, Pali and Ardhamāgadhī, the *gīti* is common and appears to be the original metre from which the others evolved : it is therefore noteworthy that of these nine names six contain the word *gīti*, suggesting that they were originally regarded as varieties of that metre.

[1] *lalitā* is (probably merely by chance) the name of one kind of *uggatā*. We shall see in Chapter IX that the *uggatā* has in effect a prior *pādayuga* of thirty-two *mattā*, but a posterior of only twenty-six *mattā* (six full *gaṇas* and a half). It thus bears some resemblance to the *vallarī*.

We have noted the rare occurrence of *uggīti* and *upagīti* in Pali ; they also occur very rarely in the Classical literature. The *ariyāgīti* appears to represent an old form from the experimental period in which the sixteen *gaṇas* of the musical strophe were filled completely by the words instead of each *pādayuga* terminating with a prolonged syllable or a rest. In the Classical period occurrences of *ariyāgīti* have been found by Ballini (1912, p. 102), together with a continuous use of it in the *Nalodaya* [1] (Cappeller 1872, 87 ff.) : this late example should perhaps be compared with Apabhraṃśa *mattāvuttas* which also show the full *gaṇa* (⏑–⏑) at the end of each *pāda* (*pajjhaṭikā*, for instance : ⏒⏒ ⏑⏑– | ⏑⏑⏑⏑⏑– | (⏑⏑– –⏑⏑) | ⏑, ⏑⏑–⏑ × 4, is practically identical with *ariyāgīti*). The *Nalodaya* metre is also related to Apabhraṃśa *mattāvutta* in its regular use of rhyme. In fact, however, the *ariyāgīti* is the dominating metre of the *Rāvaṇavaha* (5th century) and a systematic search, particularly of Prakrit literature, might reveal a regular use of this metre throughout the Classical period. We have no examples of *ariyāgīti* in our period, but we do find varieties resembling it in having the full end *gaṇas* in the so-called " hypermetre " in Ardhamāgadhī (described by Jacobi, 1885a, 389 ff.), in the metres called *mātrāsamaka* [2] in the early theory (Piṅgala IV, 42–7)—of which the only traces in the literature are those in the *Mahābhārata* discussed by Hopkins (1902, 353–4), and in the metres called *gītyāryā* in the early theory (Piṅgala IV, 48–52) but not found in the extant early literature (one strophe is found later : *Naiṣadhacarita* XXII, 148). Taking a hint from Jacobi we may suppose that as the *gīti* evolved from the *vetālīya* the proto-*ariyāgīti* was evolved from the *opacchandasaka*.

If the *ariyāgīti* is not common, only the shadows of its variations *vallarī* and *lalitā* (mixed with ordinary *gīti*), *sugīti* (cf. *ariyā*) and *anugīti* (cf. *uggīti*) are to be found. Only the *sugīti* may claim two extant examples (see Ballini, 1912, p. 102).

[1] The date of this poem may be *c.* A.D. 900, if it is by the Vāsudeva at the court of Kulaśekharavarman.

[2] On later metres of this type see Sinha, 1953, 177 f. (origin of *pādākulaka* > *caupāī*).

§ 204. Variations :

pathyā (any of the above metres having a caesura immediately following the third *gaṇa* of each *pādayuga*)

vipulā (any of the above metres not having a caesura immediately following the third *gaṇa* of the first *pādayuga* : *ādivipulā* or *mukhavipulā*, of the second *pādayuga* : *antavipulā* or *jaghanavipulā*, or of both *pādayugas* : *mahāvipulā*)

capalā (any of the above metres having ⏑ – – ⏑ in the second and fourth *gaṇas* of either or both *pādayugas* : *ādicapalā* . . . *mahācapalā*. Other rules are given which were not yet observed in Pali, although they may have developed from tendencies already present in Pali usage)

gurviṇī (characterized by having ⏑ – – ⏑ in the odd *gaṇas*. The genuineness of this metre was doubted by Cappeller (1872, pp. 78–81), and it is not mentioned by Piṅgala. The corruption which Cappeller suggests was responsible for the apparent occurrence of *gurviṇī* in the Classical literature may also be invoked to explain the more numerous apparent cases in Pali. On the other hand the " hypermetre " in Ardhamāgadhī is definitely of the *gurviṇī* type, and in the most thoroughgoing manner, the rôles of the odd and even *gaṇas* being interchanged throughout. There is thus no reason to doubt that the *gurviṇī* of the theory existed in the earlier period, although the recollection of it in the treatises on metrics is extremely vague).

§ 205. Jacobi's " Law of Vipulā " (see " Zur Kenntniss der Āryā ", ZDMG XL, 1886, 336 ff.) based on the usage from the Hāla Anthology onwards, was not yet observed in the Pali *ariyā*, although the normality of the *pathyā* had already become established in the later Canonical texts and the *vipulā* had been reduced to its secondary position.

The *gurviṇī* is perhaps more primitive than the *gīti* in that its arrangement of the *gaṇa*-rhythms more directly reflects the structure of *mattāchandas*. With the relationship between *gīti* and *gurviṇī* may be compared that between ordinary *vetālīya* and *pavattaka*. This parallel will be studied below.

Tables of Gaṇacchandas *Structure. The* Gaṇacchandas *Texts*

§ 206. In the tables the seven possible *gaṇa* structures (- -, ⏑⏑-, -⏑⏑, ⏑-⏑, ⏑⏑⏑⏑, ⏑, -), with ⏑- as a doubtful eighth, are shown separately with their occurrences in selected Canonical texts as the various *gaṇas* of the strophe :

- -

Posn. of *gaṇa*	*Upālisutta* (M I 386)	*Mettasutta* (Sn 143–151)	*Tuvaṭaka-sutta* (Sn 915–934)	*Isidāsī-gāthā* (Th II 400–447)	*Sumedhā-gāthā* (Th II 448–487 and 493–522)
1	7[1]	7?	13[2]	26	41
2				8	19?
3	7	7	12	32	43?
4			1 (-,-)	20	21?
5	7	9	8	25	41?
6					
7	6		9	26	35?
8					
9	5[1]	8	12[2]	28	41
10				9	12
11	6	6	13	32?	40?
12				15	23?
13	5	9	8	37	40?
14	1				
15	5	1	5	26	39
16					
17	8[1]				
18					
19	7				
20					
21	1 (10)				
22					
23					
24					

[1] If ⏑- was permitted as the first *gaṇa* of a *pādayuga*, distinct from - - by licence (or anceps), then - - only 6 times in 1, only once in 9, and 5 times in 17; the balance being ⏑- (or ×-).

[2] One case in 1 and two cases in 9 are perhaps ⏑- (cf. preceding note). The figures for the *Tuvaṭakasutta* are incomplete, the poem being very corrupt with a number of apparent *gurvinī* type deviations from the usual structure, which resembles that of the two preceding poems. Sn 915, 917bcd, 918b, 920d, 923b, 926–7, 929b, 932 and 933d are omitted.

§ 207. ⏑ ⏑ —

Posn. of *gaṇa*	*Upālisutta*	*Mettasutta*	*Tuvaṭaka-sutta*	*Isidāsi-gāthā*	*Sumedhā-gāthā*
1	3	2	3	13	9
2			2	8?	7
3	3	2	4	6	18
4	2	2	1	9?	7?
5	3			13	12?
6			1?[2]		
7	4	9	3	13	19?
8					
9	4	1	2	10	15
10			1	5?	7
11	4	3	2	9?	17?
12		1	1	5?	13
13	5		2[3]	9	23?
14	1		1		
15	5	8	8	18?	15
16					
17	2				
18	1				
19	3				
20					
21					
22					
23	1 (10)[1]				
24					

[1] Doubtful licence, but our scansion is certain unless the cadence was outside the *gaṇacchandas* structure (*opacchandasaka* !).

[2] Burmese MSS. and *Niddesa* read *payuttaṃ* here : ⏑–⏑.

[3] One may be ⏑––⏑ (931).

§ 208.

— ⏑ ⏑

Posn. of *gaṇa*	*Upālisutta*	*Mettasutta*	*Tuvaṭaka-sutta*	*Isidāsī-gāthā*	*Sumedhā-gāthā*
1				7	9
2			1?	5	5
3				5	4
4				6	10
5				6?	12
6			1?		1?
7				7	9?
8					
9				9	4?
10	—⏑⏑ does not occur in either the *Upālisutta* or the *Mettasutta*.			6	13
11				6	7
12				10	6
13			1		2?
14					
15				4?	10
16					
17					
18					
19					
20					
21					
22					
23					
24					

§ 209. ⏑—⏑

Posn. of *gaṇa*	*Upālisutta*	*Mettasutta*	*Tuvaṭaka-sutta*	*Isidāsī-gāthā*	*Sumedhā-gāthā*
1					
2	9	9	13	25?	27
3				1	
4	4	7	10	11?	28?
5			4		
6	7	9	11	44?	58
7					1?
8					
9					2?
10	8	9	14	23?	28?
11					1?
12	1	8	12	17?	21?
13			2		1?
14	7	8	12	1[1]	
15					
16					
17					
18	9				
19					
20					
21					
22	1 (10)				
23					
24					

[1] 401. Everywhere else we find the *ariyā* short sixth here, so this is suspect: it is one of the verses said to have been added by the recensionists.

§ 210.

⏑ ⏑ ⏑ ⏑
(⏑,⏑⏑⏑ except where otherwise noted)

Posn. of *gaṇa*	*Upālisutta*	*Mettasutta*	*Tuvaṭaka-sutta*	*Isidāsī-gāthā*	*Sumedhā-gāthā*
1					6 (mostly ⏑⏑,⏑⏑)
2	1			2	7 (sometimes ⏑⏑⏑,⏑)
3				1	
4			1?	2?	
5					
6	2			2	5
7					
8					
9			1 (⏑⏑⏑⏑)		2 (⏑⏑, ⏑⏑ and ⏑⏑⏑⏑)
10	1			5 (1 : ⏑⏑,⏑⏑)	5 (1 : ⏑⏑,⏑⏑)
11				1??	
12			1?	1 (⏑⏑⏑⏑)	5
13					
14	1	1			
15					
16					
17					
18					
19					
20	1 (10)				
21					
22					
23					
24					

§ 211.

˘

Posn. of *gaṇa*	*Upālisutta*	*Mettasutta*	*Tuvaṭaka-sutta*	*Isidāsī-gāthā*	*Sumedhā-gāthā*
6					1
8	10	3	6	13	21
14				46	64
16	10	2	4	15	28
22					
24	1 (10)				

—

Posn. of *gaṇa*	*Upālisutta*	*Mettasutta*	*Tuvaṭaka-sutta*	*Isidāsī-gāthā*	*Sumedhā-gāthā*
8	(does not occur— endings in *-assa*)	6	7	32	43
16		7	8	32	35
24					

§ 212.

˘— and ˘,—[1]

Posn. of *gaṇa*	*Upālisutta*	*Mettasutta*	*Tuvaṭaka-sutta*	*Isidāsī-gāthā*	*Sumedhā-gāthā*
1	1	(Does not occur)	2?	(Does not occur)	
4	3		3		
9	4		1?		
12	7		2?		
17	3				

§ 213. It was not practicable to scan all the *gaṇacchandas* strophes in the Canon (the total is more than 450). On the one hand the state of preservation is extraordinarily bad, but on the other hand the very great complexity of the *gaṇa* metre rules out all but a very small number of possible readings. Whereas in *mattāchandas* a large number of different metrical interpretations may fit the *mattā* count, in *gaṇacchandas* the *gaṇa* divisions and the exact rules governing their rhythmic structures leave us with far fewer doubtful alternatives. The difficulty is to find the traces of the original strophes in the

[1] ˘,- perhaps always ≡ - -. Besides these we find five cases of ˘,˘˘ apparently ≡ ˘,- with resolution (*Upālisutta* has one in fourth position and two in twelfth; *Tuvaṭaka* has two in fourth).

mangled verses which have come down to us, preserved since the 1st century B.C., it seems, by people who did not understand the metres, and edited by modern scholars who were similarly ignorant of them (which is hardly surprising in view of the state of the manuscript material) or who, at best (Sn), were not able to venture far into the realm of conjecture in the absence of general rules governing Pali metrics and of particular rules governing the ancient *gīti*. Although the restorations we can make are in most cases convincing, the time and effort needed to puzzle out these 450 enigmas proved too great for the present study. It is hoped that the sample taken is an adequate basis for discussion.

§ 214. The *gaṇacchandas* verses in the Canon are distributed as follows. There are two poems in Sn, the well known *Mettasutta* in the *Uragavagga* (*gīti*, except possibly the last strophe which H. Smith suggests is *gurviṇī* : 1949, 1164) and the *Tuvaṭaka-sutta* in the *Aṭṭhakavagga* (*gīti*). These texts seem to represent the oldest stratum of *gaṇacchandas* in the Canon. Whereas the *Mettasutta* is comparatively well preserved, the *Tuvaṭakasutta* is full of corruptions. It does not observe the *capalā* rule followed by the *Mettasutta*, and it seems to allow ⏑--⏑ in the odd *gaṇas*. The poem may represent a slightly later stage than that of the *Mettasutta*, when greater freedom was allowed, the *gaṇa* principle having become firmly established. In any case it is much earlier than the majority of our *gaṇacchandas* texts, and we cannot reconstruct its usages with any certainty in the absence of further similar examples.

The *Upālisutta* of the *Majjhimanikāya* (which otherwise contains only a few scattered verses in *anuṭṭhubha* and *tuṭṭhubha*) is also in *gīti*. This eulogy of the Bhagavant resembles the *Mettasutta* in the regularity of the *capalā* structure, but it is composed in strophes of six *pādas* instead of the usual four, the groups of six being clearly marked by a refrain throughout. It also differs from the *Mettasutta* in that the first syllable of the *pādayuga* appears to be partially anceps, i.e. any short syllable may be lengthened there to produce the full *gaṇa* (⏑- > - -). This primitive feature seems to occur a few times in the *Tuvaṭakasutta* also.

In the *Therīgāthā* we find three poems, the *Kisāgotamīgāthā*, *Isidāsīgāthā* and *Sumedhāgāthā*, and in the *ariyā* metre, but with a much higher frequency of *capalā* than in Classical *ariyā*.[1] Five *Jātakas*, in an even worse state of preservation than the *Therīgāthā* verses, are in the same metre (the *Culladhammapāla*, No. 358, the *Kāliṅgabodhi*, No. 479, the *Candakinnara*, No. 485, the *Cullasutasoma*, No. 525, and the long *Khaṇḍahāla*, No. 542). The usage of the various *gaṇas* appears to be similar to that in Th II.

Elsewhere there are only scattered examples of *gaṇacchandas*, and it is noteworthy that none are found in Dh, U, I, Vv or Pv. There are a few strophes in Th I, including *uggīti* (359) and *upagīti* (489), in the *Mahāvagga* of the *Vinaya*, in S I, in the *Buddhavaṃsa*, Th II 23–4 in a very corrupt state and one or two other strophes in the *Jātaka*. We may mention finally the *uggatā* and *pamitakkharā*, metres derived from *gaṇacchandas*, found in the *Lakkhaṇasutta* of the *Dīgha*, which would add another twenty-seven strophes to our total.

The Origin of Gaṇacchandas

§ 215. It is more than eighty years since Cappeller published his remarkable study of *gaṇacchandas*,[2] yet his theories are still very little known, much less subjected to criticism or replaced by more modern research. The question of the nature of the rhythm of the *ariyā*, regarded by many Sanskritists as most obscure—a system of arbitrary rules rather than a verse form with strongly marked rhythms which could be felt in recitation like those of the more familiar *vatta* or *upajāti*—was first properly posed by him and was very largely clarified by his keen insight. Jacobi, having additional materials at his disposal, such as the Ardhamāgadhī texts, carried the study further by his hypotheses about the history of the post-Vedic metres. His tentative conclusions, as formulated in the famous ZDMG article of 1884, have, however, achieved an authoritativeness which would astound that ingenious scholar were he alive today, for he himself pointed out later (1895, p. 271, f.n. 2) that his work had been done before he knew of the

[1] Note that the latter two poems are in the immediate context of the *Subhājīvakambavanikāgāthā* in the later style of *mattāchandas*.

[2] *Die Gaṇachandas*, Leipzig, 1872.

existence of *gaṇacchandas* in the Pali texts—thus implying that his historical conclusions might be vitiated, or might at any rate require fresh demonstrations taking the new discoveries into account. Ballini, who in 1912 published the careful collection he had made of the contributions to the study of Indian metrics, unfortunately missed this and simply copied out the old arguments, although by that time all the *gaṇacchandas* in the Pali Canon had been printed (admittedly only the Sn examples seem to have been recognized).[1] Even today, Professor H. Smith in his own work on Pali *gaṇacchandas* merely refers to the 1884 article with the remark : " Quelle qu'ait été la genèse de 8.5,01...05 [*gaṇacchandas*], il ne sera pas inutile de confronter le *śloka* (ac : 8.1.3, aux équivalences – – : ⏑⏑–) avec les *kōla* 8.5,01 et 8.5,03, qui servent de points de départ au système de [2]*gaṇa* à quatre ou à six mores..."[2]

§ 216. Before discussing the rhythms of *gaṇacchandas* in relation to actual " performance " with music, involving the ictus scheme put forward by Cappeller, it is necessary to trace the origin of the metre and of its rhythmic elements. Without a living picture of the metre such as its historical development can give us, we are in no better position than Cappeller in trying to fit a ready made theory, such as Westphal's, to the dead metrical scheme of the old treatises on metrics. That Cappeller's results were, on the whole, not illusory as Kühnau's were, can be affirmed only through our knowledge of the nature of *gaṇacchandas* gained mainly as a result of Jacobi's historical studies.

§ 217. The *gīti* strophe contains the same number of *mattā* as the *vetālīya* strophe :

⏓⏓ | – ⏑⏑ | – ⏑–⏑ ⏓ |, ⏓⏓ – | – ⏑⏑ | – ⏑–⏑ ⏓ × 2 *vetālīya*

⏓⏓ – | ⏑ – ⏑ | ⏓⏓ – | ⏑(–), – ⏑ | – – | ⏑ – ⏑ | ⏑⏑ – | ⏓ × 2 *gīti*

(we give the *vipulā capalā* form of *gīti* as found in our earliest *gaṇacchandas* texts).

[1] Ballini : " La poesia profana (Laukika)," in SIFI-I, vol. VIII, part 2, Florence, 1912 ; see p. 89. Fausbøll's edition of Sn appeared in 1885, just after Jacobi's main article.

[2] 1949, p. 1159.

—Jacobi in his 1884 article gives a theory of the evolution of *gaṇacchandas* based on this correspondence. He describes two forms of *gaṇacchandas*, a newer form found in the later Śvetāmbara Canonical texts and in the Classical literature (the *ariyā*), and an older form found in the earlier Śvetāmbara texts: *Āyāraṅgasutta* and *Sūyagaḍaṃ* (the *gīti*). The same historical sequence, as we have already suggested, appears in the Pali texts, where the *gīti* is found in association with the earlier *mattāchandas* texts in Sn whilst the *ariyā* is found alongside a later *mattāchandas* text in Th II. Whilst *mattāchandas* is more widespread in the Pali Canon, occurring in texts where *gaṇacchandas* is not found (Dh, U, Vv, Pv and the *Aṅguttaranikāya*),[1] there are altogether more strophes in *gaṇacchandas* than in *mattāchandas* (over 450 as against less than 400). This fits in very well with our picture of the older *mattāchandas*, widely used in the earlier texts, being pushed out by the newer *gaṇacchandas*, which is but rarely used in the earlier texts whilst it is very popular in the later texts.

Jacobi gives the following scheme for early *gaṇacchandas*:

⏕ – | ⏑ – ⏑ | ⏕ – | ×, ⏕/– ⏑ | ⏕ – | ⏑ – ⏑ | ⏕ – | × × 2

and points out the resemblance to *vetālīya*, the second and third, sixth and seventh, *gaṇas* being simply interchanged, and, he believes, a different principle of measurement being introduced: in place of the Vedic foot of four syllables, which he unjustifiably attributed to *vetālīya*, we have the *gaṇa* structure. Having seen only Dh as an example of early Pali poetry he supposed that *gaṇacchandas* was unknown in Pali and was not invented until a post-Pali period represented by the Śvetāmbara Canon. This is not the case, but he was nevertheless right in supposing *mattāchandas* to be the earlier metre, if the outline of the general development of the musical metres indicated in our last chapter is correct.

§ 218. If the *mattā* count is identical in the two metres (*vetālīya* and *gīti*), and proves their affinity, how are we to account for

[1] As against *gaṇacchandas* found in the *Majjhimanikāya* where *mattāchandas* does not occur.

the curious rearrangement of the *gaṇas* ? The mere carrying of the musical rhythm through the cadence as well as the free part of the *pāda* does not explain the normal form of *gaṇacchandas* as a direct descendant of the normal form of *mattāchandas*. In our study of *mattāchandas*, however, we have found a number of alternative rhythmic structures, including such a " rationalized " *pādayuga* as that of the *vegavatī*, and in *gaṇacchandas* also there were such alternatives. By putting together all the evidence at our disposal, meagre though the literary remains of our period may seem, a fairly clear picture emerges from which it should be possible to elucidate the nature, interrelationship and process of evolution of all these metres.

§ 219. In the case of *mattāchandas* we have the " syncopated " *pādayuga* called *pavattaka* :

⏑–⏑|⏖ –|⏑–⏑×,⏑⏑|⏑–⏑|⏖ –|⏑–⏑×

In the case of *gaṇacchandas* we have the *gurviṇī*, which we may also call syncopated, the eight *mattā* rhythm ⏖ –|⏑–⏑ beginning one *gaṇa* late ; in illustration of this metre we may give the Ardhamāgadhī " hypermetre " as described by Jacobi, 1885a, 389 ff. :[1]

⏓–⏓|⏖–|⏑–⏑|:|⏖–|⏑–⏑|:|⏖–|⏑–⏑|–(×)

(the part enclosed by |: :| may be repeated a varying number of times—see Jacobi's article for details).

The similarity between these two metres extends almost to identity, syllable for syllable : besides the *gaṇa* ⏑–⏑ appearing in exactly the same positions in both, the *gaṇa* ⏖– (initial long which may be resolved, final long fixed) appears twice (second and sixth positions). Only the fourth *gaṇa* changes slightly, from ×,⏑⏑ to ⏖–. The only difference is the *pāda* and strophe structure, since in place of the four *pāda mattāchandas* strophe the " hypermetre " has its curious extendable form, varying from an occasional four *gaṇa* (first, second, third, and eighth

[1] This metre is used in the *Varṇakas* of the Jaina Canon, a special type of descriptive composition.

gaṇas of the above scheme) strophe (?) to one of twenty-eight *gaṇas*, any even number in between being permitted, the eight-*gaṇa* form being the favourite. The initial *gaṇa* sometimes takes the form - -, and the final *gaṇa* generally has the full four *mattā*, like the *ariyāgīti*, but may have only the single anceps syllable. With the usage in the final *gaṇa* should be compared the *mattāchandas* usage of combining an *opacchandasaka* posterior *pāda* with a *vetālīya* prior, which results in a *pādayuga* of exactly the same length (32 *mattā*). For convenience of reference we may call a metre with the full final *gaṇa*, or the *opacchandasaka* cadence, " acatalectic " and the alternative, in which the final syllable is missing, " catalectic ".

§ 220. We can now see all the components of *gaṇacchandas* separately, with their *mattāchandas* prototypes, and the various combinations and permutations which are possible. We may construct a kind of matrix of musical metres in three dimensions : " normal "/" syncopated ", " acatalectic "/" catalectic ", *mattāchandas*/*gaṇacchandas*—in which the third pair seems to be of least significance in our theoretical analysis, their difference emerging only in practice, where the least important distinctions so often appear on the surface, obscuring the inner relationships and interconnections of things :

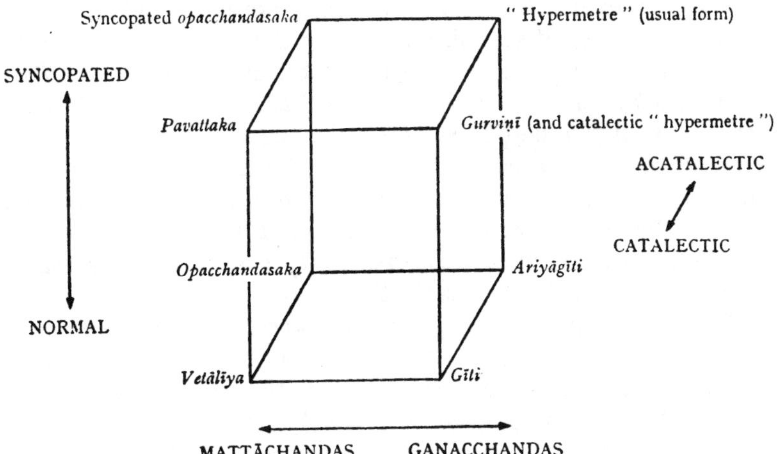

§ 221. Taking only the " catalectic " forms of the metres, we may compare their structures as follows :

⏔ | ⏔⨱⨱ | – ⏑–⏑ × |, ⏔ ⏔ | ⏔⨱⨱ | – ⏑–⏑ × × 2 *vetālīya*
⏑ –⏑ | ⨱⨱ – | ⏑–⏑ × |, ⏔ | ⏑– ⏑ | ⨱⨱ – | ⏑–⏑ × × 2 *pavattaka*
⏓–⏓ | ⨱⨱ – | ⏑–⏑ |: ⨱⨱ – | ⏑– ⏑: | ⨱⨱ – | ⏑–⏑ | × " hypermetre "
(*gurviṇī*)
⨱⨱ – | ⏑– ⏑ | ⨱⨱ – | ×, –(⏑) / (⏑–) | – – | ⏑– ⏑ | ⏑⏑– | × × 2 (or × 3) *gīti*

– | ⏓⏓⏓ | – – | ⨱⨱ – |, – | ⏓⏓⏓ | – – | ⏑⏑– – × 2 *svāgatā*
⨱⨱ | – ⏑⏑ | – ⏑⏑ | – – |, ⏔ ⏑⏑ | – ⏑⏑ | – ⏑⏑ | – – × 2 *vegavatī*
– | ⏑–⏑ | ⏑⏑ (–) – | ⏑–⏑ × × 4 *rathoddhatā*

From the conflict of the mixed rhythms of *mattāchandas* (the uneven *pādas* and the two opposing rhythms within them : – – | ⏑–⏑ together with the syncopation or two *mattā* shift of the proto-*gaṇa* divisions) a whole array of new metres was generated, the most important (the most successful solution to the rhythmic problem of creating an isochronous but not monotonous strophe) being the *gīti*, with its rich potential of further development of rhythmic variety and flexibility within the 16 *gaṇa* strophe.

§ 222. In the last chapter we considered how *mattāchandas* developed several fixed offshoots, or, more precisely, several forms in process of stabilization of rhythm in particular directions which later became fixed. In the development *vetālīya* > *pavattaka* (and > *chappadā* (*ṣaṭpadā*) > *rathoddhatā*) we reach a well-rounded *samavutta*. In the development of the *vegavatī* and the *svāgatā* the cadence rhythm is assimilated to that of the opening, in the former metre a rather monotonous strophe being produced, in the latter a fresh opposition of rhythms of the *mattāchandas* type, apparently with a " normal " prior *pāda* and a " syncopated " posterior.

The transition from the *pavattaka* to the " hypermetre " was of quite a different nature. As we have seen, there is hardly any change at all in the external, schematic, appearance of the metre. What has changed is the wider context in which the metre is situated, the way in which it is used and the " deeper " nature of the rhythms which does not appear in the superficial scheme. As far as we know, the *pavattaka* was not used as an independent metre, but only as a variant of *vetālīya*, but in any case it was a *mattāchandas* : its cadence was fixed, its strophe was divided by the cadences into four *pādas*. Used as a *gaṇacchandas*, the same rhythmic scheme acquires the following new characteristic : the division into four *pādas* is superseded by the articulation into eight similar segments of eight *mattā* each which might be called " bars " ; this perfectly cyclic rhythm is then seen to be in its essence, or simplest form, the repetition of this segment, so that a phrase of musical type may replace the old strophe, and may be of any length, within reason, from two segments or " bars " (four *gaṇas*) upwards (three " bars " = six *gaṇas*, four " bars " = eight *gaṇas*, etc., etc.). The phrase of eight " bars " or sixteen *gaṇas* which is equivalent in length to the old strophe was the most popular form, and became the stabilized form of *gaṇacchandas*, but in the late Medieval metres (e.g. in Hindī) the alternatives, especially those of eight *gaṇas* or of thirty-two, but also those of twelve, twenty, twenty-four, and so on, are still frequently used. The metre has become fully musical and can be used in the same way as a musical *tāla*.

§ 223. It is a remarkable fact that of the two ancient, basic *tālas*, *caturasra* and *tryasra*, described in the *Nāṭyaśāstra* one, the *caturasra*, has the same form as this eight *mattā tāla* of *gaṇacchandas*. It is not clear why the two fundamental musical rhythms, binary and ternary, should be defined in this curious way with complicated structures :

caturasra : *SSIŚ*[1] (*cañca*) = - -⏑⌞ (eight *mattā*)
tryasra : *SIIS* (*cāpa*) = -⏑⏑- (six *mattā*)

—whatever the musical theory may be which underlies these descriptions, it does not seem possible that the *gaṇacchandas* rhythm, whether it be - -⏑-⏑ or ⏑-⏑- - (depending merely on where the cycle is regarded as beginning), resembles the *cañca* merely by coincidence, the sole difference being the resolution of the *pluta* into a long and a short, which makes hardly any

[1] In the Indian notation *I* = short, *S* = long, *Ś* = *pluta*.

difference in the feel of the rhythm. Whether the musical theory was based on the association with metrical rhythm, or vice versa—or whether the *cañca* is an imitation of the call of the woodpigeon or of some other natural rhythm—is a question which cannot be taken up here. We may note the continuity of metrical development without, for the present, enquiring further into the interactions with the ancient music which resulted in the stabilization of the fundamental *gaṇacchandas tāla*. We may also note that the adoption of the *gīti*, with ⏑–⏑ in the even *gaṇas*, rather than the *gurviṇī*, as the standard form of *gaṇacchandas*, suggests that the metre was brought into line with the musical convention that the *tāla* began on the first *garu* : –́ –⏑⏑⏑ and not on the *lahu* : ⏑́⏑⏑– –. This is uncertain because there is no reason why the strophe should not begin *viṣama* (with an " anacrusis "), in the same way as the normal form of *mattāchandas*. It is possible that the *gaṇa* form ⏑–⏑ retained its cadence-associations and that –́ –⏑–⏑ was felt to be the form of the metrical rhythm.

§ 224. The *gīti*, or normal form of *gaṇacchandas*, stands in a somewhat similar relationship to the *gurviṇī*—" hypermetre " as the *vetālīya* does to the *pavattaka*. Since in the case of *gaṇacchandas* the " syncopation " involved is a shift of four *mattā*, whilst in *mattāchandas* it is one of only two *mattā*, the *gīti* and *vetālīya* do not coincide at all in *gaṇa* articulation. Unlike the *gurviṇī* and *pavattaka*, they show no ambiguity in their structure : one is plainly *gaṇacchandas*, the other plainly *mattāchandas*. One may here invoke the principle of stabilization of metres in their most characteristic forms, furthest removed from other metres, which we put forward in the last chapter (§ 150, end). The only cases recorded of ⏑–⏑ in *mattāchandas* in the position of the future even *gaṇas* are the " syncopated " *pāda* forms : ⏓⏓ –|⏑–⏑|⏑–⏑(⏓)(⏓), which occurs in the *Kummāsapiṇḍajātaka* (J III p. 412, 150a and others), in Sn (8a : *yo nāccasārī na paccasārī* repeated five times) and in Th II; and ⏓⏓|– –|⏑–⏑|⏑–⏑– ⏓ (in position of sixth *gaṇa*), which occurs as refrain in J 458 and doubtfully in Sn. Clearly the conjunction of ⏑–⏑|⏑–⏑ was avoided in all the metres.

The question of ⏑–⏑ in the even *gaṇas* brings us to the problem of the fourth *gaṇa*, in which the two *pādas* of *mattāchandas* were welded together to form the *gaṇacchandas pādayuga* of 7½ (or 8) *gaṇas*.

§ 225. According to Jacobi's theory the fourth *gaṇa* of the earliest *gaṇacchandas* was formed by the coalescence of the final (anceps) syllable of the prior *vetālīya*, when short, with the first two syllables of the so-called anacrusis of the posterior *pāda*, when this had the form -⏑-. This seems very neat, and it explains the *vipulā* form of *gaṇacchandas*, in which the caesura falls after the first short syllable of the fourth *gaṇa* |⏑,-⏑| (a very common form, in fact the regular form, in some of our oldest texts) as a legacy from *mattāchandas* (end of the prior *pāda*). Although there is evidently some connection here between the two metres, this argument is not satisfactory as it stands, and the fourth *gaṇa* was not derived in this direct manner. The final anceps syllable of the prior *pāda* probably counted as a long in the musical rhythm, a short syllable being lengthened : this seems to be the true nature of the final anceps of the *gaṇacchandas pādayuga* and of other final anceps syllables in Indian metres.[1] If the initial syllable of the posterior *pāda* of *vetālīya* was allowed to be anceps (which is doubtful, and in any case probably restricted to the earlier period), this should surely be limited to allowing exceptional metrical lengthening or shortening in initial position, and should not be interpreted as meaning that such an initial group as -⏑ is not quantitative (as Jacobi contended). Thus we should interpret ⏑-|-⏑⏑ . . . as - -|-⏑⏑ . . . and -⏑-|-⏑⏑ . . . as ⏑⏑-|-⏑⏑ . . . This would result, in the transition from *vetālīya* to *gīti*, in a fourth *gaṇa* form -,⏑⏑ (taking the *vetālīya pādayuga* proposed by Jacobi as the starting point). Now this form actually appears in early Pali *gaṇacchandas* (although -⏑⏑ as a *gaṇa* is unpopular in any position), in the *Tuvaṭakasutta*. More frequent (especially in the *Upālisutta*) is -,- or ⏑,- (>-, -) in the fourth *gaṇa* (cf. posterior *vetālīya* with initial long). That ⏑,-⏑ is very much commoner than these forms of the fourth *gaṇa* is evidently due to the adoption of the alternating system of - - and ⏑-⏑ as the

[1] cf. §§ 102 and 226.

basic rhythm of all *gaṇacchandas*, ⏑–⏑ occurring in the odd *gaṇas* of the "hypermetre" and the even *gaṇas* of the *gīti*. The formation of the *gīti* was certainly helped by the quantitative fitting together of . . . ×,⏓⏑ of the *vetālīya*, and the caesura following the first syllable of the fourth *gaṇa* undoubtedly originated from *mattāchandas*. The adoption of the form ⏑,–⏑ with the caesura in the fourth *gaṇa* following the short syllable, may have pleased the ancient poets, as it satisfied Jacobi's desire to find a nice correspondence of structures, but it should be regarded as the result of the impact of the regular *gaṇacchandas* rhythm on the divided *pādayuga* of *mattāchandas*, and not as the manner of generation of that rhythm from *mattāchandas*.

It was not only in the fourth *gaṇa* that a caesura appeared in *gaṇacchandas*: in the second and sixth also we have the "secondary caesura", which is the rule when four short syllables make up these *gaṇas* (⏑,⏑⏑⏑). This usage may have been as important in the fixing of the *vipulā* forms with caesura ⏑,⏑⏑⏑ and ⏑,–⏑ in the fourth *gaṇa* as the memory of the old *pāda* division. It evidently arose from the need to stress the syncopated rhythm ⏑́,⏓⏑⏑. It should be noted that in early Pali *gaṇacchandas* it was the fourth *gaṇa* which from the beginning showed a tendency to variations of rhythm, and that the second *gaṇa* maintained the ⏑–⏑ rule longer and even in the later texts (e.g. Th II) has ⏑–⏑ much more frequently than does the fourth *gaṇa*.

§ 226. One more question connected with the origin of *gaṇacchandas* is that of the initial anceps in the old prior *pāda*. We have seen in *mattāchandas* that occasionally it seems necessary to assume the exceptional lengthening of a short *pāda*-initial syllable (including root syllables), against the normal rules for licence, to preserve the *mattā* count (see Tables 1 and 2, §§ 128–9, in Chapter V: ⏑–⏑⏑ > – –⏑⏑ and ⏑– –⏑⏑ > – – –⏑⏑ in Sn). Sometimes we have to assume the same lengthening in early *gaṇacchandas* at the beginning of the *pādayuga*. Thus in the *Upālisutta* we wish to read: *n̄ahātakassa*, *p̄urindadassa*, *s̄atīmato*, *t̄athāgatassa*, etc. The same thing appears to happen in the *Tuvaṭakasutta*, but in the *Mettasutta*, which is so regular in other ways too, it is absent. The cases are limited to *gaṇas* of two syllables: ⏑– > – –. In the later texts this special licence is not found.[1]

In the initial of the old posterior *pāda* we find traces of this old anceps in three places[2] where it is apparently necessary to assume: ⏑,⏑⏑ > ⏑,–⏑ (fourth *gaṇa*).

The final syllable of the *pādayuga* (and probably of the prior *pāda* in the earliest texts) remained anceps, as seems to be the rule in almost all Indian metres, but it is of interest that in the Pali texts there is a considerable preponderance of longs in this position, indicating a strong feeling for a syllable of at least two *mattā* (half a *gaṇa*). We may conclude that any short vowel as *pādayuga* final in Pali *gaṇacchandas* underwent metrical lengthening.

The Origin of the Ariyā

§ 227. Various explanations have been attempted to account for the shortened sixth *gaṇa* in the second *pādayuga* of the *ariyā*. This metre replaces the *gīti* in the later Pali Canonical texts, and thereafter remains the dominant, almost the exclusive, form of *gaṇacchandas* in the extant Prakrit and Sanskrit literature. Although the theory places the two metres on a level as alternative structures, along with *uggīti* and *upagīti*, and does not recognize that the *gīti* is an older, discarded form, the distribution of the metres in the Pali Canon seems conclusive evidence for a historical change.[3] Jacobi (1884) was led to the same conclusion in his study of Ardhamāgadhī *gaṇacchandas*.

§ 228. Cappeller (1872, pp. 69–70), finding it impossible to accept a single short syllable as equivalent in any way to a whole *gaṇa*, regards the short sixth as merely an acciaccatura (" Vorschlag ")[4] belonging to the seventh *gaṇa*. This seems quite unjustifiable. Equally improbable is the suggestion that the *gaṇa* was completed by a musical " rest ", if only because

[1] Except for one case of *tato* (> *tāto*) initial in the *Isidāsīgāthā*.

[2] *Upālisutta*, strophes 7, 8 (twice). Alternatively we might assume > –, ⏑⏑ (lengthening the final of the prior *pāda*).

[3] cf. § 214 above and also § 203.

[4] Ballini incorrectly translated this into Italian as " appoggiatura ", which would have been " Vorhaltung " in German.

no caesura appears which would allow a break in the uttering of the words. Jacobi suggested (1884, p. 602) that for some reason the singing of the strophe required inequality of the *pādas*, and cites the *Gītagovinda* as an example in which the strophes throughout have either all four, or at least three, of their *pādas* different from one another. This much later example of musical metres, of course, belongs to the Apabhraṃśa-Hindī stage in which such inequalities in a number of metres can be seen quite clearly to be the result of the musical structures, with rests and pauses in the text as it is fitted to the *tāla* (the traditional recitation being still alive amongst the popular Hindī reciters and preachers in India we can easily verify this). However, we do not find a *gaṇa* of one *mattā* in the later technique. The only explanation which seems to fit the case is that the final cadence of the *ariyā* strophe was marked by syncopation, just as in performance of the classical music the cadence or coda (at the end of a piece and also sometimes at the end of each verse of a song) is often marked by syncopated drumming. It seems likely that this syncopation derived from the syncopation in the *gaṇa* (⏑⏑)́–́⏑ (→), the " cadence *gaṇa* " of each eight *mattā* section of *gaṇacchandas* : the syncopation, instead of being resolved by the final short syllable of the *gaṇa* . . . ⏑|–́ (→) . . . with a return to a new section, is carried on to mark the final cadence of the whole strophe . . . |(⏑⏑)́|–́ - |–́||. The assumption of a *gaṇa* of one *mattā* is merely a conventional description of this syncopated close, which might also have been described in other ways. In modern European music, especially from Scriabin onwards, the old musical " Taktgleichheit " is not infrequently swept aside by the insertion of a bar with a different time signature (see e.g. the 21st of Scriabin's twenty-four Preludes, opus 11, for an early example of mixed time signatures : 3/4, 5/4 and 6/4), and even bars containing a single beat are found. This overt notation, however, merely makes clearer syncopations which have always been used to enliven music, though more modern composers have felt freer to experiment with them and to alter the bar lines and time signatures in the score as well as the rhythms in the music. Rossbach (1854, pp. XIX f.) already has drawn attention to an interesting example by Mozart in the Overture to *Le Nozze di Figaro*. Beat shifts are very frequent in Mozart.

§ 229. In the *gīti*, strophes of both four and six *pādas*, or perhaps more precisely of two and of three *pādayugas*, are found, and we have also noted the curious indefinitely extendable strophe—if we can call it such—of the " hypermetre ". So far *gaṇacchandas* had not advanced decisively beyond *mattāchandas* in achieving a truly musical strophe, in place of the metrical organization more suitable for continuous narrative, which stops short at the *pādayuga* (cf. the epic *vatta*, in which the *pādayugas* are little more than lines of blank verse and the narrative runs on fairly freely over them, sentences not necessarily coinciding with strophes, leading to editorial difficulties in breaking up the narrative into " verses " and numbering them). With their refrains, coincidence of sentence and strophe, interplay of rhythms, and so on, *mattāchandas* and the *gīti* show a regular strophe organization, but this is of an external nature not imposed by the metre. With the *ariyā* we find a four *pāda* unity based on the metre itself, that is on the musical " sentence " of two " phrases ", the second of which " answers " and completes the first, which is the basis of the strophe. The transition to musical metrics was completed by this invention of the *visamavutta* strophe structure.[1]

The Gaṇas *and the Structure of the* Gaṇacchandas *Strophe*

§ 230. We have already observed that in what appear to be the earliest *gaṇacchandas* verses extant (*Mettasutta, Upālisutta*)[2] the structure is practically fixed. ⏑--⏑ is the rule in the even *gaṇas*, except occasionally in the fourth, where (apart from one case of ⏑,⏑⏑⏑) ⏑⏑- and ⏑,-(= - - ?) seem to be allowed and to have their origin in the transition process from *mattāchandas*.[3] ⏕- is regular in the odd *gaṇas* (in the *Mettasutta* ⏑⏑- being the rule in the seventh and - - the rule in the fifth so that the " posterior *pāda* " is practically fixed: -⏑|- -|⏑--⏑|⏑⏑-|-

[1] We may thus regard the adoption of the *aḍḍhasamavutta* structure (*mattāchandas*) as the initial stage of this transition.

[2] The early Ardhamāgadhī *gīti* is of a similar nature, but not quite so rigid as the Pali.

[3] See above, § 225.

whereas the " prior *pāda* " is allowed some alternations) ; in the first and third - - is about three times as common as ⏑⏑- in the *Mettasutta*, and in the first, third and fifth - - is about twice as common as ⏑⏑- in the *Upālisutta* (here it is of interest to note that the second *pādayuga* has most freedom and that the third *pādayuga* is most rigid) ; the *Upālisutta* has one-and-a-half times as many - - as ⏑⏑- *gaṇas* in the seventh position in the first *pādayuga*, equal numbers of these two in the second *pādayuga*, and ⏑⏑- alone in the third *pādayuga* (where, however, it is a refrain repeated throughout the poem).[1] -⏑⏑ does not occur in these two Pali poems. ⏑,⏑⏑⏑ as resolution of ⏑-⏑ occurs seven (sixteen) times (only one of which is in the *Mettasutta*), and it never appears in the odd *gaṇas*. Thus no odd *gaṇa* may end in two short syllables.

§ 231. It appears that the rigid *Mettasutta gīti* represents the earliest *gaṇacchandas*, whilst the *Upālisutta* and the Jaina texts show a slightly later stage in which, the basic *tāla* having become firmly established, some variations are introduced. Even in the Classical Period, however, - - retained its popularity as the simplest form of *gaṇa*, as Cappeller has shown, and he also draws our attention (1872, pp. 48–9) to the interesting statement in the *Prākṛtapaiṅgala* (Bollensen, 1846, Appendix, p. 536, verse 4 = Ghoṣa's edition, 1902, p. 112, verse 58) that the best *āryā* (*gāhāṇaṃ gāhā, āā*) is that consisting of twenty-seven long syllables and three shorts (a total of only thirty), which is called *lacchī* (*lakṣmī*) (the three shorts are of course those in the sixth *gaṇas* which are compulsory). In the later Pali *gaṇacchandas* - - is much the commonest *gaṇa*, but in the even positions ⏑-⏑ still predominates. -⏑⏑ has taken its place alongside ⏑⏑- as a regular but not very frequent alternative to - -, and a few cases of the complete resolution ⏑⏑⏑⏑ are also found in the odd *gaṇas*.

§ 232. The rule of the secondary caesura in ⏑,⏑⏑⏑ as resolution for ⏑-⏑ (which itself tends fairly strongly to ⏑,-⏑ in any position)

[1] AM has mainly - - in the third and seventh *gaṇas* and - - and ⏑⏑- about equally in the first.

is adhered to in all the Pali texts with very few exceptions—not more than are likely to have been produced by mere corruption. On the other hand Jacobi's " Law of *vipulā* " (1886, p. 340) does not seem to have been in force in the later Pali texts, although in the earlier ones it is not infringed because a caesura after the first syllable of the fourth *gaṇa* is produced by the division into prior and posterior *pādas* at that point. According to Jacobi's Law, in the *vipulā* metre, in which there is no caesura at the end of the third *gaṇa*, if the forms ⏑–⏑ or ⏑⏑⏑⏑ occur in the fourth *gaṇa* there must instead be a caesura after the first syllable of that *gaṇa* : ⏑,⏓⏑. In the earlier Pali texts we see the original basis for such a usage in the *pāda* division at that point to which we have just referred. In the later Pali texts, however, with the abolition of this *pāda* division the *pathyā* (with caesura after the third *gaṇa*) and *vipulā* (without this caesura) forms seem to be used without further restrictions. Just as in any *gaṇa* with ⏑–⏑, there is a tendency to ⏑,–⏑ which should probably be described as a " secondary caesura ", resulting apparently from a feeling for the strongly marked syncopated rhythm ⏑́,–́ . . . which manifested itself in a kind of staccato. In the *Isidāsīgāthā* and *Sumedhāgāthā*, however, this caesura is much less common in the fourth *gaṇa* than in the second or sixth, on account of the prevalence of the new *pathyā* form. Whilst there is usually a caesura at the end of the third *gaṇa*, the form ⏑–⏑ is still by far the commonest fourth *gaṇa*. There are thus many cases of ⏑–⏑ without caesura, but even in the *vipulā pādayugas* there are several cases where no caesura appears (e.g. Th II 478 ab, 501 ab, 522 ab, 505 cd ; 498 ab has ⏑–,⏑). In the later literature, such as the Hāla Anthology, the conflict between the prevailing *pathyā* and the ⏑,⏓⏑ rhythm in the fourth *gaṇa* was resolved by the adoption of the usage described by Jacobi. ⏑–⏑ as fourth *gaṇa* gradually lost its popularity not only with the generally increasing flexibility of the *ariyā* but also through these difficulties of structure, and it became still less common than ⏑–⏑ as second *gaṇa*.

§ 233. It is clear from the *tāla* structure underlying *gaṇacchandas* (–́ –⏑–⏑, or ⏑́–⏑– – ?) that the *gīti pādayuga* consists of four " bars ", segments or " measures " in this *tāla* and the *ariyā* strophe of eight (with syncopated close). Cappeller placed the " main ictus " on the even *gaṇas*, that is, he adopted the second of the *tāla* forms given above : ⏑̋-⏑-́ -. He tried to justify this conclusion partly by analogy with Greek metre and partly by arguments within the limits of the " normal " forms of *gaṇacchandas*. The analogy proves nothing (we have rejected Westphal's " comparative metrics " above, §§ 22 ff.) and the latter arguments were unavoidably circular : by a simple interchange of one rhythm for another throughout they could be made to prove that the main ictus fell on the odd *gaṇas*. The discovery of the " hypermetre " with its *gurviṇī* structure lends support to Cappeller's conjecture, and if the matrix of musical metres given in § 220 could be made to demonstrate that the *gīti*, like the *vetālīya*, opened *visama* (§ 223)—both being " normal " metres—but had a " bar " of eight *mattā* whereas that of the *vetālīya* contained only four *mattā*, we could say that in origin *gaṇacchandas* was organized according to Cappeller's scheme. Against this we have the musical tradition that the *tāla* is -́-⏑⌊-, and it seems unlikely that, even if in origin the *gaṇacchandas tāla* was ⏑̀-⏑- -, the metrical structure was not brought into line with this convention (and the *gīti* thereby converted into a song strophe which began *sama* with its accompanying *tāla*). In practice the difference between -́ -⏑-⏑ and ⏑̀-⏑- - is unimportant : there exist today similar differences of convention between North and South Indian music, and such regional differences very probably existed in ancient times too. Cappeller, however, deserves the greatest praise not only for recognizing the eight *mattā* cyclic (or *cakravartana*) structure of *gaṇacchandas* but also for his grasp of the nature of the *gaṇa* form ⏑̀-⏑, whether its ictus be main or secondary. The word accent falling frequently on the long syllable of this *gaṇa*, it was a bold conjecture to place the musical ictus on the first short syllable, producing a strong syncopation, but there can be no doubt now that this is the correct analysis (see § 232 above on the secondary caesura and Cappeller's correct assessment of the first kind of secondary caesura on p. 94 of his study).

§ 234. A *gīti* strophe of two *pādayugas* may be analysed as follows in pairs of four *mattā gaṇas*, those with the " cadence " rhythm and the final " half-*gaṇas* " being underlined :

4 + 4 + 4 + 4 + 4 + 4 + 4 + (4) | + 4 + 4 + 4 + 4 + 4 + 4 + 4 + (4) ||

↓
prolonged
final or
2 + rest

—if the metre were taken as *viṣama* the result would simply be changed to :

4 + 4 + 4 + 4 + 4 + 4 + 4 + (4) | + 4 + 4 + 4 + 4 + 4 + 4 + 4 + (4) ||

The *ariyā* strophe may be analysed similarly, with its syncopated close :

4 + 4 + 4 + 4 + 4 + 4 + 4 + (4) | + 4 + 4 + 4 + 4 + 4 + 1 + 4 + (4) ||

syncope

—the syncopation was perhaps accompanied by a rallentando, bringing the rhythm to a point of rest at the final syllable of the strophe.

The Historical Significance of Gaṇacchandas

§ 235. At first sight it may appear that from the multiplicity of rules *gīti* and *ariyā* are tricky metres to handle compared with, for instance, the epic *vatta*. As we have seen, however, the *gaṇacchandas* rhythm is just as natural as any other when its musical structure is grasped. Further, Professor H. Smith has shown that the infinitely variable *gaṇacchandas* strophe—" l'*āryā* bouddhique, comme celle de Varāhamihira et d'Īśvarakṛṣṇa " (1950a, p. 14)—could accommodate any technical term, whereas the old *vatta-tuṭṭhubha* technique entailed the avoidance of ⏑⏑⏑,[1] which resulted sometimes in the metrical

[1] But see below, §§ 244–5, on successions of shorts in the Pali *vatta*.

alteration of words which could not otherwise be fitted into the verses (see 1950a, p. 10).

§ 236. Besides satisfying the need for a metre which could accommodate any technical term used by the ancient religious and philosophical schools (no doubt it was used also for technical treatises dealing with science, art, architecture, poetics, and so on), *gaṇacchandas* was equally amenable to the vogue for successions of short syllables which accompanied the Apabhraṃśa tendency in the language. H. Smith has pointed out this tendency in Pali, and we have referred to his rhythmic studies several times already : here we may refer to his article on anticipations of Apabhraṃśa in Pali in the BSL 1932, 169 ff. : " Désinences verbales de type apabhraṃśa en pali." In Apabhraṃśa most conjuncts are reduced to a single consonant and the masculine nominative singular termination is abbreviated to *-u* ; in " pali assoupli " these tendencies are illustrated by *bhavissati* > *bhavihiti* and by the metrical shortening of final *-o*. The appearance of the new " mesures légères " (P″) in various metres in the later Pali texts may be interpreted as showing a desire on the part of the Buddhist poets to present their teaching in forms closer to the current popular taste than the " heavy " old rhythms.

§ 237. *Gaṇacchandas* served equally well for either rhythm, and evidently was extremely popular in the transition period. We can see in the Pali literature how from the old *gīti*, where there is little freedom of structure, the suppleness of the metre was gradually increased, as the musical form became more familiar to the listener, until entirely new possibilities were created. Cappeller has shown (1872, pp. 81–5) how the poets using *gaṇacchandas* were able to bind the form very closely to the meaning by the use of rhythms expressing the feeling of the situation described. This principle, as is well known, became very highly developed in Classical Sanskrit, in the association of various metres with different emotions, objects or events. *Gaṇacchandas*, the most important metre of the transition period from the later Pali texts to the rise of the Classical Sanskrit literature (a period of which the greatest literary monument is perhaps the Hāla Anthology), could achieve a great deal of this type of expression within the structure of a single metre. We have already noted that the repertoire of fixed classical metres was largely derived from *gaṇacchandas* rhythms, so that we can now say that it seems to have been through experiments in *gaṇacchandas*, and the growing up of usages associating the various rhythms with the various requirements of poetic expression, that the classical metres were evolved and given their various fixed patterns and the characteristics associated with them.

Chapter VII

THE VATTA

Previous Research

§ 238. The *vatta* in Pali has received more attention from scholars than the other metres. Although the analyses of Pali *vatta* usage made between 1887 (Simon) and 1912 (Ballini) were somewhat premature owing to the very imperfect knowledge of the metrical interpretation of the texts at that time, and the statistics published are often far from being as accurate as the form of presentation would suggest,[1] a rough approximation to a true understanding of the metre was obtained and two important conclusions drawn.[2] In this chapter the results of previous research will be briefly summarized, with perhaps more precision than was possible half a century ago, and some further conclusions will be drawn.

§ 239. The two conclusions already mentioned as having resulted from the old discussion are as follows :

1. The Pali *vatta* is close in structure to the *anuṣṭubh* of the *Brāhmaṇas* and *Upaniṣads*, being apparently of slightly more recent origin, whilst on the other hand it appears to be a little older than the *vaktra* of the *Bṛhaddevatā* ; this chronological sequence is continued by the *Mahābhārata* and afterwards by the *Rāmāyaṇa*.

2. The *vatta* of the *Aṭṭhaka* and *Pārāyana vaggas* of Sn appears to be older than that of Dh, Th and J.

[1] Simon, for instance, gave complete and exact figures for Th and J, implying that he had solved all the problems of doubtful scansions, variant readings, corruption, and so on in these exceptionally difficult texts. We shall never attain such precision in our statistics, for, as we have repeatedly pointed out above, the language itself possesses a certain fluidity which results in frequent metrical ambiguity.

[2] The materials available include : Simon, " Der Śloka im Pali," ZDMG, 1890, 83 ff. (statistics on about 6,000 verses in Dh, Th and J) ; Moore, JAOS, 1907, 317 ff. (figures for the *Itivuttaka*) ; Oldenberg, " Zur Chronologie der indischen Metrik," in *Gurupūjākaumudī*, Leipzig, 1896, 9 ff. ; " Zur Geschichte des Śloka," NG 1909, 219 ff. (includes statistics on *Aṭṭhaka* and *Pārāyana*) ; Smith, SnA III, 1918, 637 ff., Sd IV, 1949, 1148 ff. and its BHS continuation in 1950a, " Retractiones Rhythmicae " (1951 : system of nomenclature). Other contributions will be mentioned below.

§ 240. These conclusions are based on the frequencies of the *pathyā* form of the prior *pāda*, which are stated to be as follows:

	Text	Frequency
	Ṛgveda	*circa* 2% (part of Book V)—20% (part of Book X) . . . Arnold, 1905, Chapter VII.
	Śunaḥśepākhyāna (*Aitareya-brāhmaṇa*) and Book X of ṚVS	27%—Oldenberg, ZDMG, 1887, p. 63.
based on very small numbers of verses	*Śatapathabrāhmaṇa* (*yajñagāthāḥ*)	37%—Oldenberg, 1909, pp. 227–8.
	Bṛhadāraṇyakopaniṣad	50%—Oldenberg, 1909, pp. 227–8.
	Īśopaniṣad	52%—Oldenberg, 1909, pp. 227–8.
	Īśopaniṣad	65% [1]—Gildemeister, 1884.
	Kaṭhopaniṣad	78%—Oldenberg, ZDMG, 1887.
probably all these figures are a little too low [2]	*Aṭṭhaka* and *Pārāyana*	68–70%—Oldenberg, 1909.
	Jātaka	74–5%—Simon, 1890.
	Theratherīgāthā	76%—Simon, 1890.
	Itivuttaka	77–8%—Moore, 1907.
	Dhammapada	80%—Simon, 1890.
	Bṛhaddevatā	83–4%—Oldenberg, 1909.
	Epics [3]	87–8% Oldenberg, 1909 and Hopkins, 1902.
	Aśvaghoṣa	88·3%—Johnston, 1936, p. lxvi.
	Saddharmapuṇḍarīka	89·5%—Edgerton, 1936, p. 44.
	Raghuvaṃśa	93%—Oldenberg, 1909.

[1] The discrepancy between Gildemeister's and Oldenberg's figures for the *Īśopaniṣad* does not seem to have been explained. Oldenberg probably used a better edition and perhaps rectified some doubtful readings. Aiyar's figures (JOR, 1927, 122) show fifty-seven non-*pathyā* out of 224 (= 25·5%) prior *pādas* for the five *Upaniṣads*: *Kaṭha, Śvetāśvatara, Muṇḍaka, Kena, Īśā*. The resulting 74·5% *pathyā* is the same as that for the *Jātaka*, but the time spread of these five texts may be even greater. However, the *Upaniṣad* figures for *pathyā* would certainly be raised if we allowed for conjuncts such as *pr, br,* not making position, which Aiyar does not.

[2] Imperfect knowledge of the orthography, etc., increased the number of irregular metrical structures in these early counts. It will be seen below that the Pali texts vary from *circa* 65% to 85%.

[3] On the more primitive versification of the *Mahābhārata* see Ballini, 1912, pp. 14 (f.n. 1) and 33, and the passages there referred to in Jacobi's *Rāmāyaṇa* (1893a, pp. 80–1, etc.) and Hopkins (1902). Hopkins divides the *Mahābhārata vatta* into three main types: the "unrefined *śloka*" of certain parts "less free" in structure than the *Upaniṣad* metre; the "current *Bhārata śloka*"; the "pseudo-epic, on a par with the *Rāmāyaṇa śloka*".

Vatta *Usage. The* Vipulās

§ 241. The " rules " for the *vatta*, from the Epic usage onwards, were worked out by Jacobi in the article " Zur Lehre vom Śloka " (1885b, 442 ff.). (It is strange that we find only a garbled description of the *vatta pathyā* in Piṅgala, and that even Halāyudha in his commentary gives a very incomplete description of the *vipulā* usages). Jacobi's rules are as follows :

The *vatta* strophe or *siloka* consists of four eight-syllable *pādas*, grouped in two *pādayugas* each of which ends with the cadence ⏑-⏑×.[1]

In the *pathyā* (normal) form the prior *pāda* of each *yuga* has the cadence ⏑- - ×. Of the four opening syllables which precede this, the first, like the initial syllable of any *vatta pāda*, is anceps, whilst syllables 2–4 must not be ⏑⏑⏑ or ⏑⏑-. These rules apply also to the four opening syllables of the posterior *pāda*, but in syllables 2–4 of the latter -⏑- also is excluded.

§ 242. In the first *vipulā* the cadence of the prior *pāda* is ⏑⏑⏑(×) (the final short is rare, despite the anceps usage) ; in the opening, syllable 4 is long and usually syllable 3 as well : ×⏑- - or × -⏑-.

In the second *vipulā* the prior cadence is -⏑⏑(×) (again the final short is rare) ; the prior opening is always × -⏑-.

In the third *vipulā* the prior cadence is -,- - × with a caesura after syllable 5 ; the prior opening is × -⏑-.

In the fourth *vipulā* the prior cadence is ,-⏑- × with a caesura after syllable 4 ; this *vipulā* being rare, it is difficult to determine the rules for the opening, but syllable 4 appears to be regularly long. (This *vipulā* is extremely rare in Classical Sanskrit, not appearing at all, for instance, in the works of Bhāravi and Māgha. The first three *vipulās* appear in decreasing order of frequency, except in Kālidāsa, who uses the third most frequently.)

[1] The four *pāda* rule is frequently broken in Pali and in Epic (and Purāṇic) *silokas* : see above, § 229, and below, § 267.

§ 243. In the *Mahābhārata* the usage is much freer, as has been shown by Hopkins. Thus :

In the posterior opening –⏑– is not excluded from syllables 2–4 (i.e. we may have the " iambic " *pāda* × –⏑–⏑–⏑×, which is also found in Pali).

In the *vipulās*, the rules for the prior opening are sometimes disregarded : × – – – may occur in any *vipulā*, and ×⏑– – occasionally occurs in *vipulās* 2–4 as well as in the first. (×–⏑– is given as the regular opening for the fourth *vipulā*, which we may perhaps take as supplementing Jacobi's rules.)

A " fifth *vipulā* " occasionally appears, which is unknown in the *Rāmāyaṇa* and in Classical Sanskrit, but which is quite frequent in the *Upaniṣads*. The prior cadence is ⏑⏑– × ; there do not appear to be any special restrictions for the prior opening.

A sixth non-*pathyā* form, described as " rare ", has the prior cadence – –⏑×.

Finally we have the only other possible form of the prior cadence, which is identical with the posterior cadence ⏑–⏑×. Hopkins describes this as " sporadic ".

§ 244. The Pali usage is more archaic than that of the *Mahābhārata*. The third *vipulā* is much more common than the others [1] except in the *Aṭṭhaka* and *Pārāyana*, where ⏑–⏑× as prior cadence is commoner than any of the *vipulās*. The second *vipulā* is next in favour, followed by the first, then the " fifth ". In the Th ⏑–⏑× follows these, and is followed by the fourth *vipulā*, whilst in the other texts (except Sn IV and V) the fourth *vipulā* is commoner. – –⏑× has the lowest frequency of all ; it is regularly preceded by the opening × –⏑–. The rules for the *vipulā* prior openings are similar to those found for the *Mahābhārata*, with perhaps a little more freedom.

" Hypermetric " *pādas* may be produced by the resolution of a syllable into two shorts. This is a regular feature of the initial syllable of the *pāda* (as also in the *tuṭṭhubha*), but it happens also occasionally, and apparently as a regular usage in the metre, at

[1] It is curious that Kālidāsa should have had the same preference.

the sixth syllable of the prior *pāda*. This may lead to difficulties in scansion, since the resolved form resembles the " fifth *vipulā* " :

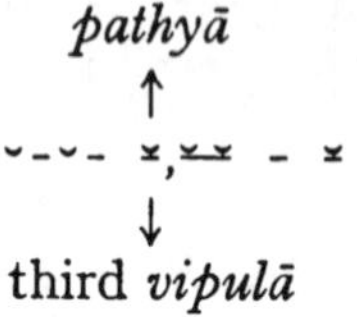

—provided the reading of the *pāda* is certain, there seems to be no doubt that the form should be classed as *pathyā* or as third *vipulā*, with resolution at the sixth. The resemblance to a *tuṭṭhubha pāda* with caesura after the fifth syllable should be noted. Smith (Sd 1148) gives " after a caesura " as a condition for resolution at the sixth, which may be correct : [1] compare the *gaṇacchandas* usage of secondary caesura when ⏑––⏑ is resolved into ⏑,⏑⏑⏑. In the case of the third *vipulā* we have the usual opening ×–⏑–, e.g. :

⏑ – ⏑ – – ⏑⏑ – ⏑
sahassabhāgo, maraṇassa | Sn 427

—whereas with the *pathyā* the opening remains free, as in the remarkable *pāda* :

– – ⏑ ⏑ ⏑ ⏑⏑ – –
nānākuṇapaparipūro | Sn 205

—this might, however, be classed as resolution at the fourth (fifth *vipulā*).

§ 245. Resolution at the fourth and resolution at the seventh seem to occur, but so rarely that mere corruption may be the cause. Thus we have :

– ⏑ –, ⏑⏑ ⏑ – – ⏑
āgataṃ na paṭipūjeti | Sn 128

[1] E.g. Sn 122a, 205, Th II 11c, 118e and 119e (but these two may be third *vipulā*), 212a, 236c, 341c ; counter case : Th II 77a. In Sn 205 and Th II 212 and 236 we have the *avyakta* caesura in a compound. The confusion of *pathyā* with third *vipulā* in cases of doubtful final quantity weakens the argument for this " secondary " caesura.

⏑ – ⏑, ⏑⏑ ⏑ – – ⏑
katassa paticayo natthi | A III 378

⏑ – ⏑ – – – ⏑⏑ –
anutthuṇanto, kālakataṃ | Sn 586

(or is this a mixture of third and second *vipulās*, 5 + 4, resembling the mixed *tuṭṭhubha pāda*, 5 + 7, in that two segments not normally associated are joined at the caesura ?)

– – ⏑ – – – ⏑⏑ –
Pañcālacaṇḍo, Ālavako | D III, p. 205

(same structure again ; this *pāda* seems clear but the rest of the strophe is interpolated).

We see that in the *vatta* as well as in the musical metres the Pali Canon shows the tendency to successions of short syllables, overcoming the avoidance of ⏑⏑⏑ which seems to have been the earlier *anuṣṭubh* usage.

Tables of Vatta *Structure*

§ 246. In the tables which follow will be found an analysis of some *vatta* texts not previously studied, together with a new analysis of some of those studied by Simon. The new analysis is required partly as a check on the figures published before and partly because Simon took the aggregates of verses in Th and J as though these were homogeneous texts, which is far from being the case. For a preliminary study of the Pali *vatta* it was useful to make a rough survey of several thousand verses, but for any serious attempt to understand the usage, and especially to understand the changes which took place during the centuries of the growth of these collections, it is necessary to present the texts broken up into their component units. Smith's classification (1951, 18 ff.) is provisionally adopted, although it is extremely clumsy on account of the separation of related rhythms. The forms are taken in their natural sequence, not in the numerical order of the classification.

§ 247. Key

cadence of prior *pāda*:

A = *pathyā* = ⏑ – – ×
N = *vip.* 1 = ⏑ ⏑ ⏑ (×)
Bh = *vip.* 2 = – ⏑ ⏑ (×)
M = *vip.* 3 = –, – – ×
R = *vip.* 4 = ,– ⏑ – ×
S = "*vip.* 5" = ⏑ ⏑ – ×
T = – – ⏑ ×
B = ⏑ – ⏑ ×

opening of prior *pāda*:

11 = ⏑ – ⏑ –
3 = – – ⏑ –
13 = ⏑ ⏑ – –
5 = – ⏑ – –
9 = ⏑ – – –
1 = – – – –
14 = ⏑ ⏑ – ⏑
6 = – ⏑ – ⏑
10 = ⏑ – – ⏑
2 = – – – ⏑
12 = ⏑ – ⏑ ⏑
4 = – – ⏑ ⏑
15 = ⏑ ⏑ ⏑ –
7 = – ⏑ ⏑ –
16 = ⏑ ⏑ ⏑ ⏑
8 = – ⏑ ⏑ ⏑

(the initial syllable of the *pāda* being anceps an eight-fold classification pairing the forms as shown would be adequate)

The opening 11/3 is in the primitive rhythm which seems to underlie the most ancient Indian metrical technique, and which became the regular opening for the *tuṭṭhubha-upajāti*. Its character as basic rhythm is shown by its compensatory function in the *vatta* as normal opening when the *vipulās* are employed, whilst with the regular Pali *pathyā* (and . . . ⏑–⏑× prior or posterior) there is great freedom in the choice of openings, 11/3 being less popular than 13/5 and 9/1. The effect of syncopation produced by 13/5, 14/6 and 10/2 (cf. A and R, and perhaps Bh, M and S) was evidently extremely popular as the main technique of variation from the primitive or basic rhythm. 12/4, 15/7 and 16/8 were little used.

§ 248. Sn : *Uragavagga*

Opening	A	N	Bh	M	S	B
	Kasibhāradvājasutta (10 *pādayugas*)					
3	2		(no *vipulās*)			
5	2					
9	2					
1	1					
6	1 (2?)					
2	1 (or 1') [1]					
8	1 (or No. 6)					
	10 (100%)					
	Parābhavasutta (50 *p.*)					
11	1		2			
3	1		1 (2?)	1?	1?	
13	13	1		1		
5	4	1	1			
9	1					
1	3 and 1'	1				
14	4					
6	4 (5?)					
10	2					
2	3 (or 2 and 1'?)					
7				1		
8	1? (or No. 6)					
	38 (and two with corrupt openings equals 40) (80%)	3	4 (5?)	2	1?	

[1] 1' signifies plus one with initial resolution.

§ 249.

Opening	A	N	Bh	M	S	B
			Vasalasutta (56 *p.*)			
11	1					
3	4 (1 r. 6th)[1]		1 (? or 5)	2 or 3 (r. 6?)	4(??)	
13	1	1				1
5	7 (and 1 r. 4th?)					
9	4					
1	6			1		1
14	1					
6	5 (6?)				1?	
10	4					
2	3					1
4	3					1
15	2					
	42 (75%)	1	0 or 5	2 or 4 (or 8)	1 or 6	4
			Hemavatasutta (56 *p.*)			
11	2?	1	1?	3?		
3	4		1			
13	3					
5	10?		1			
9	3					
1	4					
6	3 (6?)					
10	1	1?				
2	8					
12	1					
4	5					
7		1 (2?)				1
	45 (80%)	4	3	3		1
			Āḷavakasutta (21 *p.*)			
11	1			3		
3			1′	1 and 1′		
13	1					
5	1	1				
1	1				1?	
6	1 or 3					
2	2 or 4					
12	2					
4	2					
	13	1	1	5	1	

[1] "r." = "resolution at the".

§ 250.

Opening	A	N	Bh	M	R	S	B
	Vijayasutta (28 *p.*)						
11	3 (1 r. 4th)	1					
3	4 (5?)	1					
13	1						
5	1 (?) (r. 6th)					1?	
1	2 and 1′	1					1
14	1?					1	
6	2						
10	2						
2	3						
12	1						
4	1 r. 6th?					1?	
	21 or 23	3				1 or 3	1
	Munisutta (2 *p.*)						
1	1						
14 or 13							1
	1						1
Totals *Uragavagga* (223 *p.*)	172 or 174 (77–8%)	12	8 or 14	12 or 14	—	4 or 11	7

Cūlavagga

Opening	A	N	Bh	M	R	S	T	B
	Hirisutta (6 *p.*)							
11	1			1				
13					1			
5	1							
14	1							
4	1							
	4			1	1			

§ 251.

Opening	A	N	Bh	M	R	S	T	B
	Mahāmaṅgalasutta (24 *p.*)							
11	4							
3	6 (7?) and 1′	1		2?				1
13	1							
5	2	1						
9	1							
6	1 (2?)							
10	1							
4	1							
8	1 (? or No. 6)							
	19 (80%)	2		2				1
	Dhammacariyasutta (20 *p.*)							
11			1	1				
3			1	2				
13	1							
5	3 (4?)				1			1
9	1							
1	2							
14	1							
10	1							
2	1							
4								1
7	1 (or No. 3)							
	12 (60%)		2	3	1			2
	Brāhmaṇadhammikasutta (70 *p.*)							
11	3	1	1	4			1?	
3			1	3				
13	3							
5	9			1?	1	1		
9	6	1?				1?		
1	6							
6	7							
10	4							
2	4 or 5					1 or 2		
12	2							
4	5 or 7			2?			1?	1 or 2
15							1?	
	51 (73%)	2	2	9	1	2	1 or 2	1 or 2

§ 252.

Opening	A	N	Bh	M	R	S	T	B
Kiṃsīlasutta (2 *p.*)								
9	1							
1	1							
	2							
Uṭṭhānasutta (9 *p.*)								
3				1				
13								1
5	3							
9	1							
	(one corrupt *pāda*, possibly M 10)							
8								2
	4			1				3
Rāhulasutta : vatthugāthā (4*p.*)								
3	1							
1	2							
7	1							
	4							
: Sutta proper (12 *p.*)								
3	1			1 and 1′				
13	1							
5	2							
9		1						
6	1							
10	3							
4				1				
	8	1		3				

Vaṅgīsasutta (6 *p.*)

5	2							
9	1							
6	1 (? proper name upsets metre)							
10	1							
8	1							
	6							
Totals *Cūlavagga* (153 *p.*)	110 (72%)	5	4	19	3	2	1 or 2	7 or 8

§ 253. *Mahāvagga*

Opening	A	N	Bh	M	R	S	T	B
				Pabbajjāsutta (40 *p.*)				
11	1?			3	1 or 2	1?		
3	1′	2	2	1 and 1′	1			
13	1					1		
5	3 or 4							
9	3					1		
1	7 and 1′							
6	3							
10	2							
2	1							
12	2							
4	1							
	25 or 26 (63–5%)	2	2	5	2 or 3	3		

Padhānasutta (51 *p.*)

11	4			1 (and 1 r. 6th?)	1			1
3	2? (and 1 r. 6th?)			2 or 4	1′			
13	2 or 3							
5	7	2						
9	5					2		
1	6	1				1		
14	1							
6	3					1?		
10	2?							
2	3?							
12	2?			1?				
4	2							
	34 or 38 (67–74%)	3		4 or 7	2	3 or 4		1

Subhāsitasutta (8 *p.*)

11				1				
3	1 and 1′							
5	1							
1	2							
2	1							
12	1							
	7			1				

§ 254.

Opening	A	N	Bh	M	R	S	T	B
				Sundarikabhāradvājasutta (9 *p.*)				
3	1							
5	2							
9	1							
1	2	1		1				
14	1							
	7	1		1				
				Sabhiyasutta (15 *p.*)				
11				1				
3	1							
13	1?							
5	3							
9	2							
1	3							
10	1							
2	1 and 1′							
12	1			1				
4	1							
	14?			2				
				Selasutta (52 *p.*)				
11	2		2					
3	3		1′	3				
13								
5	6	3				1		
9	5							
1	7							
14	1							
6	2?							2
10	1							
2	5	1						
12	2							
4	4							
7				1 or 3				
	38 (73%)	4	3	4		1		2

§ 255.

Opening	A	N	Bh	M	R	S	T	B

Sallasutta (41 *p.*)

Opening	A	N	Bh	M	R	S	T	B
11	1		2	2				
3	1 and 1′	1	1	1				
13	3							
5	6							
9	1							
1	3			1				
14	4							
6	5							
2	4 and 1′							
12	2							
4	1							
	33 (80%)	1	3	4				

Vāseṭṭhasutta (111 (131) *p.*)

Opening	A	N	Bh	M	R	S	T	B
11	6	1	1	3				
3	7 and 1′			3	1?	3?		
13	2		1					1
5	19 (20)	1						
9	10?			1	1?			1
1	7 (14)							
14	2							
6	7 (14)							
10	8							
2	12 (17)							1
4	6							
7	3			1				
8	1							
(1 not scanned)	91 (111) (82 (84)%)	2	2	8	1	3		3

Kokāliyasutta (2 *p.*)

Opening	A	N	Bh	M	R	S	T	B
14	1							
6	1							
	2							

§ 256.

Opening	A	N	Bh	M	R	S	T	B
			Nālakasutta (51 *p.*)					
11	2		3	3	1?			
3	4	1	2	1	1 or 2	1?		1
13	5	1?						
5	2				1?			
9	2	1						
1	7			2				
14	1							1?
6	2 or 3							
10	2							
2	2							
12	1							
4		1'?						
8	1?							
	31 (61%)	3	5	6	3 or 4	1?		2
			Dvayatānupassanāsutta (76 (89) *p.*)					
11	3	1		1				1?
3	5		1	2 (6)			1?	
13	1							
5	17 (25)	1						
9	6							
1	11	2						
14	1							
6	6							
10	2							
2	4							
12	1				1			
4	3?		1					
7	1 (2)							
8	1?							
(2 not scanned)	62 (71) (84 (81·5)%)	4	2	3 (7)	1		1?	1?
Totals *Mahāvagga* (456 (489) *p.*)	344 (373) or 349 (378) (78 (77·5)%)	20	17	37 (41) or 40 (44)	9 or 11	11 or 12	1?	9

§ 257. *Therīgāthā*

Opening	A	N	Bh	M	R	S	T	B
Ekikā Theriyo (39 *p.*)								
11	1?							2?
3	6	1		1	1			
13	3							
5	4					1		
9	4 or 6			0 or 2				
1	8							
6	1							
2	1							
4	2							
15	1							
	31 or 34	1		1 or 3	1	1		1 or 2
Dukanipāta (40 *p.*)								
11	2					1		
3	2	1 or 2	1 or 2	1′			1?	1?
13	3							
5	9							
9	2	1		1				
1	4 or 5		1	1?				
14	1							
6	2	1						
2	2							
4	1							
7	1?							
	29 or 30	3 or 4	2 or 3	2 or 3		1	0 or 1	0 or 1
Tikanipāta (51 *p.*)								
11	1			2				
3	5 or 6	1	2			1		
5	7			2		1		
9	3 or 4			1 or 2				
1	7 or 9							2
6	2							1
10	1							
2	4 or 5 and 1′							
4	2							
7	1?							
8	1?							
	37 or 38	1	2	5 or 6		2		3

§ 258.

Opening	A	N	Bh	M	R	S	T	B
				Catukkanipāta (8 *p.*)				
11				1 r. 6				
3	2			1				
5	1							
9	1							
1	2							
	6			2				
				Verses 67–106 (81 *p.*)				
11	4 and 1′?	1		2	1			
3	5			3 and 1′				
13	5							
5	4			1				1
9	14		1			1		
1	15 or 16			1?				
14	1							
6	6							
10	4				1			
12	1							
4	1							
7			1?					
	1 corrupt							
	67	1	2	7	2	1		1
				Bhaddā Purāṇaniganṭhī (10 *p.*)				
11				2				
5		1	1					
9		1						
1	1′	1						
6	1							
4								1
(1 corrupt)	2	3	1	2				1

Paṭācārā and her followers (112–132, 175–181 : 62 *p*.)

Opening	A	N	Bh	M	R	S	T	B
11	2		1?				1??	2
3	4		2	1				
13	1		1?			1?		
5	11							
9	9							
1	9							
14	2							
6	6							
2	6							
12	1							
4	1′ (2′)							
15								1?
8	1							
	54		2 or 4	1		1?	1??	3

§ 259.

Opening	A	N	Bh	M	R	S	T	B
Vāsiṭṭhī (12 *p*.)								
11		1						
3	1							
13	1							
5	3							
9	2							
1	1	1						
2	2							
	10	2						
Khemā (12 *p*.)								
11	1							
3	1		1′					
13	1							
5	1							
9	1							
1	1′							1
6	1							
2	2							
4	1							
	10		1					1

Sujātā (12 *p.*)

11		1						
3	2							
5	1							
9	1?						1??	1?
1	2							
2	1							
4	2							
7				1				
	9	1		1			1??	1

Anopamā (12 *p.*)

3	1							
13	1?					1?		
5	4							
9	2							
1	1							
6	1							
10	1							
2	1							
	11					1		

§ 260.

Opening	A	N	Bh	M	R	S	T	B

Mahāpajāpatī Gotamī (12 *p.*)

3			1	1				
13	1							
5	1							
9	1 or 2							
1	3							
6	1							
10	1 or 2							
8	1							
	10		1	1				

Guttā (12 *p.*)

11	1							
3	3			2				
1	2			1				
2	1							
12	1							
4	1							
	9			3				

Vijayā (12 *p.*)

3	1							
5	2?							
9	1			1?	1?			
1	1							
6	2							
2	2							
7	1?					1?		
	10?			1?	1?	1?		

3 Cālā sisters (31 (45) *p.*)

11	1	1	1	2				
3		1						
13	5 (6)							
5	4 (5)					1		
9	1							
1	2 (4)			1				2 (4)
14	1							
6	1 (2)							
2	4 (8)							
3	3 (6)							
	22 (34)	2	1	3		1		2 (4)

§ 261.

Opening	A	N	Bh	M	R	S	T	B
				Vaḍḍhamātā (18 *p.*)				
11		2						1
3	2 and 1′				1			
5	4							
1	2							
10	1							
2	1					1		
4								1
16	1							
	12	2			1	1		2
				Uppalavaṇṇā (19 (20) *p.*)				
11			1					
3	1		1	2				
5	2							
9	1		1 (2)					
1	1							1
14				1				
6	1							
2	3							
4	1?			1?				
7			1					
	10 or 11		4 (5)	3 or 4				1
				Puṇṇikā (28 (31) *p.*)				
11	2 (3) or 6 (7)		1 (2)	1				
3	4 or 8		1					
13	1?							
5	1 or 2		1?	1?				
9	1							
1	2							
6	2			2				
10	3 (4)							
2	2							
	22 (24)		2 (3) or 3 (4)	3 or 4				

Rohiṇī (39 (42) *p*.)

Opening	A	N	Bh	M	R	S	T	B
11	1 (2)		3 (5)	1	1			
3	1		2		1	1		
13	2							
5	3	1				2		
9	1			1		1		
1	7 and 1′				1	1		
14	1							
6	1				(1 not classified)			
10	2							
4	1							
7	1							
	22 (23)	1	5 (7)	2	4	5		

§ 262.

Sundarī (51 (54) *p*.)

Opening	A	N	Bh	M	R	S	T	B
11	2 (3)					1		
3	2		3	4				
13	2							
5	9							
9	4 (6)							
1	6							1
6	8			1				
10	2							
2	3							
12	1							
4	1							
7	1?							
	41 (44)		3	5		1		1

Cāpā (44 (45) *p.*)

11	2 (3)		2	2				1
3	5	1		1				
13	2		1					
5	6							
9	1				1			
1	4							
14	2							
6	3							
10	1							
2	6							
4	2							
7	1							
	35 (36)	1	3	3	1			1

Subhā Kammāradhītā (56 (58) *p.*)

11			1	1				
3		2	5 (6)	1	1	1?		
13	1				1?			
5	5?			1?				
9	5							
1	10 (11)	2	1					
14	1							
6	1							
10	7							
2	4							
12			1					
4	2 or 3							
8	1							
	38 (39) or 40 (41)	4	8 (9)	2 or 3	1 or 2	1		
Totals *Therīgāthā* (651 (678) *p.*)	497 (517) or 505 (525)	22 or 23	37 (42) or 41 (46)	46 or 52	10 or 12	15 or 18	0 or 2	18 (20) or 20 (22)

§ 263. The overall figures approximately confirm the earlier counts by Simon in regard to the proportions of the various forms. The impression results that almost any of the larger collections of verse in the Canon taken as a whole would give about the same proportions, i.e. approximately 75% *pathyā*, with the third, second, first, fifth and fourth *vipulās* in decreasing order of frequency. ⏑–⏑× as prior cadence is most variable in employment, and may sometimes be suspected of resulting from confusion with the posterior *pāda*. The only remaining possible form for the cadence, – –⏑×, seems definitely to have been excluded, but the reason for this discrimination is not apparent. In all but a few cases, which may be corrupt, the rules for the caesura in the third and fourth *vipulās* are observed.

§ 264. As soon as we break up the collections into their constituent *vaggas* or *nipātas*, and still more so if we take single poems, we find sharp divergencies from the average usage. These are so marked that, except in some of the shortest poems, we cannot dismiss them as being due merely to the taking of samples which are too small. The differences of age thus suggested seem to agree with the general drift of subjective opinion on which sort of doctrine is earlier and which later. Thus the more " rigid " doctrine and the more minute analysis of categories of existence and its physical and psychological constituents are found in verses whose percentage of *pathyā* is higher.

The Origin of the Vatta *as Epic Narrative Metre*

§ 265. In the following tables some of the texts have been reclassified chronologically in order to show whether there is any variation in the proportions of the various *vipulās* apart from the general decrease in their combined frequency :

Total *pādayugas*	A	N	Bh	M	R	S	B	
				65% or less *pathyā*				
111 57 (61)	68 or 69 35 (36)	5 3	9 7 (9) or 8 (10)	14 8 (9) or 9 (10)	6 or 8 —	3 or 4 —	4 2	(Sn) (Th II)
				67% *pathyā*				
74 (76)	50 (51) or 52 (53)	6	8 (9)	2 or 3	2 or 3	2	2	(Th II)

70% pathyā

51	34 or 38	3	—	4 or 7	2	3 or 4	1 (Sn)

72–73% pathyā

122	89	6	5	13	1	3	4 (Sn)
82 (96)	59 (71) or 60 (72)	3	3	8 or 9	—	3	5 (7) (Th II)

75% pathyā

56	42	1	0 or 5	2 or 4	—	1 or 6	4 (Sn)
40	29 or 30	3 or 4	2 or 3	2 or 3	—	1	0 or 1 (Th II)

77–78% pathyā

28 (31)	22 (24)	—	2 (3) or 3 (4)	3 or 4	—	—	— (Th II)

80% pathyā

199	158 or 160	13	10 or 11	11	—	1 or 4	3 (Sn)
95 (99)	76 (80)	1	6	8	1	1	2 (Th II)

83% pathyā

187 (220)	153 (182)	6	4	12 (15)	2	3	4 (Sn)
165	136	4	4	12?	3?	3?	3 (Th II)

85% or more *pathyā*

101	85 or 89	1	2 or 5	2 or 4	1	2?	4 or 6 (Th II)

The first *vipulā* tends to increase in popularity, whilst the third declines somewhat, although without losing its preeminence. This is surely another manifestation of the need for successions of short syllables. The " fifth " *vipulā* is nowhere very popular. The second and fourth *vipulās* both decrease in quite a marked manner. ⏑–⏑× is used very consistently everywhere, and hardly seems to be affected by the other changes.

§ 266. The *Aṭṭhaka* and *Pārāyana* require reanalysing into their component parts. On the whole they seem to fall into two clearly distinguishable strata : the very old poems which formed the nuclei of the collections and the rather later additions, especially the frame story or *vatthugāthā* of the *Pārāyana* (and the *Kāmasutta* introducing the *Aṭṭhaka* ?), made when the two *vaggas* were assembled in approximately their present form. Thus the older stratum (which may be further subdivisible into two or more phases of composition) has a lower frequency of *pathyā* than the 70% or so given by Oldenberg for the two *vaggas*, which groups it with the earliest stratum found in other parts of Sn. The problem of the frequency of ⏑–⏑× surpassing that of any other *vipulā* remains. Probably it indicates a still earlier period than the earliest *vattas* found elsewhere, but it may alternatively represent a geographical variation in usage : perhaps a more archaic *anuṭṭhubha* lingering in Western India (i.e. Kosambī and the regions further west) under Vedic influence.

§ 267. In Chapter V, Section 5 (§ 151), we have anticipated the question of the origin or "invention" of the classical *vatta* under the impact on the *anuṭṭhubha* of the metrical transition taking place during our period. At what stage in the increase of the *pathyā* frequency we should declare the *vatta* to have come into existence is apparently an idle question, since there was a gradual development towards the uneven (*aḍḍhasama*) structure of prior and posterior *pādas* from Vedic times onwards. The confirmation of the uneven structure as a deliberately cultivated narrative metre, picturesquely compared with a pair of birds which ought not to have been separated by the shooting of the " husband " (this surely is the comparison intended in the story in *Rāmāyaṇa sarga* 2, not the strophe structure of two *aḍḍhasilokas*—which is not invariable[1] and does not suggest a truly complementary pair), may, however, date from a particular period or even from the work of one poet, such as the legendary Vālmīki. Perhaps in the post-Pali period the innovation of the complete exclusion of the cadence ⏑––⏑⏓ from the prior *pāda* may mark such a decisive point, after which the *vatta* assumed its standard classical form. The *Rāmāyaṇa*, being the oldest extant work in which the classical rules allowing only the *pathyā* and four *vipulās* in the prior *pāda* are strictly observed, might thus indeed be regarded as the first poem in the new metre.

§ 268. The Pali *vatta*, however, already exhibits the general features of this metre, and differs from it only in having a greater freedom of structure and a rather lower frequency of *pathyā*, although this latter already preponderates to the extent of accounting for at least two-thirds of the verses.

§ 269. It is instructive to compare the *vatta* with the *gīti*. In its formation a counter process took place to that which created *gaṇacchandas* out of *mattāchandas* : the four similar *pādas* of the Vedic *anuṣṭubh* were fused in pairs or *pādayugas* not by assimilation to one rhythm throughout but by differentiation of the prior *pāda* from the posterior *pāda* by a kind of interrupted cadence which suspends the full close until the end of the *pādayuga*. Thus at the two extremes of metrical development in our period—the musical technique and the technique of continuous narrative in a metre which remained on the syllable-count basis of Vedic metrics—remarkably similar developments took place : the cultivation of the uneven or *aḍḍhasama* strophe. Evidently these parallel evolutions satisfied widely divergent needs. The *gīti*, as its name implies, was the song-strophe, and owed its form to the eight *gaṇa* musical phrase underlying it. As for the

[1] The six-*pāda siloka* is quite common in Pali, as in Epic Sanskrit and the tradition of the *Purāṇas*. Indeed we might suppose that the poets paid no particular attention to strophic structure in epic narrative, being conscious only of the continuous series of *aḍḍhasilokas*. It is noteworthy, especially in connection with the remarks in the concluding paragraph of this chapter, that the *gīti* also has a six-*pāda* form, in the *Upālisutta* (cf. § 229 above).

vatta, a metre consisting of four comparatively short *pādas* equal in length and practically identical in rhythm is unsuitable for continuous narrative of any length—even the longer *tuṭṭhubha* or *upajāti pāda* soon produces a monotonous effect. The long finely balanced *pādayuga* of the *vatta*, the " speaker ", however, occasionally diversified by the tripping first *vipulā*, the sedate third, the strongly syncopated fourth or the evanescent second, became the epic narrative metre par excellence.

Chapter VIII

THE TUṬṬHUBHA

Previous Research—Evolution of Tuṭṭhubha

§ 270. The Pali *tuṭṭhubha* (the *jagatī* should be understood as included in this general term except where otherwise stated) has not been studied as extensively as the *vatta*,[1] but, as we saw in the Introduction (§§ 22–29), the general history of the Indian *tuṭṭhubha* has received more attention than that of all the other metres put together. The Introduction as just referred to gives some account and evaluation of this previous research, so we may now proceed to sum up the historical conclusions suggested by it and to tackle the enigmatic Pali form of the metre from the positions we have reached in the preceding chapters.

We may take Edgerton's articles on the Epic and Buddhist Hybrid Sanskrit *triṣṭubh* [2] as a starting point, with reference to Oldenberg's outline of the history of the metre,[3] P. G. G. Aiyar's study of the *Upaniṣad triṣṭubh* [4] and Zubatý's exhaustive collection of *triṣṭubh* variations in the Epic.[5]

§ 271. The conclusions reached by Oldenberg on the earlier phase of development are as follows:

The Vedic *triṣṭubh* had two main forms, distinguished by the position of a caesura after the fourth or the fifth syllable; the commonest schemes are:

× – × –, ⏑ ⏑ – – ⏑ – ×

× – × – × ,⏑⏑ – ⏑ – ×

[1] Besides Oldenberg's work we have Smith's survey of the Sn *tuṭṭhubha* in SnA III, pp. 638–40 and his brief notes, Sd 1151–2.

[2] "The Meter of the Saddharmapuṇḍarīka"—*Kuppuswami Sastri Commemoration Volume*, Madras, 1936, 39 ff.; "The Epic *Triṣṭubh* and its Hypermetric Varieties"—JAOS, 1939, 159 ff.; "Meter, Phonology and Orthography in Buddhist Hybrid Sanskrit"—JAOS, 1946, 197 ff.

[3] "Zur Geschichte der Triṣṭubh"—NG, 1915, 490 ff.

[4] "Upaniṣadic Metre"—*Journal of Oriental Research*, Madras, 1927, 117 ff. and 247 ff. The language, orthography, *sandhi*, etc., of the verse *Upaniṣads* requires clarification, however. For example there are conjuncts not making position (ignored by Aiyar), doubtful resolutions which would disappear if we assumed Prakrit phonology or *sandhi* (neglected by Aiyar)—*va* for *iva* and the like—and the probability of licence.

[5] ZDMG, 1889, pp. 627–52.

—the second of these is often mixed with the "pentad" metre: ×-˘-×,×-˘-×| under the influence of which it perhaps originated, the caesura at the fourth type being probably the original *triṣṭubh*.

The second type is much more regular, in conforming to the above commonest scheme, than the first. It has the variant openings ⏓- - -× and very rarely ⏓˘- -⏓, and practically no variation in the break.

The first type has the secondary openings ⏓˘- -,⏓- -˘,×-˘˘ and ×˘-˘. The break has the secondary forms -˘-,˘˘˘,-˘˘ and exceptionally ×-⏓ (but this usually in . . . ⏓,-⏓-,˘-⏓| as a special metre in *Maṇḍala* VII).

§ 272. In the *Brāhmaṇas*, and in the earlier *Upaniṣads* which are mainly in prose, we find the beginning of the transition ˘˘- > -˘˘ in the break of the first type, bringing it closer to the second. We also find the first occurrences of the *pāda* without caesura (Oldenberg regards the type with "caesura" after the sixth as accidental and as belonging to this category). Thus we have the tendency to the long fifth and short sixth syllables associated with the tendency for the caesura to disappear. Oldenberg (1915, p. 504) sees here a kind of transfer of the break from the opening to the cadence, since (with the additional tendency -˘- > -˘˘) according to his interpretation of the rhythms the "anapaestic" break which followed naturally after the "iambic" opening is transformed into the "dactyl" which leads on to the "trochaic" cadence. The break in the rhythm thus made at the end of the opening renders the caesura superfluous.

§ 273. This use of Greek terms is objectionable, for the reasons stated in the Introduction. Recognizing that there is some truth in Oldenberg's interpretation we should try to restate it in line with the conceptions of Indian metrical rhythms outlined in the Introduction and elsewhere, with special reference to § 150 above. In the old metrics (Vedic, etc.) we find variation of rhythm effected by substituting one short syllable for one long one, or vice versa, in certain positions. We are here probably close enough (for historical reasons: common origin of certain Indo-European metres ?) to Greek rhythms to suggest some resemblance between, say, iambic rhythm and the commonest opening rhythm of the Vedic *triṣṭubh*. Already, however, there is present in the old Indian metre the germ of the new metrics based on the exact quantitative opposition of two short syllables to one long one. The component parts of the second form of the Vedic metre separated by the caesura suggest at once, and especially when compared with the " pentad " or *virāja*, the new metrics : ⏓⏓ (⏑) -⏑- ⏓. What is even more remarkable here is the suggestion of the actual *gaṇacchandas* unit : |⏓⏓-|⏑-⏑| × 8 (even the strophe of 8 units is of the same length—4 *tuṭṭhubha pādas* each of 2 units). How do we apply Greek theory in describing the relationship between these two Indian metres, so different yet in this analysis apparently so similar ?

§ 274. The Vedic *triṣṭubh* may have had a common origin with similar ancient Iranian, Greek and other Indo-European metres, but already it is an Indian metre, a characteristically Indian metre with the whole of Indian metrics implicit in it and, if we may add a subjective argument, having the essentially Indian ring of the verses describing Indra's exploits. We cannot say whether in the hypothetical Indo-European metrics an " iambic ", or other rhythm of which Greek preserves the archaic quality, existed, or whether as in Chinese and Tibetan metrics only the number of syllables was significant (together with their grouping in " feet " or lines of four or some other number of syllables and of multiples of such units). In the earliest Indian metrics we find a certain interplay of quantities of which the ictus theory cannot give an adequate description. In the *triṣṭubh* we find already in this earliest stage the germ of the new metrics (which will include in its development Classical Sanskrit metrics and Apabhraṃśa metrics) of exact quantitative oppositions. In Greek metrics a system of inexact quantitative oppositions, with the ictus, developed. In the newer Indian metrics we find the system of exact oppositions with, in the musical metres, the new ictus (which may fall on a long or a short syllable) derived from the music. In the older Indian metrics we have apparently an inexact, perhaps originally non-quantitative, system developing towards the exact system, with no ictus in the Greek sense or in the later Indian sense. In *gaṇacchandas* we have a clear, exact, musical structure: ⏖- isochronous with ⏑-⏑. In the *tuṭṭhubha*, even in Pali, it is most unlikely that a division of the *pāda* : ×-|⏑-×,|⏑⏑-|⏑-× would yield four units of exactly equal length, although the opposition of the pair of short syllables to the other syllables of the *pāda*, and also to the other form of the *pāda* with this pair interchanged with the (long) fifth syllable, does indicate the exact ⏑⏑/-.

§ 275. The *tuṭṭhubha* derives its character not from the units from which the *pāda* may be built up, as does a musical metre (or a Greek metre), but from the *pāda* as a whole. This character it retains, in a modified form, in the classical *upajāti*. It is to the combination of this indivisible *pāda* system with the musical character of the new rhythms that the fixed classical metres owe their wonderful diversity. Only the *tuṭṭhubha* retained the *pāda* as its unit throughout the Early Middle Indian Period, when all the other metres show the uneven structure of *pādayugas* of two unequal *pādas* and the musical metres the new unit, the *gaṇa*. This was its very important rôle in that period, and we should seek to interpret its rhythmic structure, including its suddenly "advanced" appearance (in some respects—primitive in others) as found in our texts, in this light.

§ 276. Edgerton and Oldenberg reached the following conclusions concerning the later development of the *triṣṭubh* :

The *Mahābhārata triṣṭubh* lies in two clearly distinguished strata, apparently belonging to two different periods of composition. The older stratum, found for instance throughout the *Sabhā Parvan* (II), shows the continuation of the tendencies of the *Brāhmaṇa* period, together with the special feature of hypermetric *pādas*. It should be noted further that *jagatī pādas* frequently alternate with *triṣṭubh pādas* within the strophe. There are three types of hypermetre, that produced by adding a seven-syllable break plus cadence (as in the first Vedic type given above) to a five-syllable opening (second type) being by far the commonest. The other types are produced by resolution at the fifth after the (early) caesura and by resolution at the first, which however is extremely rare in the Epic. To the same stratum appear to belong, besides the *Bhagavadgīta* and many other parts of the Epic, the later *Upaniṣads* such as the *Kaṭha* and *Śvetāśvatara* and perhaps the *Baudhāyana* and *Vāsiṣṭha Dharmasūtras*. It would appear that the Canonical Pali *tuṭṭhubha* [1] is associated with this same stratum, although the proportions of the various structures are different. The Ardhamāgadhī metre resembles the Pali, but more regularly approximates to the Classical *upajāti* form.

The later stratum in the Epic, found for instance throughout the *Virāṭa Parvan* (IV), shows the pure *upajāti* type without mixture of *triṣṭubh* and *jagatī pādas* and without hypermetres. Licence, even, may be used to obtain the fixed *upajāti* scheme. Many other sections of the Great Epic and the entire *Rāmāyaṇa* conform to this type.

§ 277. The *triṣṭubh* in Buddhist Hybrid Sanskrit, for instance in the *Saddharmapuṇḍarīka*, conforms to the *upajāti* type except for the occurrence of mixed *triṣṭubh* and *jagatī* and of hypermetres by resolution at the first, fourth [2] and fifth syllables (as in the *upajāti* type, there is no evidence for a caesura). As to its chronological position, Edgerton says no more than than it may derive from the metrics of the " original Prakrit " dialect of the Buddhist Canon.[3] We may suggest that the BHS *triṣṭubh* represents a transition phase between the older Epic (or the Pali) metre and that of the later Epic.

Oldenberg relies on the evidence of the *anuṭṭhubha* (see our Chapter VII) to demonstrate that the Pali Canon is older than the Great Epic, and would regard the apparent " lateness " of the form of the Pali *tuṭṭhubha* as perhaps a local development

[1] i.e. the freer *tuṭṭhubha* of the majority of the texts. In the latest texts we find the classical *upajāti* and *vaṃsaṭṭhā*.

[2] cf. Régamey, 1938, pp. 12 and 66. See Smith, 1950a, 17 ff. for a survey of BHS *triṣṭubh* forms.

[3] He would perhaps revise this statement today in the light of his investigation of Buddhist dialects (1953). If the Buddhists did not use a special dialect it is unlikely that they used a special metrics (i.e. one peculiar to themselves and not whatever was current in the countries where they were active).

in Eastern India. We must look for a more convincing explanation by developing our theories of the evolution of the metre in the light of Edgerton's results.

Tuṭṭhubha *Structure in Pali*

§ 278. The types of *tuṭṭhubha* found in the Canon are as follows:

Caesura at fourth

breaks:
- -⏑⏑
- ⏑⏑-
- -⏑-
- ⏑⏑⏑
- --⏑

Caesura at fifth

breaks:
- -,⏑⏑
- -,⏑⏑- (hypermetre 5 + 7)
- -,-⏑⏑ (hypermetre 5 + 7)
- -,⏑-
- -,-⏑- (hypermetre 5 + 7)
- ⏑,⏑⏑ (frequently > -,⏑⏑)
- -,-⏑

Caesura at sixth and/or third

breaks:
- -⏑,⏑
- -⏑,-

Caesura at third and/or seventh (Sn 239a ?)

break ⏑⏑⏑

(alternatively these last two classes have been described as having no caesura; Oldenberg also gives - - - and - -⏑ without caesura)

Openings

×-⏑-(-) the only common opening in all the above types
×- - - very rare (break -⏑⏑)
×⏑- - very rare (breaks -⏑⏑,-⏑-)
- -⏑⏑- extremely rare (Sn 214a)
-⏑ ⏑--⏑ extremely rare (Sn 243, 247, 252)

Hypermetres

Besides the 5 + 7 types above, any form may have resolution of the first syllable. In the commonest forms, with break -⏑⏑, we may have resolution at the fifth so that the break becomes ˘˘˘˘. Resolution at the fourth, as found in BHS, does not seem to occur in Pali.

The break ×-× is extremely rare (Smith ignores it in his classification Sd 1151–4) and should perhaps always be corrected (e.g. Sn 177b, 211c and 239b > -˘˘; 214a ?). But cf. ,- -˘ above.

§ 279. All these types, it appears, may occur either as *tuṭṭhubha* proper or as *jagatī* (which, for instance, shows the hypermetre 5 + 8, and so on). It was not possible within the scope of the present study, which was devoted mainly to the new metres, to take up the question of the differences between the two metres, as has been done in the case of *opacchandasaka* and *vetālīya*. The results might be no less interesting: as the two metres separated out from more or less indiscriminate mixing into the classical *upajāti* and *vaṃsaṭṭhā*, which are found in the latest Canonical texts, we might find that although in these two classical metres there is no superficial difference other than the cadence (but we do feel a difference in reading them, since the *vaṃsaṭṭhā* cadence rhythm is reflected in the opening, for instance), in the development of other fixed metres, such as the *rucirā*, the interplay of cadence and opening visibly played a part.

§ 280. As Oldenberg has pointed out (1915, p. 515) there is a strong predominance of the break -˘˘ regardless of the caesura: in other words a strong anticipation of the classical *upajāti* form. The opening also is "normal" (×-˘-) in the great majority of cases. As he says, however, (p. 516) it is impossible to believe that Sn and Dh are younger than the *Bhagavadgīta*, and we must rely on the *vatta* evidence, which shows that the Pali texts are earlier. Although there is a smaller percentage of non-*upajāti* forms in our texts than in the earlier Epic samples, we may point out that there is on the other hand a wider range of different structures.

§ 281. The table opposite shows *tuṭṭhubha* structure in some of the texts:

---

[1] Oldenberg states merely that in the 5 + 7 the break -,˘-˘- predominates, which he regards as a sign of antiquity.

Breaks	*Aṭṭhaka* (Oldbg.)	*Devatā* S (Oldbg.)	*Munisutta*	*Khagga-visāṇa*	Dh (Fausbøll)
,-˘˘	112	26	12	27 (68)	Caesura not recorded by Fausbøll
,˘˘-	5	6	4	3	
,-˘-	12	3	3	5	
,˘˘˘	2			1?	
,--˘	7		2		
,˘-˘				1	
-,˘˘	167	33	12 (20)	43	
-,˘˘-	no figures given[1] (see footnote, p. 208)				
-,-˘˘					
-,-˘-					
-,˘-	5	3	3	1?	
˘,˘˘	25	9	3?		
-,-˘	3				
-,- (= *virāja*)				1 (2)	
-˘(,)˘	100	36	13?	28	
-˘(,)-	3	1		1?	
--(,)˘			1?		
˘˘˘(,)					
---	1				
--˘	4				
Total -˘˘	379 85%	95 81%	37 (45) 70%	98 (139) 80%	107 75%
Total *upajāti-vaṃsaṭṭhā*	359	86	31 (39)	88 (129)	
Total	446	117	53 (61)	123 (164)	143
Openings other than ×-˘-(-)					
˘˘--	1				
×-˘˘	3	2	1		3
˘˘-˘˘		1			
-˘˘-	7	4			
×- - -	10	5		5	1
-˘- -	2				1
˘˘- - -	1			1	
-˘-˘-					1

Initial resolution occurs about sixty times in the approximately 1,600 *tuṭṭhubha pādas* of Sn (after allowing, of course, for the illusory cases with *svarabhakti* vowels which do not make extra syllables). There is no restriction on the words which may fill this position.

The History of the Tuṭṭhubha *in the Early Middle Indian Period*

§ 282. In order to reconstruct the history of the *tuṭṭhubha* in our period we must understand the relationship between the Pali and Epic (and BHS) forms of the metre. Despite the predominance of the *upajāti* rhythm which gives it a classical, late appearance, we can find marks of antiquity in the Pali metre which confirm our previous conclusion that most of the Pali Canon is older than the extant Epic. In the period of the origin and development of *mattāchandas* the initial alternation ⏑⏑ would be very popular, whilst in the period of the establishment of the fixed metres in their classical forms, when the true *mattāchandas* had been replaced by the fixed metres such as *aparavatta* and the classical *vetālīya*, it would be natural to discard such a usage.

§ 283. Now it is precisely in the Pali *tuṭṭhubha* that we find frequent initial resolution, which is very rare in the Epic.[1] On the other hand, resolution at the fifth is more common in the Epic, whereas in Pali it is extremely rare.[2] In this case the resolution was evidently connected not with *mattāchandas* but with the development of the classical fixed metres such as *rucirā*. In BHS also resolution at the fifth is commoner, and here too we are on the threshold of classical metrics. In the earlier phases, during which the caesura might fall after the fourth, and the fifth syllable be then regularly short, such internal resolution would have destroyed the structure of the metre, and it seems clear that the establishment of approximate *upajāti* rhythm with the fifth syllable almost invariably long was the essential prerequisite for resolution at the fifth. The 5 + 7 hypermetre was a union of two familiar components

[1] It is also quite common in the *Upaniṣads*.
[2] In the *Upaniṣads*, again, it is less common.

and did not require such a basis, whilst the initial resolution not only does not result in the rhythmic confusion which would follow internal resolution in the earlier phases but was probably catalysed by parallelism with the second half of the *pāda* in the regular form with caesura after the fifth and by parallelism with the *virāja*: ⏓–⏑–⏓ × 2 (*virāja*)//⏑⏑–⏑–⏓ × 2 (initial resolution). This initial resolution is likely to have been the first manifestation of the transition to the new metrics of exact quantitative oppositions.

§ 284. The possibility of some geographical differentiation, suggested by Oldenberg, cannot be entirely ruled out, although, as we have said in the Introduction (§ 13), Aryan-speaking India must be regarded as developing as a fundamentally homogeneous cultural unit and local variations (which are nevertheless of great importance and interest) must be seen as secondary. We might thus conclude that *mattāchandas* and initial resolution was an Eastern development, remembering that the *vetālīya* was also called *māgadhikā* or *māgadhī* (Jacobi, 1884, p. 593), and suggest that as the new technique radiated to Western India it underwent modification into the fixed forms such as *aparavatta* and classical *vetālīya*, initial resolution in the *tuṭṭhubha* not finding favour in the West, or at any rate in the North-West. Buddhist Hybrid Sanskrit and then the *Rāmāyaṇa* would show the further development in the East, whilst the *Mahābhārata* would show the development in the North-West immediately following the *Brāhmaṇa* stage.[1] The Ardhamāgadhī literature would be an additional illustration of Eastern developments in the Pali period.

Such divisions, however, seem too sharp and artificial, since we know that the Pali literature at any rate was not confined to the East, and the BHS literature may be partly of non-Eastern origin. Even if the new developments we have studied originated in Magadha, they spread so rapidly to the other regions that it seems impossible to distinguish the time-lag in the West before they were adopted there. It is unlikely that such a lag would amount to as much as fifty years, and our

[1] The (verse) *Upaniṣads* have the Eastern feature of initial resolution.

chronology may never be able to mark off such short periods with any certainty.

§ 285. It seems certain that the verse parts of the Pali Canon represent quite a long period of composition, overlapping some of the other literature to which we have referred. Whereas the old *tuṭṭhubha* verses we have studied here are certainly pre-BHS, we find on the other hand the prototypes of classical *upajāti* and *vaṃsaṭṭhā* in a minority of later Canonical texts, alongside other proto-*akkharacchandas*. These may be later than the earliest BHS texts and later than the older stratum of the Epic. Although all the stages in the evolution *tuṭṭhubha—upajāti* are not yet clear, we can see the approximate interrelations of the various texts to which we have referred, and the process of limitation of the metre to its classical forms in the context of the rise of the new metres. In the next chapter we shall describe these fixed classical forms and note the contribution of the *tuṭṭhubha* to the establishment of the Classical metrics, in which *upajāti* and *vaṃsaṭṭhā* were especially favoured as elevated narrative metres.

CHAPTER IX

AKKHARACCHANDAS

Structures of the Samavuttas, Aḍḍhasamavuttas *and* Visamavuttas

§ 286. We have already noted, especially in studying *mattāchandas,* the origin in our literature of some of the fixed syllabic metres which later played a predominant rôle in the Classical literature. The Pali Canon uses as many different metres as such a *mahākāvya* as the *Śiśupālavadha,* and we propose here to attempt a complete survey of the fixed, or at any rate fixescent, metres to finish our survey of Pali metres found in the Canon.[1] We may follow the usual classification into *samavuttas, aḍḍhasamavuttas* and *visamavuttas.*

§ 287. *Samavuttas*

No. of syllables in *pāda*	
6	⏑ ⏑ ⏑ – – x × 4 (metre of Th I 381, not named)
10	⏑–⏑–⏑–⏑–⏑– × 4 (metre of S I 14, not named)
	– – ⏑⏑–⏑⏑–⏑x × 4 *upaṭṭhitā* I
11	– ⏑⏑– ⏑⏑– ⏑⏑– x × 4 *dodhaka*
	x – ⏑ – – ⏑⏑ – ⏑ – x × 4 *upajāti* (or *jāti*)
	– ⏑–⏑⏑⏑– ⏑– ⏑ x × 4 *rathoddhatā*
12	x – ⏑ – – ⏑⏑ – ⏑ – ⏑ x × 4 *vaṃsaṭṭhā* (or *upajāti*)
	⏑̲⏑̲ – ⏑–⏑ ⏑⏑– ⏑⏑x × 4 *pamitakkharā*
	– – – – – ⏑⏑⏑⏑ – – x × 4 metre of Th I 111
13	x – ⏑ – ⏑⏑⏑⏑ – ⏑ – ⏑ x × 4 *rucirā*
	x – ⏑ – –, ⏑⏑⏑⏑ – ⏑ – x × 4 *ānandajāta* [2]

[1] Only those which occur as complete strophes are given, thus the *meghavitāna pāda* J *nipāta* VII verse 149a is not classifiable as illustrating the *meghavitāna* metre, although it shows the origin from *mattāchandas* of the independent *meghavitāna* metre. An attempt to list all such anticipations would probably not go beyond Smith's Sd Index, to which the reader is referred for this supplementary information.

[2] This name is suggested for the metre of the introduction (a late addition) to the *Nālakasutta* (Sn 679 ff.), where it is mixed with *vaṃsaṭṭhā* strophes, from the first word of the *Sutta* : *ānandajāte tidasagaṇe patīte* . . . The metre occurs also in three BHS texts : *Mahāvastu* II, 293–397, *Lalitavistara,* 229–34, *Śikṣāsamuccaya,* 89–90 and 297–308 (Edgerton, 1953, *Grammar,* p. 8 ; Smith, 1950a, p. 18).

Aḍḍhasamavuttas

⏑⏑– ⏑⏑– ⏑⏑– x | – ⏑⏑– ⏑⏑– ⏑⏑– x × 2 *vegavatī*
– ⏑–⏑/⏑⏑– – – ⏑⏑ x | – ⏑–⏑/⏑⏑– – – ⏑⏑ – x × 2 *svāgatā*
⏑⏑⏑⏑⏑⏑ – ⏑ – ⏑ x | ⏑⏑⏑⏑ – ⏑⏑ – ⏑ – ⏑ x × 2 *aparavatta*[1]
⏑⏑⏑⏑⏑⏑ – ⏑ – ⏑ – x | ⏑⏑⏑⏑ – ⏑⏑ – ⏑ – ⏑ – x × 2 *pupphitaggā*

Visamavuttas

upaṭṭhita-ppacupita
– – – ⏑⏑– ⏑–⏑ – ⏑⏑ – – | ⏑⏑– ⏑⏑⏑⏑ – ⏑–⏑ – – |
⏑⏑⏑⏑⏑, ⏑⏑⏑– | ⏑⏑⏑⏑⏑⏑⏑, ⏑⏑⏑– ⏑⏑– x × 1 *upaṭṭhitappacupita*
– – – ⏑⏑– ⏑–⏑ – ⏑⏑ – – | ⏑⏑– ⏑⏑⏑⏑ – ⏑–⏑ – – |
⏑⏑⏑⏑⏑, ⏑⏑⏑–, ⏑⏑⏑⏑⏑, ⏑⏑⏑– | ⏑⏑⏑⏑⏑⏑⏑, ⏑⏑⏑– ⏑⏑– x × 1 *vaḍḍhamāna*
– – – ⏑⏑– ⏑–⏑ – ⏑⏑ – – | ⏑⏑– ⏑⏑⏑⏑ – ⏑–⏑ – – |
– – ⏑⏑– ⏑–⏑ – | ⏑⏑⏑⏑⏑⏑⏑, ⏑⏑⏑– ⏑⏑– x × 1 *suddhavirājosabha*

uggatā
⏑⏑– ⏑–⏑ ⏑⏑– ⏑ | ⏑⏑⏑ ⏑⏑– ⏑–⏑ – |
– ⏑⏑⏑⏑ ⏑⏑– ⏑⏑– | ⏑⏑– ⏑–⏑ ⏑⏑– ⏑–⏑ x × 1 *uggatā*
⏑⏑– ⏑–⏑ ⏑⏑– ⏑ | ⏑⏑⏑ ⏑⏑– ⏑–⏑ – |
⏑⏑⏑⏑⏑⏑ ⏑⏑– ⏑⏑– | ⏑⏑– ⏑–⏑ ⏑⏑– ⏑–⏑ x × 1 *lalita*
⏑⏑– ⏑–⏑ ⏑⏑– ⏑ | ⏑⏑⏑ ⏑⏑– ⏑–⏑ – |
– ⏑–⏑ ⏑⏑– ⏑⏑– | ⏑⏑– ⏑–⏑ ⏑⏑– ⏑–⏑ x × 1 *sorabhaka*

It must be noted that a certain fluidity of structure prevails in most, and perhaps in all, of these metres, which are still in process of crystallization out of the *mattāchandas* > *gaṇacchandas* system in which *mattā* and *gaṇa* equivalents were substituted for one another fairly freely. Two shorts may often be substituted for a long, especially initially (as even in the old *vatta* and *tuṭṭhubha*), and in several of the metres the initial syllable is anceps (the *upajāti*, for instance, does not yet appear to be further divisible into *indavajirā* and *upendavajirā*).

The Origins of the Akkharacchandases

§ 288. We have already discussed the origin of the *pupphitaggā* (§§ 144 and 167), the *aparavatta* (§§ 144 and 165 ff.), the *vegavatī* (§§ 179 f.), the *rathoddhatā* (§ 178), the *dodhaka* (§ 179) and the *svāgatā* (§§ 179 ff.). This disposes of the *aḍḍhasamavuttas*, which developed from *mattāchandas*.

Upajāti and *vaṃsaṭṭhā* are the fixed forms of *tuṭṭhubha* and *jagatī* to which these metres became limited during our period. In some of the later Canonical texts we find these metres very nearly in their strict classical form, e.g. *upajāti* Th I, 776 ff. = M II, 72–4; *vaṃsaṭṭhā* D III, 147 ff., 156 ff., 161 f., 165,

[1] It is not certain that this metre occurs independently in the Canon. The only example seems to be J IV 443 (XV 190), a tag verse which may be commentatorial.

A III, 40, and Bv I, 1 ff. (with occasional *rucirā pādas* : in the *Lakkhaṇasutta rucirā* is used independently). The *rucirā* is simply *vaṃsaṭṭhā* with the fifth syllable regularly resolved, we see its origin in the texts just mentioned (Bv and D III).[1] The *ānandajāta* originated in a very similar way, through the regularly resolved sixth in the 5 + 7 hypermetric *tuṭṭhubha*.

§ 289. Let us now consider the group of metres clearly related to *gaṇacchandas*, in which the *caturasra* or " woodpigeon " rhythm (⏓⏓–⏑–⏑) appears. The *pamitakkharā* [2] is evidently derived from a *gaṇacchandas pāda* made up to four full *gaṇas* by completing the fourth *gaṇa*, but with the rhythm of the third *gaṇa*, not the second. It thus resembles such Apabhraṃśa metres as the *pajjhaṭikā*, and also the *mattāsamaka* or *ariyāgīti* type of ancient metre with a full strophe of 64 *mattās*. Note the initial alternation (in the classical metre the initial long is not found) :

⏓⏓–|⏑–⏑|⏑⏑–|⏑⏑– × 4.

The *uggatā* can be understood only by analysis into segments of the 8 *mattā caturasra* rhythm. Jacobi (1889, 464 ff.) saw the *gaṇacchandas* origin of the metre, but apparently he was baffled by the number of *gaṇas* forming the strophe (14.5) and could see no reason for this curious length. Nevertheless he noted the regular alternation of the two basic types of *gaṇa* rhythm. In fact the structure is clear and natural when measured by the *tāla* :

⏑⏑–|⏑–⏑| ⏑⏑–|⏑’,⏑⏑⏑| ⏑⏑–|⏑–⏑| –’,⏓⏓|⏑,⏑⏑⏑| ⏑⏑–|⏑⏑–| ’,⏑⏑–|⏑–⏑|
1 2 3 4 5 6

⏑⏑–|⏑–⏑|⏓
7 8

—eight " bars " of eight *mattā* (the apostrophes indicate the *pāda* junctions).

[1] See also J II 269–270. On p. 220 of the same volume we find a *pāda* 5 + 8 with resolved sixth (cf. *ānandajāta*) = fourteen syllables. *Rucirā* occurs also at S V 400 = A II 55 = A III 52 (three *pādas* or originally a whole strophe ?).
[2] Found in the *Lakkhaṇasutta*, D III, 169 f., 172 ff.

§ 290. For the second half of the fifth bar compare the fourth *gaṇa* of the *pamitakkharā*, and notice that this is the only bar the end of which coincides with the end of a *pāda* and is marked by a caesura. From the position of the end of the first *pāda*, which coincides with the secondary caesura required by the *gaṇa* ⏑,⏑⏑⏑ when equivalent to ⏑––⏑, we connect this metre with the old *gīti vipulā* (first *pāda* ending with the first syllable of the fourth *gaṇa*). The curious variations in the fourth bar (the seventh *gaṇa* again resembles some forms of the *gīti* fourth *gaṇa*, with the *pāda* junction, but in the odd position), with caesura and end of the second *pāda* after its first syllable and the remainder of the bar subject to the variations *lalita* and *sorabhaka*, can be explained by parallelism with the eighth bar : we are here at the end of the first *pādayuga*, but whereas the second *pādayuga* ends with a bar containing just the one syllable and a " rest ", in the first the bar is filled up with the usual rhythm. At this point, however, before the final return to the strict opening rhythm in the last *pāda*, the strophe is diversified by variations within the rhythm of the *tāla*, leading to a kind of break at the end of the fifth bar which, as we have noted, ends like a *pamitakkharā pāda*. Evidently the basic structure of the strophe is as follows. We begin with the main rhythm, like a *dhruva* (modern *sthāyī*) in musical form ; this *pāda* may thus be called the *dhruva*. The rhythm is then varied increasingly up to the break at the end of the third *pāda*, which contrasts strongly with the first ; this section resembles the *ābhoga* in musical form. Finally the *dhruva* is repeated or " recapitulated " to close the strophe, again as in music.[1] This structure is the prototype of the medieval *tāḷavuttas* of Apabhraṃśa and the Modern Languages. It seems to have been inspired by the tendency to " ternary " form which appears to be inherent in Indian and European music alike. Comparativists might find it interesting and instructive to compare the history of sonata form with that of the *păda*.

§ 291. Only the *upaṭṭhitappacupita* is equal in complexity to

[1] cf. § 230 on the three *pādayugas* of the *Upālisutta gīti* : 1 = *dhruva*, 2 has most freedom, 3 is most rigid.

the *uggatā*, even the Classical Sanskrit poets not having employed a more elaborate metre, although they used *pādas* of much greater length than those of Pali. This metre, however, again belongs to the strictly musical and *deśī* tradition which led to the Apabhraṃśa *pāda*, where we see its true continuation and a further elaboration of strophe structure. It does not appear to have been used in Classical Sanskrit literature after Aśvaghoṣa (*Saundarananda* II, 64–5, where it is followed by the *udgatā* of *sarga* III), being replaced by the *śārdūlavikrīḍita*, a *samavṛtta* with the same opening - - -⏑⏑-⏑-⏑ . . . .

§ 292. If we apply the *caturasra tāla* to the *upaṭṭhitappacupita* we obtain this result :

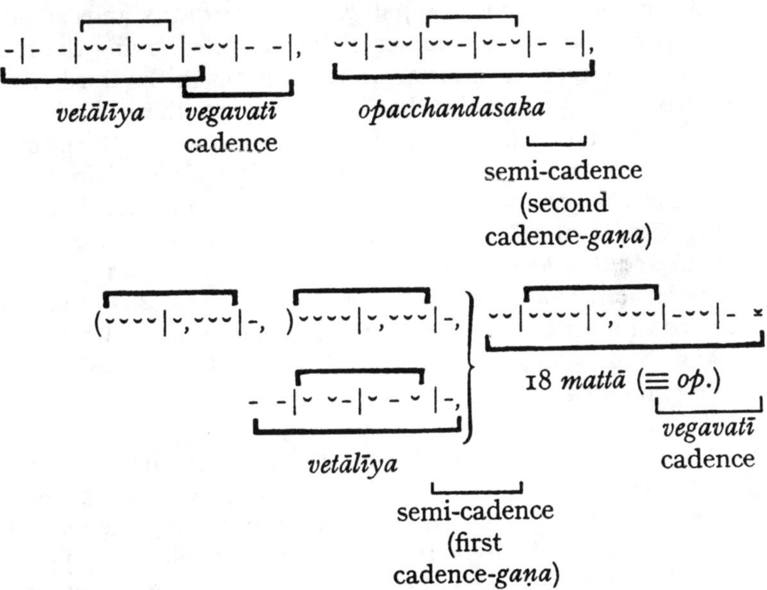

—to which we have added the comparison with mixed *mattāchandas* mentioned in § 182. We see in the first place that the original structure was that of the *vetālīya—opacchandasaka* strophe of Sn : *vet.* + *op.* × 2 ; the *suddhavirājosabha*, being the earliest form of *upaṭṭhitappacupita*, having a prior *vetālīya* for its third *pāda*. Next we see the rationalization of the cadence rhythms previously observed in *vegavatī* and *svāgatā*, in which the whole strophe is assimilated to a regular underlying measure. The metre was not assimilated completely to the *gaṇacchandas tāla*, and retained its *mattāchandas* characteristics in the same way as the *svāgatā* did, but the *caturasra* rhythm appears in each *pāda* (the secondary caesura in ⏑,⏑⏑⏑ seems to be regular in the Pali examples [1] in so far as they could be scanned ; it is not regularly observed by Aśvaghoṣa).

§ 293. We may thus describe the metre as more primitive than the *uggatā*, and probably as a prototype for the special *păda* characteristics of that metre. On the other hand it has certain definite *tāḷavutta* characteristics, being even more advanced than *uggatā* in some ways. Thus, as described by Piṅgala (V 28 : *pṛthag ādyam*), the first *pāda*, or *dhruva*, stands somewhat apart from the remainder of the strophe, having the full cadence. We then have far greater variations in the third *pāda* than has the *uggatā* (notice that in both metres these variations occur in the third *pāda* only), which is limited within the framework of the 14.5 *gaṇas* (note also that Piṅgala describes the recitation of *uggatā* as *ekataḥ* = in one piece in contrast to the *pṛthag ādyam* of the *upaṭṭhitappacupita*). Thus whereas the normal *upaṭṭhitappacupita* third *pāda* contains only 10 *mattās*, the *suddhavirājosabha* contains 14 and the *vaḍḍhamāna* 20 (or perhaps 22 if, as seems possible, the first half of it is followed by a pause of 2 *mattās*)—or we may describe the *vaḍḍhamāna* as having an extra *pāda*.

§ 294. The other details of the structure are not so clear. There seems to be no particular reason why the first *pāda* should contain 22 *mattā*, and be formed by adding the *vegavatī* cadence to that of the *vetālīya* with one syllable overlapping, whilst in the other *pādas* the cadence ends where the original *vetālīya* or *opacchandasaka* cadence ended. Some cause external to the metre must be sought : presumably in the musical setting. The first and second *pādas* begin in parallel like posterior *pādas* : this might be said to emphasize the reopening or new beginning at the second *pāda*. The remaining *pādas*

[1] D III, 159 f., 175–9. It is usually a " concealed " caesura in a compound.

apparently follow on without a break. The first two short syllables of the fourth *pāda* combine with the final syllable of the third to make up one *gaṇa* similar to the first half of the *vegavatī* cadence, the rhythm of the third *pāda* is then repeated in the fourth *pāda*, but ends with the full *vegavatī* cadence.[1] There is thus a kind of crescendo leading up to the end of the strophe, the succession of eight shorts being repeated two or three (*vaḍḍhamāna*) times.

In the Pali *upaṭṭhitappacupita* there appears to be further flexibility of structure, such as the initial long permitted in the second *pāda*, and a more thorough analysis of the few strophes in the *Lakkhaṇasutta* should eventually enable us to work out the earlier usages in this metre. Unfortunately this task could not be carried out within the scope of the present study.

§ 295. Four metres remain, all *samavuttas*. In Th I 381 we have a single strophe of ⏑⏑⏑⏑– –⏒ × 4 (cf. Smith in Sd 1170). The last syllable is perhaps always short (two *pādas* end with short vowels, the others with *niggahīta*), so that we could scan as a kind of *gaṇacchandas* : ⏑⏑⏑|– –|⏑,⏑⏑⏑|– – . . . (a strophe of eight *gaṇas*). In the absence of further examples we can do no more than speculate about the origin of this metre, it may even be a chance spontaneous outburst :

> *atihitā vīhi*
> *khalagatā sāli*
> *na ca labhe piṇḍaṃ*
> *katham ahaṃ kassaṃ* ||

—it is a *bhikkhu's* " lament " attributed to the inspiration of Māra, the first verse of the *Tekicchakānigāthā*, which continues (382–6) in an unusual form of *gaṇacchandas* (see Smith, Sd 1164 and 1171 for an attempt to describe this). The poem is of great interest in that it is dated by the Commentary : *ettha ca Bindusārarañño kāle imassa therassa uppannattā tatiyasaṅgītiyaṃ imā gāthā saṅgītā ti veditabbā* (Dhammapāla). We have already been led (e.g. § 142) to associate the Moriyan period with perhaps the most important phase in the development of

[1] i.e. part of the *dhruva* only : this too has parallels in the musical practice.

Pali metrics, and these possibly experimental verses fit in well with such a supposition ; we may regret that they are not in one of the better known of the new metres, which might give us a more exact notion of the chronology of *gaṇacchandas.*

§ 296. Also in Th I we find another single strophe in an unknown metre :

duppabbajjaṃ ve duradhivāsā gehā
dhammo gambhīro duradhigamā bhogā
kicchā vutti no itarītaren' eva
yuttaṃ cintetuṃ satatam aniccataṃ | |
Th I 111 (*Jentagāthā*).

(no variant readings recorded by Oldenberg ; Siamese edition and Sinhalese edition, Colombo 1930, identical).[1]

—Smith gives - - - - -,⏑⏑⏑⏑- - - as the scheme, evidently assuming *vuttī, aniccātaṃ, duradhivăsā* and *itaritarena* m.c., all of which are quite legitimate according to our findings on Pali usage, with the possible exception of the third, which, however, may have been influenced by *adhivasati.* The metre may have originated from the *tuṭṭhubha*, except for the cadence, which may be related to *gaṇacchandas* : . . . ⏑|- -|- or to Th I 381. We may suppose again that this was a more or less experimental metre belonging to the period of the limitation of the *tuṭṭhubha* and the establishment of exact quantitative opposition, and perhaps the first in which long successions of longs and shorts were contrasted—a favourite expedient of Classical metrics. The nearest Classical metres are *paṇava* :

- - -⏑⏑⏑⏑- - - × 4

and *asambādhā* :

- - - - -⏑⏑⏑⏑⏑⏑⏑- - - × 4

which may have been derived from our metre by the loss or addition of two syllables.

[1] Compare, however, Dh 302 ab ; *duppabbajjaṃ durabhiramaṃ, durāvāsā gharā dukhā.*

§ 297. In J I 125. 20–1 we find the *upaṭṭhitā* 1 (Sd 1169; not to be confused with the *upaṭṭhitā* 2, Sd 1166, which is ⏑–⏑⏑⏑– – –⏑– – × 4):

– –⏑⏑–⏑⏑–⏑– × 4

—it may be a prototype of *ujjalā*, *hariṇaplutā* or *dutavilambita*. The origin of the cadence is not clear.

Finally we have the metre of S I 14 (two strophes):

⏑–⏑–⏑–⏑–⏑– × 4

—this might be classified as a variety of *tuṭṭhubha* having only ten syllables and the normal opening rhythm carried on throughout the *pāda*. The effect was no doubt too monotonous to become popular in Indian metrics, although something like it (⏑–⏑–⏑–⏑– × 4) is used in Hindī and it may be a popular and persistent dance rhythm which occasionally infiltrated the domain of metrics.

The Formation of the Classical Metrics of India

§ 298. To conclude this chapter we may state that all these Pali metres are at the very beginning of their development in the context of the new metrical techniques, and that they are the prototypes and forerunners of the magnificent repertoire of the Classical Sanskrit fixed metres. The development of such metres was made possible only by the establishment of the principle of exact quantitative opposition through the cultivation of the musical metres, and many of them bear traces of *mattāchandas* and *gaṇacchandas* rhythms which in crystallized form became independent metres.[1]

§ 299. The *tuṭṭhubha*, but not the *vatta*, was assimilated to the new system in various forms, but the majority of the new metres originated from *mattāchandas* and *gaṇacchandas* forms. In the early stages it was *mattāchandas* which gave rise to various *akkharacchandases*; in the later stages, and still more so in the post-Pali period, it was from *gaṇacchandas* that most

[1] We have noted in § 237 the *gaṇacchandas* origin of the poetic associations of various types of rhythm in the Classical metrics.

new metres were derived. It may be suggested, however, as has already been mooted in Chapter VIII (§ 275), that the contribution of the *tuṭṭhubha* to the new Classical metrics was the quatrain structure of four similar *pādas*, as units of rhythmic structure, which it preserved in opposition to the assimilation of the *pāda* structure to a musical strophe subdivided into *gaṇas* in the musical metres. As was stated there, it is to the combination of these two opposed elements, the indivisible *tuṭṭhubha pāda* and the endless musical rhythms of the new metres, that the Classical Sanskrit metres owe their wonderful diversity and subtlety of rhythm.

CONCLUSION

§ 300. The apparently simple task originally proposed for this study (" so slight a task to any scholar with leisure that we may fairly expect it to be accomplished before long "—Rhys Davids in 1903, D II p. viii) turned out to be in fact a major research project too great to be completed within the time available or within the scope of a single monograph. There are far more verses in the Pali Canon than Rhys Davids reckoned in 1903, and only a small fraction (selected as the most important and most typical) of them have been scanned for this work. In order to achieve even this we were led far afield into research on the language, on related Indo-Aryan dialects and their metrics, on Indian music, and not least on the general problem of the nature of rhythm in poetry (cf. Kühnau, 1886, pp. v–x and 1–18). This study is therefore no more than a preliminary outline in which we have tried to present and settle the main problems of Pali metre, leaving the fuller working out of the usages in the various texts to future research. Only the chapter on *mattāchandas*, which was considered to be of the greatest importance (the first new metre), comes anywhere near completeness as a survey of its subject, whilst that on the *tuṭṭhubha* is a mere sketch to prepare for the task of scanning hundreds more verses in this metre and describing its usage in detail.

§ 301. On the other hand we have gained inestimably from being side-tracked in carrying out Rhys Davids' project by a host of interesting questions which could not have been foreseen by him. The work became a historical project. Only as a phase—as it turns out, perhaps the most decisive phase—in the general history of the Indo-Aryan languages and their literature can Pali metre be understood. The problems accordingly acquire much wider interest than they possessed as obscure questions concerning a single somewhat remote dialect. If the problems of the most decisive phase of the transition to Middle and Modern Indian and the new metrics can be solved, then a fuller understanding and appreciation of Sanskrit, Apabhraṃśa, Ardhamāgadhī and Māhārāṣṭrī poetry will follow. Even the study of Hindī, Gujarātī and other modern literatures may gain, although they have the advantage of living traditions. The most important conclusions to draw in this connection concern the origin of the new metres and their strictly musical organization from *gaṇacchandas* onwards, including their close conformity to musical forms and conventions (the *dhruva—ābhoga—dhruva* system of ternary form superseding the *aḍḍhasama* structure even whilst maintaining the four *pāda* strophe ; the syncopated coda, etc.). At the same time we note the musical rhythmic basis of the Classical *varṇavṛttas*, despite the maintenance of the strict four *pāda* metrical form and of the *pāda* as the unit in opposition to the *gaṇa* organization of the musical metres.

§ 302. It follows naturally from this historical analysis of the metres that we should hope to be able to arrange our texts in chronological order, using a criterion more objective than any proposed hitherto. A brief summary of the chronological results of our study is given below. The analysis according to the proportion of long to short syllables might be used with success on the prose texts, which were as much subject to the changing language-rhythm as the verse, to enable us to relate them also to our chronological framework.

In Chapter V (§ 193) we arrived at a division of some of the Canonical texts into five periods of composition, on the basis of the development of *mattāchandas*. Let us try to combine the results obtained in the other chapters with this division (see p. 225.)

§ 303. The *Aṭṭhaka* and *Pārāyana* are omitted : according to Oldenberg's figures the *Aṭṭhaka tuṭṭhubha* is 85% *upajāti*-rhythm, which would make it later than S I (81%), whereas we have suggested that the *vatta* of these *vaggas* is extremely old. The problem of these texts remains, but it seems certain that they cover a very wide range of time. The *Aṭṭhaka* may be much later than the *Pārāyana* (it includes the *Tuvaṭakasutta* in *gīti*) : whilst the *Aṭṭhaka* is almost entirely in *tuṭṭhubha*, the *Pārāyana* contains a good many *vattas*, although these are mainly in the frame story. A careful comparison with the metres of the *Brāhmaṇa* literature might settle this difficulty (see also the discussion in §§ 282–3).

Approximate date	Period	*Mattāchandas*	*Gaṇacchandas*	*Vatta*	*Tuṭṭhubha*	*Akkharacchandas*
	o			earliest Sn (65%)[1] and earliest Th II *Cūḷavagga* (72%)	most of Sn ?	
	i	Sn 1–34, 83–90, 359–75 most of J	Sn, M	most of *Uragavagga* and *Mahāvagga* (77–8%) (*Kaṭha*)		
300 B.C.	i a	Dh, U part of J (AM : *Sūyagaḍaṃ*)			*Munisutta* ? (Early Epic ?) Dh ?	
Moriyan Period	ii	Sn *vegavatī* poem ? Th II part of Th I S I	Th II, J	Dh (80%), later Sn and Th II (> 83%)	S I ? part of J and M Sn 679–98	part of Th I, S I part of J and M Sn 679–98
200 B.C.	ii a	*Lakkhaṇa* part of Vv	*Lakkhaṇa*	latest Th II (85%)	*Lakkhaṇa* Bv	*Lakkhaṇa* Bv
100 B.C.	iii	most of Vv, Pv, Ap, Cp	Ap	(Epic average 87–8%) (*Rāmāyaṇa*)	(Late Epic)	(BHS : *Mahāvastu*)

[1] % of *pathyā*.

§ 304. We shall not here attempt to draw detailed conclusions about the development of Buddhist doctrine, although we may make one or two observations which indicate the changes in some aspects of it. Thus we may contrast the Buddha legend of the very early *vatta* texts of Sn (405–24, 425–49) with the elaborate contents of the *Lakkhaṇa* or Bv, or the admonitions of Sn 699–723 with those of Sn 724–64. With the earlier group we may compare Sn 83–90 and 359–75, whilst in the later period we have the dramatic episodes of S I, the stories of the last three Th II poems, and later still the theory of *kamma* as illustrated in Vv and Pv. Of great importance are the verses attributed to disciples and later monks : Th I seems to cover a long period of development and many different techniques of composition, some of them dated by the Commentary.

§ 305. The Pali Canon grew from a collection of simple, direct poems (and no doubt also prose narratives of the *Brāhmaṇa* type, which perhaps preponderated) characterized by a forceful, rather abrupt diction, to a greatly enlarged chrestomathy of literary compositions of all types, in which the direct style had been superseded by every kind of calculated aesthetic manoeuvre. The religion growing in popularity attracted the best philosophers and poets of India to give it a literature superior to those of its rivals. Its character, however, was thereby changed to a complex, learned system, the best aspects of which were not so much the content of the literature as the beauties of its presentation : highly developed metrics and poetics. Finally the Canon grew still further, and became imposing in mere size: in the *Abhidhamma* the implications of the philosophy were worked out to the last theoretical permutation, in the *Vinaya* a corresponding elaboration of disciplinary rules and regulations took place, whilst in the more " popular " section of the Canon the laity were provided with endless legends in which creation had been superseded by repetition, and the quest for enlightenment by pietism.

Bibliography and References

(The editions of texts used are those of the PTS except where otherwise stated and for the *Vinaya*, ed. Oldenberg, and the *Jātaka*, ed. Fausbøll. The best general bibliography for Pali and related studies is that given by Helmer Smith in his " Epilegomena ", 1948, to Vol. I of the *Critical Pali Dictionary*. For a bibliography of the Indian treatises on Sanskrit metrics see M. Krishnamachariar, *History of Classical Sanskrit Literature*, Poona, 1937, pp. 897–912. The same work contains a bibliography of the Indian treatises on music : pp. 810–884.)

ADIKARAM, E. W., 1946. *Early History of Buddhism in Ceylon* (Migoda : Puswella).

AGGAVAṂSA, 1928–30. *Saddanīti*, ed. H. SMITH (Lund : Gleerup) with Index Volumes, 1949 in progress.

AIYAR, G., 1927. " Upaniṣadic Metres," JOR (Madras : Kuppuswami Sastri Research Institute), Vol. I, 117 ff. and 247 ff.

ALLEN, F., 1879. " Über den Ursprung des homerischen Versmasses," ZVSIS, 556 ff.

ALLEN, W. S., 1953. *Phonetics in Ancient India* (London : Oxford University Press).

ALSDORF, L., 1928. " Der Kumārapālapratibodha " (Hamburg : No. 2 of *Alt- und Neu-Indische Studien*), 10 ff.

—— 1936. *Harivaṃśapurāṇa* (Hamburg), of PUṢPADANTA.

—— 1937. *Apabhraṃśa-Studien* (Leipzig : *Abhandlungen für die Kunde des Morgenlandes* 22.2).

ANDERSON, 1913. " Stress and Pitch in Indian Languages," JRAS, 867 ff.

ĀPTE, 1891. *Practical Sanskrit–English Dictionary* (Poona : Shiralkar), Appendix II on Sanskrit Prosody.

ARISTOXENUS. (See Rossbach and Westphal.)

ARNOLD, E. V., 1905. *Vedic Metre* (Cambridge University Press).

BAKE, A. A. (Lecture notes.)

BALLINI, A., 1912. *La Poesia Profana* (*Laukika*) (Florence : SIFI-I, Vol. VIII, part 2).

BATHOLOMAE, C., 1886. " Zur Metrik " (Halle : Niemeyer, *Arische Forschungen* II), 1 ff.,—16 ff. on caesura after the seventh in *triṣṭubh*, etc.

BASHAM, A. L., 1951. *History and Doctrines of the Ājīvikas* (London : Luzac).

BELLONI-FILIPPI, F., 1912. *La Poesia Religiosa* (Florence : SIFI-I, Vol. VIII, part 1 of *La Metrica degli Indi*).

BENFEY, T., 1874–80. " Die Quantitätsverschiedenheiten in den Saṃhitā- und Padatexten der Veden " (Göttingen : *Abhandlungen der Königlichen Gesellschaft der Wissenschaften* XIX–XXVII).

BERGAIGNE, A., 1889. JA Huitième série XIII, on Vedic metres.

BHARATA, 1929. *Nāṭyaśāstra*, ed. BAṬUKANĀTHAŚARMAN and BALADEVOPĀDHYĀYA (Varanasi : Chowkhamba, Kashi Sanskrit Series, No. 60).

BLOCH, J., 1920. *La formation de la langue marathe* (Paris).

BLOCH, J., 1934. *L'Indo-Aryen du Veda aux temps modernes* (Paris : Adrien — Maisonneuve).

—— 1950. *Les Inscriptions d'Asoka* (Paris : Les Belles Lettres).

BÖHTLINGK, O., 1877. *Sanskrit Chrestomathie* (St. Petersburg : Academy of Sciences, second edition), p. 342 on irregular hiatus (= p. 445 of the first edition, 1845).

BOLLENSEN, F., 1846. *Vikramorvaśī*, Appendix to edition of (St. Petersburg).

—— 1859. " Über die Aufhebung der Sperrung (Position) vor Doppelconsonanten im Indischen," ZDMG, Vol. XIV, 291 ff.

—— 1881. " Zur Vedametrik," ZDMG, 448 ff.

BROCKHAUS, H., 1865. " Die sechszeiligen Strophen in Sanskrit-Gedichten," ZDMG, Vol. XIX, 594 ff.

BROWN, 1837. " A Familiar Analysis of Sanskrit Prosody " (London).

—— 1869. " Sanskrit Prosody and Numerical Symbols Explained " (London).

BÜHLER, G., 1883. *Leitfaden für den Elementarkursus des Sanskrit* (Vienna).

CAPPELLER, C., 1872. *Die Gaṇachandas* (Leipzig).

CHÉZY, A. L., 1827. " Théorie du śloka ou mètre héroique " (Paris : JA).

CHIBA, 1935. *A Study of Accent* (Tokyo).

COLEBROOKE, H. T., 1811. " On Sanscrit and Pracrit Poetry " (*Asiatic Researches*, Vol. X).

DĀMODARA (MIŚRA), 1925. *Vāṇībhūṣaṇa*, ed. PARAB and PAṆŚĪKAR (Bombay—second edition).

DAVE, T. N. " Gujarātī Prosody " (typescript).

EDGERTON, F., 1936. " The Meter of the Saddharmapuṇḍarīka " (Madras : *Kuppuswami Sastri Commemoration Volume*), 39 ff.

—— 1939. " The Epic Triṣṭubh and its Hypermetric Varieties," JAOS, 159 ff.

—— 1946. " Meter, Phonology and Orthography in Buddhist Hybrid Sanskrit," *JAOS*, 197 ff.

—— 1953. *Buddhist Hybrid Sanskrit Grammar* and *Dictionary* (New Haven : Yale University Press).

EWALD, H., 1827. " Über einige ältere Sanskrit-Metra " (Göttingen).

FAUSBØLL, V., 1855. *Dhammapada*, Appendix to edition of (Copenhagen).

FELBER, E., 1912. " Die indische Musik der vedischen und der klassischen Zeit " (Vienna : *Sitzungsberichte der Kais. Akademie der Wissenschaften*, philosophisch-historische Klasse, Vol. 170, part 7).

FOX STRANGWAYS, A. H., 1914. *The Music of Hindostan* (Oxford : Clarendon).

GEIGER, W., 1916. *Pāli Literatur und Sprache* (Strassburg : Trübner).

—— 1938. *A Grammar of the Sinhalese Language* (Colombo : Royal Asiatic Society, Ceylon Branch).

—— 1943. *Pāli Literature and Language* (Calcutta University) (= English edition of 1916).

GELDNER, K., 1877. *Über die Metrik des jüngeren Avesta* (Tübingen).

GILDEMEISTER, J., 1844. " Zur Theorie des Śloka," ZKM, Vol. V, 260 ff.

GRASSERIE, 1892. " Essai de mètres " (Paris : *Revue de linguistique et de philologie comparée*, No. 25).

GRIERSON, G. A., 1895–96. Articles on the accent (ZDMG, Vol. 49, 393 ff., Vol. 50, 1 ff.).

HEMACANDRA, 1949. *Chandonuśāsana* (Apabhraṃśa metrics), ed. H. D. VELANKAR in *Jayadāman* (Bombay : Haritoṣa Samiti, Poona Oriental Book House).

HENDRIKSEN, H., 1944. *Syntax of the Infinite Verb-Forms of Pali* (Copenhagen : Munksgaard).

Hopkins, E. W., 1902. *The Great Epic of India* (New York/London).

Jacobi, H., 1877. " Das Quantitätsgesetz in den Prakritsprachen," ZVSIS, Vol. XXVII, 594 ff.

—— 1879. " Über den Śloka im Pali und Prakrit," ZVSIS, 610 ff.

—— 1883. " Noch einmal das prakritische Quantitätsgesetz," ZVSIS, 292 ff.

—— 1884. " Über die Entwicklung der indischen Metrik in nachvedischer Zeit," ZDMG, Vol. 38, 596 ff.

—— 1885a. " Indische Hypermetra und hypermetrische Texte," IS, Vol. XVII, 389 ff.

—— 1885b. " Zur Lehre vom Śloka," IS, Vol. XVII, 442 ff.

—— 1886. " Zur Kenntniss der Āryā," ZDMG, 336 ff.

—— 1889. " Über die Udgatā," ZDMG, 464 ff.

—— 1891. WZKM (on accent and ictus).

—— 1893a. *Das Rāmāyaṇa* (Bonn).

—— 1893b. " Über die Betonung im Klassischen Sanskrit und in den Prakritsprachen," ZDMG, Vol. 47, 574 ff.

—— 1895. *Sacred Books of the East.* Vol. XLV (translations of Jaina texts).

—— 1912–13. " Über eine neue Sandhiregel im Pali und im Prakrit der Jainas und über die Betonung in diesen Sprachen," IF, Vol. XXXI, 211 ff.

—— 1918. *Bhavisattakaha* (Munich : *Abhandlungen der Königlichen Bayerischen Akademie der Wissenschaften*, Phil. Kl., Vol. XXIX, part 4).

—— 1921. *Sanatkumāracarita* (Munich : *Abh. Bay. Ak. Wiss.*, Ph. Kl., Vol. XXXI, part 2).

Jain, Banarsi Das, 1923. *Ardhamāgadhī Reader* (Lahore : Panjab University).

—— 1926–28. " Stress Accent in Indo-Aryan " (London : *Bulletin of the School of Oriental Studies*, Vol. IV), 315 ff.

Johnston, E. H., 1936. *The Buddhacarita*, Part II (Lahore : Panjab University).

Jungmann, J., 1821. " Krátký přehled prosodie a metriky indické," *Krok*, Vol. I, part 1.

Keith, A. B., 1906. " The Metre of the Bṛhaddevatā," JRAS, 1 ff.

Kellogg, S. H., 1893. *A Grammar of the Hindí Language* (London, second edition).

Kühnau, R., 1886. *Die Triṣṭubh-Jagatī-Familie* (Göttingen).

—— 1887. *Rhythmus und indisches Metrik* (Göttingen).

Kuryłowicz, J., 1928. " Quelques problèmes métriques du Ṛgveda," *Rocznik Orjentalistyczny*, Vol. IV, 196 ff.

—— 1949. " Les racines seṭ et la loi rythmique ĭ/ī," *Rocznik Orjentalistyczny*, 1 ff.

—— 1952. *L'accentuation des langues Indo-Européennes* (Krakov).

La Vallée Poussin, L. de, 1936, 1930 and 1935. *Histoire de l'Inde* (3 vols., second edition of Vol. I, Paris : Boccard).

Lacôte, F. (1909, published in :) 1926. JA, Vol. 209, 101 ff. (on scansion).

Lanman, C. R., 1880. " Catalectic verses of 7 syllables," *Proceedings of the American Oriental Society.*

Leumann, E., 1924. " Zur indischen und indogermanischen Metrik," *Festschrift für Wackernagel*, 78 ff.

Lin Li-Kouang, 1949. *L'aide mémoire de la vraie loi* (Paris : Adrien-Maisonneuve).

Macdonell, A. A., 1904. *Bṛhaddevatā*, Introduction (Cambridge, Massachusetts : Harvard University).

MAJMUDAR, 1930. *Metres in the Old Upaniṣads* (London University thesis).
MAYRHOFER, M., 1951. *Handbuch des Pali* (Heidelberg : Winter).
MEHENDALE, M. A., 1948. *Historical Grammar of Inscriptional Prakrits* (Poona : Deccan College Dissertation Series).
MEILLET, A., 1903/1949. *Introduction à l'étude comparative des langues Indo-Européennes* (Paris : Hachette, references are to the 8th edition, 1949).
—— 1913/1948. *Aperçu d'une histoire de la langue grecque* (Paris : Hachette, 6th edition, 1948).
—— 1920. " Sur le rythme quantitatif de la langue védique," *Mémoires de la Société de Linguistique* (Paris), Vol. XXI, 193 ff.
—— 1923. *Les origines Indo-Européennes des mètres Grecs* (Paris).
MINAYEFF, J., 1869. " Vuttodaya," edited in *Mélanges Asiatiques*, Vol. VI (St.-Pétersbourg : L'Académie Impériale des Sciences), 195 ff.
MOORE, J. H., 1907. " Metrical Analysis of the Itivuttaka," JAOS, 316 ff.
MÜLLER, F. M., 1869. *Rig-Veda-Sanhita*, translation, Vol. I, Preface (Vedic scansion) (London : Trübner).
NITTI-DOLCI, L., 1938. *Les grammairiens prakrits* (Paris : Adrien-Maisonneuve).
NORMAN, H. C., 1909. *Dhammapada Commentary*, Vol. I, part 2, Preface (PTS).
OLDENBERG, H., 1881. ZDMG (on the *śloka* in Manu, etc.), 181 ff.
—— 1883. " Das altindische Ākhyāna," ZDMG, 54 ff.
—— 1887a. ZDMG (on the *śloka*).
—— 1887b. *Deutsche Literaturzeitung*, 196 (criticism of Kühnau).
—— 1888. *Die Hymnen des Ṛgveda*, Vol. I : Metrische und textgeschichtliche Prolegomena (Berlin).
—— 1896. " Zur Chronologie der indischen Metrik," *Gurupūjākaumudī* (Festgabe . . . Weber) (Leipzig : Harrassowitz), 9 ff.
—— 1906. ZDMG, Vol. LX, 741 (criticism of Arnold).
—— 1909. " Zur Geschichte des Śloka," NG, 219 ff.
—— 1915. " Zur Geschichte der Triṣṭubh," NG, 490 ff.
PIṄGALA, 1874 and 1938. *Chandaḥsūtra*, ed. V. N. SHASTRI (Calcutta : Bibliotheca Indica, 1874) and KEDĀRANĀTHA (Bombay : Nirnaya Sagara Press, third edition, 1938).
PISANI, V., 1949. *Archiv Orientální*, Vol. XVII, part 2 (question of Indo-European "parent language ") (Prague).
PISCHEL, R., 1897. ZVSIS, Vol. 34, 568 ff. (against Jacobi).
—— 1899. ZVSIS, Vol. 35, 140 ff. (against Jacobi).
—— 1900. *Grammatik der Prakrit-Sprachen* (Strassburg : Trübner).
POUCHA, P., 1943. " Vom vedischen zum Sanskrit-Akzent," *Archiv Orientální*, Vol. XIV, 129 ff.
Prākṛtapaiṅgala (ANON.), 1902. Ed. GHOṢA (Calcutta : Bibliotheca Indica).
Prātiśākhyas. (See ALLEN, W. S., 1953.)
PṚTHVĪDHARA, 1936. Commentary on the *Mṛcchakaṭika*, ed. PARAB and PAṆŚĪKAR (Bombay—7th edition).
PRZYLUSKI, J., 1923. *La légende de l'empereur Açoka* (Paris : Annales du Musée Guimet).
—— 1926–28. *Le concile de Rājagṛha* (Paris : Geuthner, " Buddhica," Vol. II).
PULLÉ, 1912. " Le dottrine metriche degl'Indi " (Florence : SIFI-I, Vol. VIII).
RANDLE, H. N., 1949. " Sanskrit and Greek Metres," JOR (Madras : Kuppuswami Sastri Research Institute), Vol. XVII, 33 ff.

RAVIKARA. (Commentary on the *Prākṛtapaiṅgala*.)
RÉGAMEY, K., 1938. *Three Chapters from the Samādhirājasūtra* (Warsaw: Society of Sciences and Letters), pp. 12 and 66.
REGNAUD, P., 1880. *La métrique de Bharata* (Paris: Annales du Musée Guimet).
RHYS DAVIDS, T. W., 1903. *The Dīgha Nikāya*, Vol. II, Preface (PTS).
ROSSBACH, A., and WESTPHAL, R., 1854–65. *Metrik der griechischen Dramatiker und Lyriker*, 3 vols. in 4 (Leipzig: Teubner).
Śāṅkhāyanaśrautasūtra, 1886–89. Ed. HILLEBRANDT (Calcutta: Bibliotheca Indica)—rules for Vedic recitation.
SCHUBRING, W., 1910. *Ācārāṅgasūtra, Erster Śrutaskandha* (Leipzig), p. 60 on AM *tuṭṭhubha*.
—— 1923. *Zeitschrift für Indologie und Iranistik*, Vol. II (Leipzig), 178 ff. on *veḍha* or *veṣṭaka* hypermetre.
—— 1927. *Worte Mahāvīras* (Göttingen: Quellen der Religionsgeschichte), 3 ff. on *veḍha* metre (hypermetre).
SIEVERS, 1893. *Festgruss an Rudolf von Roth*, 203 ff. (ictus).
SIMON, R., 1890. "Der Śloka im Pali," ZDMG., 83 ff.
SINHA, 1953. *The Historical Development of Medieval Hindī Prosody* (London University thesis).
SMITH, H., 1918. *Sutta-Nipāta Commentary*, Vol. III (PTS), 637 ff.
—— 1932. "Désinences verbales de type Apabhraṃśa en Pali," BSL, 169 ff.
—— 1948. "Epilegomena" to CPD, Vol. I.
—— 1949. *Saddanīti*, Vol. IV, 1148 ff. (cf. AGGAVAṂSA).
—— 1950a. "Les deux prosodies du vers bouddhique" (Lund: *Bulletin de la Société Royale des Lettres/Årsskrift Kungl. Humans. Vetens.*), 1 ff.
—— 1950b. "Archaic Verses in the Daśabhūmīśvara," *Journal of the Ceylon Branch of the Royal Asiatic Society*, 123 ff.
—— 1951. "Retractationes Rhythmicae" (Helsinki: *Studia Orientalia*, edidit Societas Orientalis Fennica), Vol. XVI.5, 3 ff.
—— 1952. "Le futur moyen indien et ses rythms," JA, 169 ff.
—— 1953. "Inventaire rythmique des Pūrva-Mīmāṃsā-sūtra," *Uppsala Universitets Årsskrift*.
STEDE, W., 1924–27. "The Pādas of Thera- and Therī-gāthā," *Journal of the Pali Text Society*.
STENZLER, A. F., 1890. ZDMG (his metrical collections published posthumously by Kühnau), 1 ff.
TAGARE, G. V., 1948. *Historical Grammar of Apabhraṃśa* (Poona: Deccan College Dissertation Series).
TURNER, R., 1916. JRAS (on the accent), 203 ff.
VARMA, S. *Critical Studies in the Phonetic Observations of Indian Grammarians*.
VELANKAR, H. D., 1949. *Jayadāman* (Bombay: Haritoṣa Samiti, Poona Oriental Book House)—contains many references to other recent Indian publications.
VENKATASUBBIAH, 1935. "Some Rare Metres in Sanskrit," JOR (Madras: Kuppuswami Sastri Research Institute), Vol. IX, 46 ff. (with reference to Telugu).
VIŚVANĀTHA. 1902. Commentary on the *Prākṛtapaiṅgala* (edited with the text, see above).
WACKERNAGEL, J., 1896, 1905 and 1930. *Altindische Grammatik* (Göttingen: Vandenhoeck und Ruprecht).
—— 1909. "Akzentstudien," NG, 50 ff.

WEBER, A., 1863. " Über die Metrik," IS, Vol. VIII.

WESTPHAL, R., 1860. " Aufsätze zur vergleichenden Metrik der indogermanischen Völker," ZVSIS, Vol. IX.

—— 1865. *Allgemeine griechische Metrik* (= Vol. II, part 2, of ROSSBACH and WESTPHAL, see above).

WINTERNITZ, M., 1927. 1933. *History of Indian Literature*, Vols. I and II, English edition, revised (Calcutta University).

ZIMMER, 1879. " Zur Pali-Grammatik," ZVSIS, 220 ff.

ZUBATÝ, J., 1885. *Listy filologické a paedagogické* (Prague), Vol. XII, 24 ff.

—— 1886. " Některé myšlénky o vývoji metrické formy," *Listy filologické*, Vol. XIII, 19 ff.

—— 1888a. " O literatuře vēdské," *Listy filologické*, Vol. XV, 180 ff.

—— 1888b–1890. WZKM (series of articles on the accent, variation of quantity and Vedic metres: 1888 pp., 53–62, 133–40, 309–18; 1889 pp., 86–92, 151–62, 281–312; 1890 pp., 1–16, 89–112—publication not completed, because Arnold's work was forthcoming, for which Zubatý placed the unpublished part at Arnold's disposal).

—— 1889. " Der Bau der Triṣṭubh- und Jagatī-Zeile im Mahābhārata," ZDMG, Vol. XLIII, 619 ff.

INDEX OF PALI AND RELATED FORMS DISCUSSED

(The numbers refer to §§)

General Index

(The numbers refer to §§)

ABBREVIATIONS

A	*Aṅguttara*
xA	The *Aṭṭhakathā* on x
AM	Ardhamāgadhī
Ap	*Apadāna*
Bv	*Buddhavaṃsa*
BHS	Buddhist Hybrid Sanskrit
BSL	*Bulletin de la Société de Linguistique* (de Paris)
Cp	*Cariyāpiṭaka*
CPD	*Critical Pali Dictionary*
Cy	Commentary
D	*Dīgha*
Dh	*Dhammapada*
Dīp.	*Dīpavaṃsa*
gen.	genitive
I	*Itivuttaka*
IF	*Indogermanische Forschungen* (Strassburg)
IS	*Indische Studien*
J	*Jātaka*
JA	*Journal Asiatique*
JAOS	*Journal of the American Oriental Society*
JOR	*Journal of Oriental Research*
JRAS	*Journal of the Royal Asiatic Society*
Kh	*Khuddakapāṭha*
loc.	locative
M	*Majjhima*
m.	masculine
m.c.	*metri causa*
MI	Middle Indian
MSS	manuscripts
n.	neuter
NG	*Nachrichten von der Königl. Gesellschaft der Wissenschaften zu Göttingen* (Philologisch-historische Klasse)
nom.	nominative
NŚ	*Nāṭyaśāstra*
p. or pl.	plural
PED	*Pali English Dictionary* (of the PTS)
PTS	Pali Text Society
Pv	*Petavatthu*
ṚVS	*Ṛgvedasaṃhitā*
s.	singular
S	*Saṃyutta*
Sd	*Saddanīti*
SIFI-I	*Studi Italiani di Filologia Indo-Iranica*
Th	*Theragāthā* and *Therīgāthā*
Th I	*Theragāthā*
Th II	*Therīgāthā*
U	*Udāna*
Vin	*Vinaya*
Vv	*Vimānavatthu*
WZKM	*Wiener Zeitschrift für die Kunde des Morgenlandes*
ZDMG	*Zeitschrift der Deutschen Morgenländischen Gesellschaft*
ZKM	*Zeitschrift für die Kunde des Morgenlandes* (*Göttingen*)
ZVSIS	*Zeitschrift für vergleichende Sprachforschung auf dem Gebiete der indogermanischen Sprachen* (ed. Kuhn: Berlin, then Gütersloh, then Göttingen)